Henry Widdowson
On the Subject of English

Trends in Linguistics Studies and Monographs

Editors
Chiara Gianollo
Daniël Van Olmen

Editorial Board
Walter Bisang
Tine Breban
Volker Gast
Hans Henrich Hock
Karen Lahousse
Natalia Levshina
Caterina Mauri
Heiko Narrog
Salvador Pons
Niina Ning Zhang
Amir Zeldes

Editor responsible for this volume
Chiara Gianollo

Volume 330

Henry Widdowson

On the Subject of English

The Linguistics of Language Use and Learning

DE GRUYTER
MOUTON

ISBN 978-3-11-076430-7
e-ISBN (PDF) 978-3-11-061966-9
e-ISBN (EPUB) 978-3-11-061710-8

Library of Congress Control Number: 2019945524

Bibliographic information published by the Deutsche Nationalbibliothek
The Deutsche Nationalbibliothek lists this publication in the Deutsche Nationalbibliografie;
detailed bibliographic data are available on the Internet at http://dnb.dnb.de.

© 2021 Walter de Gruyter GmbH, Berlin/Boston
This volume is text- and page-identical with the hardback published in 2020.
Typesetting: Integra Software Services Pvt. Ltd.
Printing and binding: CPI books GmbH, Leck

www.degruyter.com

For Barbara Seidlhofer

Acknowledgements

Most of the chapters in this book are revised versions of previous publications.
The original versions were published as follows:

Section 1
The entries on Text and Discourse and Context and Co-text in Hogan, Patrick C. 2010. *The Cambridge Encyclopedia of the Language Sciences.* Cambridge: Cambridge University Press.

Section 2
Paper 1. As a classic book review: 'J.R. Firth 1957 Papers in Linguistics 1934–51'. *International Journal of Applied Linguistics.* 2007. 17 (3). 402–413.
Paper 2. 'Language creativity and the poetic function. A response to Swann and Maybin'. 2008. *Applied Linguistics* 29 (3). 503–508.
Paper 3. Chapter in Bruthiaux, Paul, Dwight Atkinson, William G. Eggington, William Grabe & Vaidehi Ramanathan (eds.). 2005. *Directions in applied linguistics. Essays in honor of Robert B. Kaplan.* Multilingual Matters.
Paper 4. *European Journal of Applied Linguistics.* 2013. 1 (1). 4–21.

Section 3
Paper 5. Chapter in Dontcheva-Navratilova, Olga & Renata Povolná (eds.). 2012. *Discourse interpretation: approaches and applications.* Newcastle upon Tyne: Cambridge Scholars.
Paper 6. Chapter in Hopkinson, Christopher, Renáta Tomaskova & Gabriela Zapletalova (eds.). 2012. *The interpersonal language function.* Ostrava: Universitas Ostraviensis.
Paper 7. *The Canadian Modern Language Review.* 2003. 60 (1). 89–97.
Paper 8. Chapter in Sarangi, Srikant & Malcolm Coulthard (eds.). 2000. *Discourse and social life.* London: Longman.
Paper 9. Chapter in Gerbig, Andrea & Oliver Mason (eds.). 2008. *Language, people, numbers. Corpus linguistics and society. A Festschrift for Michael Stubbs.* Amsterdam & New York: Rodopi.
Paper 10. Chapter in Bex, Tony, Michael Burke & Peter Stockwell (eds.). 2000. *Contextualized Stylistics. A Festschrift for Peter Verdonk.* Amsterdam/Atlanta GA: Rodopi.

Section 4
Paper 12. *Journal of English as a Lingua Franca.* 2012. 1 (1). 5–25.
Paper 13. *Journal of English as a Lingua Franca.* 2015. 4 (2). 359–372.

Paper 14. Chapter in Pitzl, Marie-Luise & Ruth Osimk-Teasdale (eds.). 2016. *English as a lingua franca: Perspectives and prospects. Contributions in honour of Barbara Seidlhofer*. Berlin: Mouton de Gruyter.
Paper 15. *Lingue e Linguaggi* 2016. 19. 73–78.
Paper 16. Chapter in Frauke Intemann & Frank G. Königs (eds.). 2006. *.Ach!texte – Didak-Tick der (modernen, unmodernen uknd aussererirdischen) Sprachen. Eine etwas andere Festschrift für Claus Gnutzmann*. Bochum: AKS Verlag.

Section 5
Paper 17. Chapter in Juliane House (ed.). 2014. *Translation: An multidisciplinary approach*. London: Palgrave Macmillan.
Paper 19. *Journal of Asia TEFL* 2014 11 (4)
Paper 20. Chapter in Fill, Alwin, Georg Marko, David Newby & Hermine Penz (eds.). 2006. *Linguists (don't) only talk about it. Essays in honour of Bernhard Kettemann*. Tübingen: Stauffenburg.

Papers 3, 5 and 10 were also reprinted in a selection of my work in 2009 published by the Foreign Language Teaching and Research Press, Beijing.

For the preparation of these papers for publication, I am grateful to Judith Brockmann for her secretarial help, especially indispensable in my case, by making order from my uncollated reference lists and the typographical untidiness of my text.

As to the discourse textualized in the book (as I would put it!), most of the chapters in it were written after the University of Vienna, on my retirement, made me Honorary Professor in the Department of English Studies. I think it unlikely that they would have been written otherwise, for this in effect gave me a new lease of academic life and the opportunity to be actively involved with colleagues in their teaching and research. This involvement has been a continual and invaluable source of intellectual motivation, and I am greatly indebted to my colleagues in the Department for the stimulation and support they have given me over so many years.

To one of these colleagues, I owe a particular personal and professional debt. Two of the chapters in this book were jointly authored by Barbara Seidlhofer, but she has participated in all of them. For one thing, her comments on earlier drafts resulted in the revised versions in which they now appear. But much more significantly, it has been her own innovative academic work that has provided the main inspiration and direction for my own thinking. Almost all of the issues I explore in these chapters relate in one way or another to her original insights about the nature of English as a lingua franca, and how it calls for a radical reappraisal of accepted assumptions about the pragmatics of communication and the pedagogy of language teaching.

This book, an outcome of our collaboration, is dedicated to her because it is her book as well as mine.

Contents

Acknowledgements —— VII

Introduction: Only connect! —— 1

Section 1: **Theoretical bearings**

Preamble —— 6

Section 2: **Linguistics and applied linguistics**

Preamble —— 18

1 Contextual meaning and the legacy of J. R. Firth —— 19

2 Linguistic creativity and Jakobson's poetic function —— 31

3 Applied linguistics, interdisciplinarity and disparate realities —— 37

4 On the applicability of empirical findings —— 51

Section 3: **The analysis and interpretation of language use**

Preamble —— 66

5 The pretext of interpretation —— 67

6 Interpersonal positioning and genre conventions —— 82

7 "So the meaning escapes". On literature and the representation of linguistic realities —— 96

8 Critical practices: On representation and the interpretation of text —— 103

9 The novel features of text. Corpus analysis and stylistics —— 118

10 The unrecoverable context —— 129

11 Macbeth and the third murderer. An exercise in forensic stylistics —— 139

Section 4: English as a lingua franca

Preamble —— 150

12 ELF and the inconvenience of established concepts —— 152

13 ELF and the pragmatics of language variation —— 171

14 ELF, adaptive variability and virtual language —— 183

15 The cultural and creative use of English as a lingua franca —— 189

16 Creative incompetence —— 196

Section 5: Linguistics in language learning and teaching

Preamble —— 206

17 The role of translation in language learning and teaching —— 207

18 Bilingual competence and lingual capability —— 222

19 Competence and capability: rethinking the subject English —— 233

20 Reversions —— 244

References —— 256

Name Index —— 267

Subject Index —— 269

Introduction: Only connect!

> Only connect! That was the whole of her sermon ... Live in fragments no longer
> E. M. Forster *Howard's End*

This book is a selection of papers that I have written over the past 10 years or so with the exception of two of them, which were jointly authored by Barbara Seidlhofer, and that have, again with two exceptions, already appeared in print in different places. They were written on and for various occasions: some originated as presentations at conferences, some as journal articles, some as Festschrift contributions. And as these occasions varied, so of course did the topics that were addressed and the manner of their treatment. The papers vary considerably, therefore, in their recipient design and although I have made minor revisions, I have not attempted to reformulate them as chapters that combine into a stylistically consistent connected line of argument. All I have done is to sort them into different sections according to the different areas of enquiry they relate to.

But although, in bearing the marks of their origin, these papers are diverse, they are nevertheless connected by the recurrence of common issues which lends them an underlying coherence. It is indeed central to the purpose of the book to show how these issues arise and take on particular significance as related to different areas of enquiry. Hence the same theoretical and descriptive issues about language and language use recur, as do references to the scholars who have been prominent in engaging with them. Thus, such topics concerning language variation, corpus analysis, linguistic and communicative competence, text analysis and discourse interpretation appear on the agenda or as matters arising in one paper and re-appear in another. This discursive overlap and inter-textual repetition are intrinsic to the design of the book: my intention in retaining this recurrence, rather than editing it out as redundant, is to show how these general issues about the nature of language use and learning take on a more particular significance in different contexts of discussion.

So although the papers in the book are not combined, they are associated, and the associative links are made not only by the repeated reference to familiar work in the field but also by a number of concepts which represent my own theoretical bearings on the nature of language use and learning. These are explicitly discussed or implicitly presupposed in many of the papers and so it seemed to make sense to expound them in advance in the first section of the book as a conceptual framework of reference within which the different discussions in the sections that follow can be located.

The primary purpose of this book then is to establish conceptual connections across what are so often taken to be different areas of language enquiry. Hence the deliberate ambiguity of its title. These papers are on the subject or topic of the English language and its use and in this sense are studies in linguistics. They are also about English as a school subject and the ways in which it is pedagogically designed and in this sense they can be seen as studies in applied linguistics. The two areas of enquiry are generally taken to be quite different, even opposed: theory and description on one side, practice and prescription on the other. The ambiguity of the book title is intended to reflect my view that the two areas can be so conceived as to be crucially complementary, that descriptions of how language is actually used have a direct bearing on how it can be pedagogically designed for learning, and that it precisely this relationship between language use and learning that it is the business of applied linguistics to explore.

Another opposition that these papers seek to reconcile is that which has long been institutionally enshrined in the sectarian divide between linguistics and the study of literature, with each enclosed within its own disciplinary conventions. If one looks for an urgent need for overlap, for a thematic congruence of enquiry, here surely is an obvious case. For both areas of study are centrally concerned with how language is used, with the pragmatics of text interpretation. As I argue in Section 3 of this book, whatever the text, the same issues of the indeterminacy of meaning arise. The interpretation of texts as different as *The American Declaration of Independence* and Shakespeare's *King Lear* are similarly dependent on contextual factors in that in both cases meanings will be assigned to them in accordance with assumptions and purposes which are likely to be at variance with those originally presupposed. In both cases too, the issue arises as to what are the textual constraints that set limits on interpretation, and how far particular interpretations can be privileged or disallowed by fiat. It is for these reasons that literary texts figure more prominently in these papers than might be expected in a book that purports to be about linguistics. They are, in my belief, just as relevant to linguistics as they are to literary criticism, because an exploration of how they are variably interpreted provides insights into the pragmatics of language use in general. I take the view that a linguistics that cannot account for literary uses of language, or a study of literature uninformed by linguistics are both bound to be of limited validity.

Another opposition that this book sets out to efface is that between past and present scholarship. Throughout these papers I make frequent reference to publications that are far from recent, some out of print and so, quite literally, past their sell-by date. The first two papers in Section 2, for example, discuss publications that are now more than half a century old. It might be said that being myself of advanced years, I am naturally inclined to nostalgic retrospection and so find it hard to accept that such publications have had their day, and had their say, and though perhaps of some historical interest have been superseded by subsequent developments in the study of language. Not surprisingly, I would want to challenge this view. There does indeed seem to be a pervasive assumption in the academic world, at least as far as linguistics is concerned, that thinking that is dated must necessarily be outdated and that the acceptability of academic writing, whether it takes the form of a student thesis or journal article, is conditional on the work citing references which are up to date; and the more numerous and more recent the citations the better in creating the illusion of scholarship. Citing work from the past is not likely to be given much credit; on the contrary it may well be taken as evidence of scholarly incompetence. It is a common tendency, not only in academia, to embrace innovation and keep up with current fashion and to disregard the past as irrelevant to the immediate concerns of the present. But of course, it is the past that informs the present, whether we like it or not, whether we acknowledge it or not, and this is as true in linguistics as it is in other kinds of human activity. So we need to recognize that how we think about language now is a dependent development on how others have thought about language in the past, that for all the appearance of innovation, what seems to be new may on closer and more critical scrutiny, really only be a contextual realignment of old ideas.

There is one further opposition that is not recognized in this book and this again has to do with the conditions that the genre of academic writing is conventionally required to meet. The last papers in Sections 3, 4 and 5 are different in genre from those that precede them and would not normally be found in a collection of so-called learned papers. They are satirically fanciful in key, tongue in cheek *argumenta ad absurdum*. But although these are not meant to be taken seriously at face value, they are designed to serve a serious purpose. They too engage with the issues of language use and learning that recur throughout this book, but do so by adopting an alternative perspective on things that exposes the fault-lines of accepted straight-faced ways of thinking and such dissident disrespect can have the salutary effect of prompting a critical re-appraisal of taken-for-granted assumptions. They make a serious point, one might say, because they are not serious – they are relevant precisely because they are irreverent. And so I believe there is a rightful place for them in this book.

In general, then, the aim of this book is to bring together disparate ways of thinking and talking about language into conceptual relationship. To refer to the quotation from E. M. Forster cited on the titlepage, "Only connect!". This may not be the whole of my sermon, but it is a central theme that runs throughout this book.

Section 1: **Theoretical bearings**

Preamble

As indicated in the introduction, much of the discussion in the papers in subsequent sections is informed by certain concepts, and conceptual distinctions (expounded more fully in Widdowson 2003, 2004) which represent my particular theoretical take on the nature of language use and learning. These are explained in this section as a set of personalized encyclopedia entries. This section is intended to serve as a kind of prospective priming or pretextual setting (see below) for the reading of the particular papers that follow, or as a kind of extended glossary that can be retrospectively be referred as and when the need might arise.

Text & discourse
(revised from an entry in Hogan 2010)

A fundamental distinction needs to be made between an act of communication and the language which is used to enact it. The distinction becomes clear by considering the ambiguity of the word "speech", as it occurs, for example in the title of the film "The King's Speech" where the term refers both to the speech impairment of the sovereign, and to the public address he has to make. On the one hand, reference is made to the features of the language that is produced, to the physical textual manifestation of the spoken medium. On the other hand the reference is to how this is a discoursal realization of a mode of communication. The word used as a count noun would conventionally signal the second sense and not the first, a difference effaced in the ambiguous fusion of the film title. So speech as spoken text, as linguistic manifestation, has to be distinguished from a speech, an instance of spoken discourse.

But speech as spoken text does not, of course, only involve the physical articulation of speech sounds, but the production of forms that encode semantic meaning at lexical, morphological and syntactic levels of language. So text can be defined generally as the language that people produce in the process of communication. It is the linguistic expression of intended meaning, the overt trace of covert communicative purpose. In the spoken medium, this expression takes the form of audible signals produced by one or more participants, which are ephemeral and leave no trace unless recorded. In the written medium, the text is durable and is itself a participant record of intention. Spoken text is of its nature incomplete and dependent in that it is accompanied by other, paralinguistic, expressions of intended meaning. Much of it, as in conversation, is jointly produced on line by reciprocal interaction. Developments in digitalized communication now allows for such reciprocal interaction in the written medium, as in the online exchanges in text messaging, where aspects of the spoken mode are retained by replacing face-to-face paralinguistic signals by such semiotic devices as emoticons.

Text has no independent existence for language users: it is produced only to realize some communicative purpose or other, and is a reality to recipients only to the extent that they pragmatically activate it. As a linguistic product, however, it can be analysed in dissociation from the communicative process that gave rise to it. Over recent years, vast quantities of text have been collected in corpora and analysed by computer. Most of this has been written text for the obvious reason that this can be easily scanned and stored in its original form. Spoken text can only be analysed in this way in a derived version, if it is first transcribed, that is to say transformed into a kind of writing.

Text analysis by computer, as now extensively carried out in corpus linguistics, reveals properties of language usage in detail not immediately accessible to intuition. It provides profiles not only of the frequency of occurrence of lexical and grammatical forms, but patterns in their co-occurrence. It reveals idiomatic regularities in usage over and above those required by grammatical rule (Sinclair 1991a). Such analysis is often referred to as discourse analysis, and indeed the terms text and discourse are often taken to be synonymous, both referring to actual and attested language behaviour or performance as distinct from the abstract knowledge of the language code, or competence. Since competence has generally been defined as a knowledge of sentences, this has led some scholars to suggest that text analysis and discourse analysis are terminological variants, both referring to the study of language beyond the sentence.

There are difficulties about this conflation of text and discourse. In the first place, if texts are to be defined as naturally occurring usage, they often take the form of single and separate sentences, and even of language below the sentence. Examples would be public notices like KEEP LEFT, WAY OUT, DANGER, PRIVATE and so on. Though we can analyse these notices in terms of their formal properties as sentences or sentence constituents, this is not how we experience them as uses of language. We identify them as texts not because of their form, but their function, because we recognize that they are the expression of an intention to communicate. This seems obvious in the case of these simple minimal texts, but the same would apply to any texts whatever their linguistic form: food labels, recipes, menus, book reviews, newspaper articles and so on. We identify textuality by recognizing intentionality.

This does not mean that we recognize what the intentions are that are being expressed. I can identify a piece of language as a text, even as a type of text, without being able to understand what is meant by it – a public notice in a foreign language, for example, or a complex set of instructions in my own.

This is where a distinction between text and discourse becomes crucial. Discourse can be defined as the underlying meaning of the message: what the first person text producer means by the text, and what the second person makes of it. Texts are only a partial record of the intended discourse since, in their design, assumptions will be made about a shared context of knowledge and belief, and recognition of purpose on the part of presumed recipients that do not need to be made linguistically explicit. In many cases, like the public notices mentioned earlier and other text types of a basic utilitarian kind, these assumptions will be readily ratified, and then intention and interpretation will correspond so closely that it can lead to the mistaken supposition that pragmatic meaning is inscribed in the text itself.

The meaning that is inscribed in texts is semantic. Texts are made out of the semantic resources that are encoded in a language and as such will always provide indicators of the pragmatic intention of the discourse they textualize, but the extent to which these indicators can be acted upon will vary considerably and will to a large extent depend on how far the actual recipients correspond with the presumed recipients the text producer had in mind when designing it. Of course there is always likely to be some correspondence between the intended discourse and that which is derived from the text, or otherwise no communication would take place at all. The semantics of the text will always provide a basis for, and set limits on, pragmatic inference. But since a text is necessarily an incomplete record of what its producer means to say, the meaning inferred will always be approximate. It will also depend on how far recipients are prepared to be co-operative: they may choose to disregard intention indicators and derive a discourse from the text to suit purposes of their own. In some cases, especially with literary texts, intentions may be difficult to infer from textual evidence, and may indeed be considered irrelevant to interpretation. What the text means to the receiver then overrides whatever the producer might have meant by it.

So what discourse is interpretatively derived from a text depends on how the interpreter relates the text to a context of familiar knowledge and belief.

Context & co-text
(revised from an entry in Hogan 2010)

The term context is used to refer very generally to the extra-linguistic circumstances in which language is produced as a text, and to which the text is related, the setting in which the language is used, for example, and the participants involved.

But such circumstances are many and indeterminate and only when they relate to the text in the realization of discourse do they count as context. Many circumstantial features may have no bearing whatever on what meaning is intended by a text or how it is interpreted. The question is: how does one establish which attendant circumstances are contextually significant and which are not.

The importance of taking context into account as a matter of principle in the definition of meaning has been long established. Early in the last century, the anthropologist Bronislaw Malinowski argued that an understanding of how language functions as "a mode of action" depends on establishing a relationship with its "context of situation" (Malinowski 1923). Subsequently, the linguist J. R. Firth reformulated the notion as "a suitable schematic construct to apply to language events" (Firth 1957). This construct makes mention of "the relevant features of participants" and "the relevant objects", but leaves unanswered the key question of how relevance is to be determined.

Context is a selection of those extra-linguistic features that are recognized by the language user as relevant in that they key into text to achieve communication. One set of criteria for determining relevance can be found in the conditions for realizing pragmatic meaning as proposed in the theory of speech acts (Searle 1969). A piece of text, the uttering of a particular linguistic expression, for example, can be said to realize a particular illocutionary force to the extent that situational features are taken to satisfy the conditions that define the illocution. The recognition of relevance comes about because language users are familiar with such conditions as part of their extra-linguistic socio-cultural knowledge.

But familiarity with illocutionary conditions is only one kind of socio-cultural knowledge that is brought to bear in the recognition of contextual significance. The world we live in is made familiar by projecting two kinds of order on to it: linguistic encoding on the one hand, and socio-cultural convention on the other. Communication involves an interaction between them: we make texts with the first with a view to keying them into the second. Socio-cultural conventions take the form of schemata: customary representations of reality in various degrees, culture-specific, modes of behaviour and thought which are socially established as normal. Contexts are features of a particular situation that are identified as instantiations of these abstract configurations of experience which are realized and recognized by users as discoursally relevant. These schematic constructs are not, however, static and fixed, since once they are engaged they can be extended and changed. Though communication depends on some schematic convergence to get off the ground at all, it can then develop its own creative momentum.

Although context is generally understood as an extra-textual phenomenon, apart from text but a crucial concomitant to it, the term is also often used, misleadingly, to refer to the intra-textual relations that linguistic elements contract with each within text. An alternative, and preferable, term for this is co-text.

Co-textual relations occur between linguistic elements at different levels. At the morpho-phonemic level, for example, Labov shows the tendency for segments of spoken utterance to vary according to the phonetic and morphological environment in which they co-textually occur, and is able to specify variable rules for their occurrence. These are distinct from other variable rules that Labov postulates which have to do with contextually motivated variation – where speakers, intentionally or not, adjust their pronunciation in relatively formal situations in approximation to prestige social norms (Labov 1972).

Co-textual relations at the lexico-grammatical level have attracted particular interest over recent years in the field of corpus linguistics. Computers now provide the means for collecting and analysing vast quantities of text and for identifying in detail what regularities of co-textual patterning occur. One such pattern is that of collocation, the frequency of occurrence of one word in the environment of another. But co-textual patterning extends beyond the appearance of pairs of words in juxtaposition and is also manifested in word sequences of relative degrees of fixity. The identification of such co-textual relations has led to the recognition that text is essentially idiomatic in structure (Sinclair 1991a).

Cohesion & coherence

Whereas contextual relations have to do with the pragmatics of discourse, co-textual relations of this lexico-grammatical kind have to do with the semantics of text, with the inter-connection and mutual conditioning of encoded meanings which provide a text with its internal cohesion. As exemplified in Halliday and Hasan (1976), there are a number of linguistic devices that can be identified as having a cohesive function. One example is where one or more semantic feature is copied from an antecedent expression and carried over to those that follow. Thus, a pronoun like *she* would link cohesively with a noun phrase like *the woman in white* occurring earlier in a text in that it copies the features of singular and female. It should be noted however that the co-textual link of cohesion, being semantic, does not guarantee that the appropriate pragmatic reference will be achieved. There may be more than one antecedent to which the copying expression may semantically relate, or even if the semantic link is recognized, it may fail to indicate the referential connection because this depends on extra-textual schematic assumptions. In such cases one can only make sense of the text as discourse by invoking extra-textual contextual factors. Co-textual cohesive links, therefore, do not themselves result in referential *coherence*, which is contextually dependent and a matter of pragmatic interpretation. A use of language may be co-textually cohesive as text but contextually incoherent as discourse, and vice versa.

Pretext

Acts of communication occur in contextual continuity. Speech act theorists tend to describe the pragmatics of language use in terms of separate utterances each with its own propositional content and illocutionary force. But although this may be methodologically convenient, particularly since it allows for a correlation with sentences, it nevertheless is bound to misrepresent to some degree the indeterminate and cumulative nature of communicative process itself. The texts that people produce, in speech or writing are the realizations of a discourse that is related to the continuity of social and individual experience. Acts of communication are essentially expressions of that contextual continuity. They are projections from the past in that the discourse that first person speakers/writers (P1) textualize is informed by their own knowledge of the world based on previous experience including assumptions about what it is appropriate to say on a particular occasion. And they anticipate the future in that their purpose is to act upon a second person recipient (P2) in one way or another. So the textual realization of discourse intentions presupposes a pretext in two senses. On the one hand, they draw on a knowledge of preceding communicative contexts, knowledge which P1 assumes to be shared. On the other hand they are designed to serve a perlocutionary purpose. Whenever we engage in communicate activity, it is to have some effect on our interlocutors – to make a favourable impression on them, get them to see things as we do, to have them act or think in some way. In this respect, the primary purpose of communication is perlocutionary – to bring about some effect on the second person recipient. If this were not the case, it is hard to see why we would bother to communicate at all. We always have a communicative pretext.

And just as pretext is central to the textualization of the discourse intentions of P1, so it is also central to P2's discourse interpretations of text. Whatever a P1 might intend to mean by a text, whatever effect it might be designed to have, is variously interpreted depending on the extent to which P2's previous contextual experience corresponds with that of P1 and crucially how far P2 recognizes and ratifies P1's pretextual purpose. Communication involves the approximate reconciliation of the disparity between what P1 intends to mean by a text and what the text means to P2. Where there is close pretextual correspondence, such reconciliation will be easy to achieve but in other cases, negotiation will be needed to bring the different interlocutor positions into whatever degree of approximate convergence is taken to be appropriate to the occasion. This negotiation of position in spoken interaction will in many cases be subject to constraints that restrict the individual's room for manoeuver, most obviously in socially sanctioned unequal encounters where interlocutors have pre-assigned roles they are required to conform to. In writing, where no such overt negotiation is possible, P1 has to design texts which incorporate negotiation by proxy by presupposing and anticipating the interpretative positioning of the reader.

Co-operative & territorial imperatives

Since pragmatic meaning is not linguistically inscribed in text but can only be inferred from it, communication can only happen when there is a degree of convergence of the contextual and pretextual presuppositions of P1 and P2. So communication depends on a readiness of both parties to co-operate, in other words to subscribe to the Co-Operative Principle that Grice has proposed (Grice 1975). But co-operative convergence, the establishing of common ground, necessarily involves intrusion into the separate individual spaces of the interlocutors, the personal territory in which they are secure and which they are naturally disposed to defend as representing their identity. The common ground that provides the basis for mutual understanding then becomes a site of potential contention with each participant jockeying for position. In all communication, therefore, there is a tension between the co-operative and territorial imperatives, between the social need for participants to relate to each other and the impulse to defend their individual space. There are of course some kinds of communication in such unequal encounters as interviews or interrogations, when one participant is conventionally entitled to assert territorial rights and the other to concede the intrusion, where, that is to say, positioning is non-negotiable and that of P1 is effectively an imposition on P2. More generally, however, individual communicators have room for manoeuver in reconciling the competing demands of the co-operative and territorial imperatives in reciprocally acting upon each other to persuasive effect.

Competence & capability

The term competence was famously introduced by Chomsky (1965) to identify the central concern of linguistics as a discipline, competence being defined as the abstract knowledge that native speakers have of the sentences of their language as distinct from the ways they might act upon this abstract knowledge in actual performance. Although Chomsky's focus of attention is on the rules of syntax that determine whether sentences are well-formed or not, the concept also applies to the formal properties encoded at other levels of language such as the phonological and morphological rules of word formation.

Subsequently, the term was extended, notably by Hymes (1972), to refer not only to this knowledge of the linguistic properties of a language, but to how this was put to use in communication, thereby extending the concept of competence to include aspects of performance. This extension, however, still retains the defining feature of the concept as having to do with what users know about their language which enables them to make a judgement about whether (and to what degree) a particular sample of it is normal or not. Hymes' argument for proposing the extension is summarized in his much quoted dictum: "There are rules of use without which the rules of grammar would be useless". Thus to be competent in a language is to know the rules, of use as well as grammar, and the extent to which a particular sample of performance conforms to them. This, of course presupposes that there are rules that determine the appropriate contextual use of the language, and the extent to which performance conforms to them can only be recognized by reference to what is accepted as the norm in a particular community. As Hymes says in reference to the aspects of communicative competence he proposes: "There is an important sense in which a normal member of a community has knowledge with respect to all these aspects of the communicative systems available to him. He will interpret or assess the conduct of others and himself in ways that reflect a knowledge of each ..." (Hymes 1972: 282). Competence, in other words, is taken to be the knowledge that a community of native speaking users have of both the encoding rules of their language and the rules that apply to its contextual use.

What this does not account for, however, is the fact that communication is not simply a matter of conforming to such rules but a creative process of exploiting them. When "normal members" of a native-speaking community communicate they take their bearings from what they know of these rules, but they act upon them in various ways. Their performance is rule-referenced, one may say, but not rule-governed. And users of English do not need to have the knowledge of "normal members" of a native-speaking community to be able to put the language to effective use. They do not have to be *competent* on native speaker terms to be communicatively *capable*. Some grammar rules may be redundant to the expression of their meaning and the "rules of use" that are identified as appropriate in native-speaking contexts may be quite inappropriate in their contexts and for their purposes. So we need to think of users of English as having the strategic capability to draw on the meaning potential that is virtual in the language as an adaptable resource, as having, in short a communicative capability.

Virtual language

This term refers to the meaning potential inherent in the encoding principles of a language which is not, and can never be, exhausted by any set of actual realizations. The concept of competence in a language usually presupposes a knowledge of the particular encodings that are realized in native-speaking communities. Thus grammarians will provide descriptions only of syntactic and morphological forms that are attested as conventionally conforming to these encoding principles and which are taken as representing the language. But these principles allow for an infinite range of realizations that are not attested, which do not therefore conform to the conventions of usage but which are entirely consistent with code rules. It is the ability to exploit these latent possibilities of the virtual language that I refer to as capability beyond competence.

So the descriptions of Standard English that are to be found in reference grammars are descriptions only of conventionalized realizations of virtual encoding possibilities – usually associated with the usage of educated native speakers. Take the case of pluralization. In Standard English the plural suffix can be attached to some mass nouns – for example *transformations, pretences, practices*. But in principle this suffixation also applies more generally to other nouns so that expressions *informations, evidences* and *advices* are formations entirely consistent with encoding rules. It happens that they have not been attested in native speaker usage and so are not assigned Standard English status. But although they may be stigmatized as errors, and so "not English" with reference to the actual language, they are nevertheless "in English" with reference to the virtual language and have indeed been attested in the use of English as a lingua franca. Similarly, the recategorization of nouns as verbs is restricted in Standard English to certain nouns and not others. But, in principle it applies to all nouns. The verbal use of the nouns *table* and *floor* is well attested and so recorded in standard descriptions of the language. But the use of the nouns *window* and *door* as verbs, for example, is not less consistent with the encoding principles of the virtual language.

The same point can be made about virtual morphological principles of word-formation. Affixes like the prefix *un-* and the suffixes *-less*, for example, are in actual English conventionally attached to certain lexical forms but not to others. But there is the virtual possibility of extending this affixation principle to other forms as well. Word formations like *unsad* and *unsick* or *acheless* and *prideless* are just as consistent with this virtual encoding principle as are those that happen to have become conventionally established like *unhappy* and *unhealthy* or *painless* and *shameless*.

Variation & variety

Communication involves the variable use of encoding resources available in the virtual language. This variation will generally be the individual's use of the code that has become conventionalized. This is what Chomsky refers to when he talks of the knowledge of grammatical rules as providing for creativity. There are frequent occasions, however, when users will exploit virtual possibilities for meaning making that have not hitherto been realized. Here creativity conforms to the principles of the virtual language but without conforming to their conventionally accepted realization. Variation of both kinds have always been central to sociolinguistics mainly because it provides evidence of the existence or emergence of a language variety, in other words when variants become regular and socially conventionalized. But the variable use of linguistic resources, whether conformist or not, is pragmatically motivated and variants are by no means always regular but are rather the individual's expedient use of linguistic resources to meet an immediate communicative contingency. Some variants may of course be taken up and become regular as features of a variety within a particular community and in this sense variation can be seen as the precursor of change. But variation is also a pragmatic process the significance of which is independent of what it might indicate about varieties of language.

Authenticity

This is a fashionable term which has been much used over recent years to refer to language that has actually been attested in native speaker use. Now that the features of authentic language in this sense are recorded in detail in language corpora, it has been proposed that they should be directly incorporated into language teaching materials. Thus, it is claimed, learners of English, for example, will be enabled to learn real English rather than some artificially contrived version of the language. This, of course, is an appealing idea, and this appeal of the real has been extensively exploited in reference books based on corpora of native speaker usage: a dictionary, for example, that carries on its cover the slogan "Helping the learner with real English", a grammar which bears the logo "Real English Guarantee" as a seal of approval.

The appeal of the idea is hard to resist, especially when it promoted by reputable publishers and endorsed by the authority of linguists. But the idea is misconceived. It is based on the assumption that reality is absolute and authenticity is transferable. But reality is relative: the contextual conditions that make the language real as use for its native speakers do not obtain in the very different realities of classroom contexts. Contexts have to be contrived in one way or another to make the language real for learners: if they cannot themselves authenticate the language, it has no authenticity for them.

Rather than think of authenticity as an intrinsic property of native speaker usage, it makes more sense to think of it as a property of any purposeful use of language whatever the context. Thus, anybody using English as contextually appropriate to their purposes authenticates it as a means of communication. The use of English as a lingua franca, for example, which draws on the resources of the language in non-conformist ways is no less authentic than uses that do conform to norms of native speaker usage.

Section 2: **Linguistics and applied linguistics**

Preamble

Although in its original conception, applied linguistics was more or less exclusively concerned with the pedagogy of language teaching, its scope of enquiry has now extended to include, in principle, all manner of problematic issues that arise in the use of language. And as its activities have become more diverse, so has its range of disciplinary reference, so that its very name has become something of a misnomer. The name applied linguistics indicates a dependent subaltern relationship with linguistics, and its proponents have been anxious to declare their independence and to claim equality by asserting the academic status of their work as an inter-disciplinary field of enquiry. As a consequence, applied linguistics has tended also to get dissociated from what purports to be its primary purpose: to engage with problematic issues concerning language that are actually experienced by people in the real world.

Although an engagement with these issues necessarily involves the consideration of many factors – socio-political, economic, cultural – factors usually associated with other disciplines – a disciplinary perspective only has relevance to the extent that it can be shown to have a direct bearing on the problems that people actually encounter in the practical domain. And the problems that applied linguistics lays claim to address are those which involve language in one way or another, and so it seems reasonable to suppose that linguistics, broadly defined as the study of language cognition and communication, is the area of enquiry that in principle is most immediately relevant to its purpose. So the position I take is that rather than downplay the link with linguistics by asserting the independent inter-disciplinarity of applied linguistics, we need a more rigorous and critical exploration of how far the discipline of linguistics can be made relevant and accountable in the practical domain. It is this view that is explicitly expounded in this section, and which informs the discussion in other papers in this book in one way or another.

Much of the uncertainty about what applied linguistics is, or should be, all about can be attributed to a lack of agreement on how the constituent terms of its name are to be understood: what kind of linguistics is it that is to be applied, and what is does it mean to apply it? The papers in this section address this question by tracing the development of different ways in which language has been conceived in linguistics and by considering how far they are relevant, or can be made relevant, to the real-world issues that applied linguistics claims to deal with, and in particular the issues relating to language learning and teaching.

1 Contextual meaning and the legacy of J. R. Firth

When his collected papers were published in 1957, the status and prestige of J. R. Firth as the father of British linguistics and its most influential theorist seemed secure. Colleagues and students were almost reverential in their deference to his authority. One might have supposed that this book, a compilation of almost all of his publications, and the written record of his thinking over 25 years and more, would have served to confirm his predominance and provide the essential source of reference for the subsequent development of his ideas.

But 1957 was also the year of publication of a book by another linguist, Chomsky's *Syntactic Structures*, and it was this, not Firth's volume, that was to be the dominant influence on future developments in mainstream linguistics in the following decades. 1957 can be said to mark the beginning of the confrontation of opposing approaches to the study of language – the Chomskyan formalist, the Firthian functionalist – and though the latter still had its adherents and retained some influence at the time, it was the formalist that found increasing favour in the subsequent years.

The two books are in striking contrast with each other, too, in the manner in which these alternative positions are presented. Chomsky's book takes the form of a coherent, if complex, argument for radical change, and represents a manifesto for a new conceptual order. Firth's book, on the other hand is a collection of thematically diverse papers arranged in chronological order of publication recording the history of his scholarship but with no explicit coherent connection between them at all. It is indeed a motley collection. Very general reflections about phonetics mingle with particular accounts of the phonological features of certain Indian languages and, even more specifically, the description of the structure of the Chinese monosyllable in a Hunanese dialect. Between papers like *The Semantics of Linguistic Science* and *Personality and Language in Society*, that promise to reveal something of general theoretical significance, we have technical notes on *Word-Palatograms and Articulation* and *Improved Techniques in Palatography and Kymography*, which do not. How these papers together constitute a linguistic theory is left for readers to discover for themselves. Firth himself suggests that they might use the Index of his book for this purpose. In his introduction he remarks: "In these selected papers,

---

Note: Revised from a classic book review: 2007. J.R. Firth 1957 Papers in Linguistics 1934–51. *International Journal of Applied Linguistics* 17 (3). 402–413.

https://doi.org/10.1515/9783110619669-004

which have appeared over a period of twenty-five years, a developing linguistic theory is presented, as may be apparent from the entries in the Index" (xi).

Just how readers are to construct the developing linguistic theory by consulting the index is, however, not made apparent. What *is* apparent is that with the index as the only guide, it is difficult to establish just what this theory actually is.

Readers of these papers, then, are left to work out the theory for themselves by following whatever clues they can find in the index. Elsewhere Firth is rather more considerate of his reader: in a paper promisingly entitled *A Synopsis of Linguistic Theory 1930–55*, he does provide his own summary account. This was also published in 1957, but separately in a special volume of the Philological Society, *Studies in Linguistic Analysis*, and subsequently reprinted in Palmer (1968). How far its inclusion in the book under review would have provided the necessary guidance to readers in their understanding of Firthian thinking is, however, open to doubt. Although it is the most complete and authoritative account we have, Palmer describes it as "a most disappointing paper": "It is less easy to read than many of his other articles and although Firth assured me on one occasion that he had carefully weighed every single sentence in it, it looks today even less coherent and consistent than de Saussure's Cours de linguistique générale" (Palmer 1968: 4).

The fact that Firth's theory seems to have eluded even his own attempts at elucidation, naturally gives rise to the suspicion that there might not actually be any coherent and consistent theory to elucidate. It is not surprising, therefore, that John Lyons is prompted to comment (though perhaps surprisingly in the volume *In memory of J.R.Firth*): "there are those who would deny that Firth ever developed anything systematic enough to be described as a theory" (Lyons 1966: 607). Even linguists well disposed to Firth, including colleagues who would not have had to depend only on the evidence of his writing, seem not to have been entirely clear about the theory they inherited from him. Palmer, for example, makes the comment: "Firth was, as is well known, misunderstood and largely ignored by almost all his contemporaries except those in his immediate circle, and alas, he was misunderstood by some of these too" (Palmer 1968: 2). Even that most celebrated of neo-Firthians, Michael Halliday, was apparently mistaken in claiming that his model of grammar derived from Firth: according to Palmer, the two approaches to linguistic description have "little in common". Palmer concludes: "Given that the theory supposedly represented in Papers in linguistics is so elusive of description, and apparently so susceptible to variable interpretation, even by those most closely acquainted with it, it is not to be wondered at that it succumbed to the invading force of a new theory, so explicitly propounded by Chomsky in Syntactic Structures" (Palmer 1968: 8–9).

But for all that, it is the content of Firth's book that in many ways has more sturdily stood the test of time and makes the more lasting contribution to linguistic thinking. Not only did many of his ideas anticipate later developments and the restoration of a more humanistic and socially oriented approach to the study of language, but, more importantly, his very failure to bring these ideas within the confines of an integrated theory raises crucial issues about the nature and scope of linguistic theory itself which remain unresolved to this day, and which have a direct bearing on the recurrent concerns of linguistics and applied linguistics alike.

Perhaps the clearest indications of Firth's way of thinking are to be found in one of the later papers in this collection, *Personality and Language in Society*, first published in 1950. Here he states quite explicitly that for him linguistics is essentially the study of "linguistic events in the social process" (181) and as such it is directly opposed to what he calls the "structural formalism" of Saussure which reduced language to "a system of signs placed in categories" (180). It is opposed too, of course, to the structural formalism of generative linguistics, which, for all its novelty of formulation, is informed by the same reductionist principles. Chomsky indeed explicitly acknowledges that his approach is traditional in that it adopts "the position of the founders of modern general linguistics", and he adds "and no cogent reason for modifying it has been offered" (Chomsky 1965: 3–4). The reason that Firth offers is that such an approach, in defining language in terms of abstract systems, misrepresents reality. "Actual people do not talk such a language", he says, "However systematically you talk, you do not talk systematics" (180). This would appear to be a fairly cogent reason – certainly cogent enough for Labov to adduce it some 15 years later:

> it is difficult to avoid the common-sense conclusion that the object of linguistics must ultimately be the instrument of communication used by the speech community; and if we are not talking about that language, there is something trivial in our proceeding.
> (Labov 1972: 187)

Firth would have heartily agreed. For him, as for Labov, "the study of language in its social context" is what linguistics should be all about. When Firth said so in 1957, it seemed outdated, superseded by a very different view of what linguistics should be all about. When Labov said so, after a decade or so during which the "trivial proceeding" of formalist linguistics had been dominant, it struck a dissident, even revolutionary note and was taken to be a radical change of approach. In the early 1970s, circumstances had become favourable for the emergence of the kind of linguistics that Firth had spent a lifetime proposing. But by then he had been dead for over 10 years and his work apparently forgotten, if it was ever known at all. Labov makes no reference to it.

For Firth, then, as for Labov, linguistics is essentially the study of language in its social context. And it is the concept of context that he proposes as providing the central unifying principle of his theory. Perhaps the best known notion that has survived from this collection of papers is that of the context of situation. As Firth acknowledges, the phrase is taken over from Malinowski, but he gives it a somewhat different meaning. Whereas Malinowski thinks of it as an actually occurring state of affairs, "an ordered series of events considered as *in rebus*" (182), Firth conceives of it in more abstract terms:

> My view was, and still is, that "context of situation" is best used as a suitable schematic construct to apply to language events, and that it is a group of related categories at a different level from grammatical categories but rather of the same abstract nature. A context of situation for linguistic work brings into relation the following categories:
>
> A. The relevant features of participants: persons, personalities.
>   (i) The verbal action of the participants.
>   (ii) The non-verbal action of the participants.
> B. The relevant objects.
> C. The effect of the verbal action. (182)

Firth's concern for the description of "language events" anticipates Hymes' discussion of "speech events" in his paper *The Ethnography of Speaking* first published 7 years later in 1962 (and reprinted in Fishman 1968). Hymes' description of factors in the speech event and their corresponding functions can be said to be a more specific formulation of these "features" that Firth refers to here. Hymes does not see it in this way, however. He represents his description as a development of the ideas of Jakobson (Jakobson 1960), and Firth is only given a nod of recognition in passing. One can see why. Jakobson's schematic construct is a model of coherence compared with Firth's, and much easier to interpret and to apply.

For it has to be said that although Firth prefigures future developments, his schematic construct does not give us much to go on. The specification of categories clearly depends on which features are to be identified as relevant and which are not, and Firth gives no indication of how this might be determined. In applying this schema, how do we know which features in the situation to disregard as simply contingent and which to take as typical of the category? How do we know what a particular language event is an example *of*. With the crucial condition of relevance left in conceptual limbo, it is hard to see how this construct can be put to procedural use. For all that, the kind of programme that

Firth was proposing was remarkably innovative at the time and a precursor of future enquiry. What he was trying to get at was a set of contextual factors that act upon linguistic forms to give them their communicative significance. In doing so he anticipated not only the study of language in its social context in general, but developments in pragmatics, in particular as related to speech act theory (Searle 1969).

What speech act theory does is to take up this issue of relevance. The features that Firth refers to become relevant as realizations of conditions on speech acts, which can themselves be identified as particular configurations of speech act factors as described by Jakobson and Hymes. Thus we process what is said, and who says it in the light of our social knowledge of what counts as particular acts of communication. We regulate our attention to attend only to those features of the participants and their actions that lead us to determine what propositional and illocutionary acts they are performing. What features of the language event are relevant in a particular case are those factors in the speech event which are assigned significance as actualizations of abstract speech act conditions. And what Firth refers to as "the effect of the verbal action" is precisely the third kind of pragmatic meaning that Searle discusses, namely its perlocutionary effect.

There are indications that Firth himself thought at times along speech act lines, or at least in terms of speech functions rather than the situations in which they typically occur. In his paper *The Technique of Semantics*, written in 1935, 15 years earlier than *Personality and Language in Society*, having anticipated his later paper by arguing the need for "the adequate description and classification of contexts of situation" (28) he goes on to concede that "It is perhaps easier to suggest types of linguistic function than to classify situations", and then provides a list of such functions in a passage that could have been written by Hymes himself, and which might indeed serve as the programmatic agenda for current work in pragmatics.

> Such would be, for instance, the language of agreement, encouragement, endorsement, of disagreement and condemnation. As language is a ways of dealing with people and things, a way of behaving and of making others behave, we could add many types of function – wishing, blessing, cursing, boasting, the language of challenge and appeal, or with intent to cold-shoulder, to belittle, to annoy or hurt, even to a declaration of enmity. The use of words to inhibit hostile action, or to delay or modify it, or conceal one's intention are very interesting and important "meanings". Not must we forget the language of social flattery and love-making, of praise and blame, of propaganda and persuasion (31).

While recognizing that it is easier to classify functions, Firth, somewhat perversely one might think, preferred not to do so but to attempt the more difficult task of classifying situations instead. The result, as we have noted, is far from satisfactory. Nevertheless, his "schematic construct" can be seen as a rough and provisional draft for a pragmatic account of language, and the subsequent and more explicit enquiry into speech acts and functions, one might suggest, took on where he left off.

It is unlikely that Searle, for one, would see it in this way (he makes no mention of Firth). It is unlikely too that Firth would either. He makes no reference to pragmatics anywhere in his writing, and the term itself does not appear in his Index, so we must assume that it has no part in his theory. The term that does occur *passim* in these papers, and that does figure in his Index is "semantics".

And here we come to the central question of how this schematic construct of context of situation figures in Firth's general linguistic theory. The answer is indicated in the way he describes this construct: its categories are, he tells us, of "the same abstract nature" as grammatical categories but at a different level. For him, levels of language are ordered along a single scale, from phonology to context of situation, each with its own meaning as a linguistic event, and without any discontinuity of description. Thus all linguistic statements are statements of meaning. As he puts it:

> The context of situation is a convenient abstraction at the social level of analysis and forms the basis of the hierarchy of techniques for the statement of meanings. The statement of meaning cannot be achieved by one analysis, at one level, in one fell swoop. Having made the first abstraction and having treated the social process of speaking by applying the above-mentioned set of categories grouped in the context of situation, descriptive linguistics then proceeds by a method rather like the dispersion of light of mixed wave-lengths into a spectrum ... ..Descriptive linguistics is thus a sort of hierarchy of techniques, by means of which the meaning of linguistic events may be, as it were, dispersed in a spectrum of specialized statements. (183)

This view of meaning as an inherent feature of language at all levels would seem on the face of it to be in stark contrast with Chomsky's "clear statement of the independence of grammar from meaning" (Cook 2007: 124). But the contrast is, in some respects at least, only apparent. For Firth's notion of meaning is very broad and embraces not only what linguistic items denote semantically, but the relationships they contract with others. Thus part of the meaning of a word is how it collocates with other words, but as formal and not as lexical items. As Firth puts it in his paper *Modes of Meaning*: "Meaning by collocation is an abstraction at the syntagmatic level and is not directly concerned with the conceptual or idea approach to the meaning of words. One of the meanings of night is its collocability with dark, and of dark, of course, collocation with night" (196).

But if this meaning is non-conceptual and simply a function of syntagmatic lexical co-occurrence, then there seems no reason why we should not extend this principle and apply it to grammatical relations as well. Thus we can say that the meaning of *night* is that it contracts a syntagmatic relationship with *the* to form a noun phrase *the night*, which then itself relates syntagmatically to a verb phrase *was dark*, and so on. So meaning, it would seem, can also be the property of syntactic constituency, and on this account, Chomsky is making statements of meaning all the time.

Meaning for Firth, then, is essentially a function of co-occurrence at any level of language, and the general term he uses to refer to it was "context". The co-occurrence that relates linguistic forms to external factors is accounted for by the schematic construct of the context of situation. But this is seen as related to all other realizations of context in the internal co-occurrence relations of linguistic items. So, the "spectrum of specialized statements" involves identifying contextual relations within and between all levels of linguistic description. As Firth puts it:

> Meaning, that is to say, is to be regarded as a complex of contextual relations, and phonetics, grammar, lexicography, and semantics each handles its own components of the complex in its appropriate context. (19)

This statement appears in the early paper, *The Technique of Semantics*, but is repeated in Firth's synopsis of his theory published in 1957 (Palmer 1968). Later in the same paper, he describes the technique of analysis as

> [a] serial contextualization of our facts, context within context, each one being a function, an organ of the bigger context and all contexts finding a place in what may be called the context of culture. (32)

There is no further elaboration in this, or in any other paper, of what the context of culture consists of – certainly no schematic construct of it is provided – so how all the other contexts find a place in it remains unclear.

What *is* clear is that for Firth context is the central integrating concept in his theory: there is meaning at all levels of linguistic description, and this meaning is related in that it is always a function of contextual co-occurrence. The different bands of the spectrum are all of the same kind, whether they have to do with social situation or lexis or phonetics – context within context, it is contexts, so to speak, "all the way down". The difficulty is that, although Firth has extremely insightful things to say about co-occurrence at different levels, there is a notable absence of any demonstration as to how they are to be related. He states that they should be, and leaves it at that.

Firth, then, believed that in these papers he was presenting an integrated theory whereby language would be dispersed into different bands like the dispersion of light in a spectrum, with each band alike in kind, consisting of categories of the same type and conforming to the same contextual principle. But the integration is largely an illusion brought about by a terminological sleight of hand, namely by the use of the term context to cover quite different kinds of relation: intra-linguistic on the one hand, extra-linguistic on the other. Though some linguists have subsequently given a token terminological recognition of the distinction by using "co-text" to refer to the former, the term "context" is still quite commonly used in synonymous reference to both. However, a failure to make the distinction, as I have argued in some detail elsewhere (Widdowson 2004) leads to a good deal of confusion, and, of particular relevance to a consideration of Firth and his linguistic heritage, unwarranted claims about what a linguistic theory can account for.

As we have noted, Firth deplored the kind of abstract systematic formalism that he associated with Saussure, and believed that linguistic theory should engage with the experienced reality of language and be concerned with "linguistic events in the social process", hence his insistence on the primacy of the context of situation. But in conceiving of this as a level of language in the same abstract categorical terms as all other levels, as another band in the spectrum, Firth is in effect being a systematic formalist himself, and his engagement with the actual reality of language use is really only apparent. For this reality cannot be reduced to the categorical terms of a linguistic system. What people know of their language, the encoded semantic resource for making meaning, or what Halliday calls "meaning potential" is one thing. How they draw on this resource to make meaning pragmatically, the manifold ways in which they realize this potential is an entirely different matter. You can pin down the potential in systematic, indeed systemic, terms, but not its realizations, for these crucially depend on how internal linguistic categories relate to extra-linguistic contextual factors. It was the recognition of the essential difference between the potential, which you can describe as a system, and its realizations, which you cannot, that motivated Saussure to make the distinction between *langue/parole* that Firth objects to so strongly. But he gets rid of the distinction by effectively reducing everything to *langue*: what people know of their language and what they actually do with it are of the same order of categorical abstraction. Thus, for Firth, linguistic potential subsumes its realization in language events, and so there is no such thing as pragmatics: all meaning is semantic.

Such a view perhaps represents Firth's most influential legacy to subsequent linguistic thinking, especially in the work of Michael Halliday. For Halliday too, it would seem, thinks of meaning along similar semantic lines, as encoded in intra-linguistic categories. His grammar, he says, is "at once both a grammar of the system and a grammar of the text" (Halliday 1994: xxii). It is thus both systemic and functional and the claim seems to be that in accounting for the meaning potential of clauses as abstract systems it provides the means at the same time for describing its functional realization in the production of actual texts. I have argued that Firth is able to bring extra and intra-linguistic into the same integrated system by invoking the unifying concept of context. Halliday does the same by invoking the concept of function. But just as the term "context" can mean two very different things, so can the term "function". Halliday's grammar is functional in the sense that its categories reflect the social functions that the language has evolved to serve. They are the semantic encodings of past pragmatic processes and represent the potential that has been generalized from former realizations, and as such can be seen as a closer approximation to experienced language than the categories of a formalist grammar. But in the actual use of language, this potential is realized anew in different pragmatic ways under the influence of various language-external contextual factors. Though what people mean by what they say must to some degree be constrained by the semantics of their language, it cannot be determined by it. The pragmatic functions of language use cannot be equated with the semantic functions in a systemic grammar.

That would seem to be obvious enough. And yet it is not uncommonly assumed that these functions *can* be equated. A good deal of critical discourse analysis, for example, seems to proceed on this assumption. Critical discourse analysts like Fairclough, for example, explicitly state that they take their linguistic bearings from Halliday, and so, unknowingly perhaps, follow Firthian tradition. They take Halliday's theory of language as particularly well-suited to their enquiry on the grounds that it "stresses its multifunctionality, which sees any text as simultaneously enacting what Halliday calls the 'ideational','interpersonal' and 'textual' functions of language" (Fairclough 1995: 131). But these are external pragmatic functions: the internal semantic functions that encode them in the grammar are formalized as systems of transitivity, mood and theme. But Fairclough fuses the two and takes the grammar as providing descriptive categories that are functional and textual as well, and carries out his analysis by applying them. In consequence, interpretation is derived from an analysis of texts in dissociation from extra-linguistic contextual considerations as if the texts were indeed a direct projection of semantic encodings (for further discussion see Widdowson 2004).

Firth's distrust of formalism and his conviction that linguistics should engage with language as it actually occurs are nowadays widely shared. It has become almost axiomatic for many linguists that the closer their enquiry can get to the reality of language as experienced by its users the better. Such realism has its obvious attractions. But it raises the tricky question of just how close linguistics can get without compromising its basic principles of enquiry. And how far the closeness is apparent rather than real. Linguistics as a discipline must always deal in abstractions of one kind or another and can never replicate what makes language real for its users. Some particulars are always lost in general statements, and only when data is filtered through some kind of theoretical abstraction can it become evidence. All this is obvious, but obvious or not, it does not prevent linguists making claims that their particular line of enquiry captures the reality of language whereas others do not.

Corpus linguistics is a case in point. Analysis of corpora by computer have now revealed detailed patterns of idiomaticity, of collocation and colligation in texts hitherto unsuspected, and in so doing have provided descriptive substantiation of the insights that Firth expressed over fifty years earlier. But though this undoubtedly reveals new linguistic facts about one aspect of language, namely the texts people produce, it does not represent the discourse process, the pragmatic interplay of linguistic and contextual factors that make the texts a reality for their producers.

This is not to say that linguistics should not deal with actually occurring language, what Firth refers to as "linguistic events in the social process". As Labov says: "It seems natural enough that the basic data for any form of general linguistics would be the language as it is used by native speakers communicating with each other in everyday life" (Labov 1972: 184).

But using the communication of everyday life as basic data is not at all the same thing as representing the speakers' communicative experience (whether native or not). More than once in *Papers in Linguistics*, Firth stresses how important it is for theory to make a "renewal of connection" with actually occurring language, and it is, of course, essential for linguistics as an empirical enquiry that its abstract categories should be validated by drawing on actual language data as evidence. But this is bound to be a selective process: linguists will, naturally enough, extract from the data what is relevant to their particular theoretical perspective and disregard the rest. They might, like Labov and Firth, prefer a broad functional perspective that takes in social aspects of language use, or a narrow formalist one that does not. But there must always be a limit on what can be taken in, and the question is the essentially ideological one of what that limit should be. The very process of converting data into evidence by extraction and abstraction inevitably puts any linguistic statement at a remove from the reality of language as experienced by its users. As we saw earlier, Firth objected to Saussure's notion of *langue* on the grounds that "actual people do not talk such 'a language' ". But actual people do not talk in the abstract categories that he proposed either and he can only cope with "language events in the social process" by removing them from the social process and transforming them into a theoretical construct.

But if linguistics cannot of its disciplinary nature deal with language events in the social process as they are actually experienced by people in everyday life, the claim of applied linguistics is that it can. This is an area of enquiry that is "concerned with the relation of knowledge about language to decision making in the real world" (Cook 2003: 5) Here, the renewal of connection is reversed. It is not a matter of establishing how far the data of actual language experience can be adduced to substantiate abstract categories, but of how these categories can be referred back to the experienced reality from which they were abstracted so as to present it in a different light. The question for applied linguistics is not how far models of linguistic description can be empirically validated, but how far they can be used to give us a different take on reality, to enable us to make sense of experience, and reformulate our "real world problems" in ways that might make them more amenable to solution. This, as I have argued elsewhere (Widdowson 2005) involves a process of mediation between disciplinary expertise and the "folk" experience of language in domains of actual use.

What is particularly interesting, and instructive, about these *Papers in Linguistics* is that they exemplify so clearly these issues about the relationship of linguistics to the language of everyday life as experienced by its users. Firth had insightful things to say about language at different levels, many of which anticipated later developments, but the problem was that he felt the need to integrate them into one comprehensive and unitary theory of contextual meaning.

In reading these papers, noting how strikingly perceptive and prescient particular observations are, and how vague and elusive the general theory that supposedly informs them, one is reminded of the old Greek saying about the hedgehog and the fox that Isiah Berlin cites in his celebrated essay on Tolstoy (Berlin 1953): "The fox knows many things, but the hedgehog knows one big thing". Berlin uses the saying to distinguish what he sees as two fundamentally different kinds of "intellectual and artistic personality". On the one hand, we have the hedgehogs "who relate everything to a single central vision, one system less or more coherent or articulate, in terms of which they understand, think and feel – a single, universal, organizing principle in terms of which alone all that they are and say has significance".

Chomsky, with his quest for a universal organizing principle, is the hedgehog of linguistics *par excellence*. He knows one big thing. The foxes, on the other hand

> pursue many ends, often unrelated and even contradictory .... their thought is scattered or diffused, moving on many levels seizing upon the essence of a vast variety of experiences and objects for what they are in themselves, without consciously or unconsciously, seeking to fit them into, or exclude them from, any one unchanging, all-embracing, sometimes self-contradictory and incomplete, at times fanatical, unitary inner vision.
>
> (Berlin 1953: 7–8)

This sounds very like Firth, moving on many different linguistic levels, the fox who knows many things. The problem was that he aspired to be a hedgehog. He was not content to focus on things "for what they are in themselves" but sought to fit them into his "all-embracing unitary inner vision", which if not "incomplete" was elusive of formulation, and, as I have argued, "self-contradictory" into the bargain. But it is this very effort to reconcile these contraries that makes Firth so interesting, and so relevant to our current concerns. For his attempt to bring so many things, so many disparate aspects of language, within one big thing, one comprehensive abstract linguistic system, raises fundamental issues about what linguistics can in principle account for and what it cannot, and about what the role of applied linguistics might be in making linguistics relevant to problems that arise from people's actual experience of "language events" in the real world.

2 Linguistic creativity and Jakobson's poetic function

As with a number of terms current in linguistics, "creativity" can be defined in different, indeed contradictory ways. One of them, that of Chomsky (1965), defines it as an intrinsic generative property of the linguistic code which provides for the production of an infinite number of sentences in conformity with the same set of rules. In Carter (2004), on the other hand, creativity is defined quite differently as a property of the communicative use of language in context, and it is this conception of creativity that is the focus of attention in a special issue of *Applied Linguistics* (Vol. 29.3) As the editors put it: "[I]t can be identified broadly as a property of all language use in that language users do not simply reproduce but recreate, refashion, and recontextualize linguistic and cultural resources in the act of communicating ..." (Swann and Maybin 2007: 491).

In this definition, creativity is not a function of reproductive conformity, but of the pragmatic exploitation of communicative possibilities. Interestingly, however, having defined creativity in these general pragmatic terms, the editors then introduce a third definition: "Our focus in the special issue", they say, "is more specific" in that it deals with "creativity in its poetic sense" (491). The question arises as to how then this poetic creativity is to be defined and how (or) whether it can be related to creativity of a more general pragmatic kind.

The theorist who is cited to give authority to this more specific focus on poetic creativity is Roman Jakobson and his celebrated specification of factors in the speech event (Jakobson 1960). Such creativity is equated with his notion of the poetic function as coming about by a "focus on the message for its own sake". The first thing we need to be clear about, however, is that the factor that Jakobson is referring to here is the message *form*, its linguistic wording, and not its content. This distinction between message content and form is not only crucial to an understanding of what Jakobson is proposing, but, as we shall see, central to the general question of the relationship between pragmatic and poetic creativity. For if creativity is to equated with the poetic function in this Jakobsonian sense, it follows that it will come about whenever there is a focus on the form of a particular message, whatever its content. One might note, in passing, that such a conclusion is not likely to be welcome in SLA circles where focus on form is seen as counter-productive and responsible for deflecting focus away from meaning, and arresting the natural process of language

---

Note: Revised from the article 2008. Language creativity and the poetic function. A response to Swann and Maybin. *Applied Linguistics* 29 (3). 503–508.

https://doi.org/10.1515/9783110619669-005

acquisition. How can it be, one might wonder, that a focus on form can be commended as essentially creative on the one hand, and condemned as essentially uncreative on the other? This is, surely, a question worth pondering.

But Jakobson has more to say about the poetic function. He goes on to suggest how this focusing on form is brought about: "The poetic function projects the principle of equivalence from the axis of selection into the axis of combination" (Jakobson 1960: 358).

This perhaps calls for a little elucidation. Linguistic elements at any level (sounds, words, grammatical constituents, phrases) are paradigmatically classified by their equal potentiality of occurrence in a syntagmatic combination. Thus, to take a simple example, all words that can occur as adjectives in the noun phrase *the ... sea* are equivalent in that any one that is selected would complete the grammatical combination:, *the deep sea, the salt sea, the cruel sea* and so on. If more than one is selected over and above syntactic requirement, this equivalence is then projected into the axis of combination and the poetic function realized: *the deep, salt, cruel sea*. This principle, simple enough in itself, can of course result in complex patterns when it operates across linguistic levels, as in the combination of recurrent sounds, words and phrases in this quotation from Dylan Thomas's *Under Milk Wood*: "... the sloe black, slow, black, crow black, fishing boat-bobbing sea."

What needs to be noted is that on this Jakobsonian account the poetic function is essentially a matter of repetitive conformity to rule. The linguistic elements involved are formally equivalent, but they are equivalent only at one level and not another: phonologically but not lexically equivalent like *sloe/slow/crow*, grammatically but not lexically equivalent like *sloe black /slow/black* and so on. So the sameness and difference interrelate in a creative complementarity. Jakobson, then, defines the poetic function in strictly formalist terms: it is a function of focus on form, and this focus comes about by the non-canonical operation of linguistic rules. It is based on the assumption that the normal, unmarked combination consists of one filler per slot as formally required, and no more. If you use more than one filler – a sequence of adjectives, for example, rather than just one, as in the examples cited earlier, then there is a transfer of equivalence, the form is recognized as a departure from the canonical norm, and the poetic function is automatically achieved.

The first point that might be made about this is that this transfer of equivalence is not the only way in which a message form can be marked as abnormal and draw attention to itself. A single filler in the slot can serve the purpose, as would be the case if Dylan Thomas had selected only the word *slow* as the adjective in the noun phrase slot *the ... sea*. The unusual, unexpected. collocation would focus attention on form. Or consider Matthew Arnold's line: *The unplumbed, salt, estranging sea*. Here it is the selection of the words *unplumbed* and *estranging* that makes the message form marked, as much if not more than their formal equivalence as adjectives. Conversely, of course, one can have instances of multiple slot filling (*silly old fool, bright young thing*) that are not collocationally marked at all. But notice that collocational markedness is not a feature of the poetic function in Jakobson's definition, for he is only concerned with the formal properties of the language code and not with how these are realized in actual co-textual usage.

Not only is he not concerned with co-text, but he is not concerned with context either, and this can be said to make his poetic function even less satisfactory as an account of creativity. The essential point here is that when language is put to contextual use, the message form is not focused on formally *for its own sake*, but pragmatically for the sake of the message as a contextually dependent formulation of communicative intent. We mark the form in some way for some purpose – to give some point to what we say, to create an effect. So if we are to deal specifically with "poetic" creativity, it is difficult to see how this can be done without taking more general pragmatic considerations into account. The question is: how can this be done – how can Jakobson's focus on the message form be defined in pragmatic terms so that his poetic function actually functions to poetic effect.

Message form is of course only one of the factors in Jakobson's account of the speech event, the others being addresser, addressee, context, contact and code. Though the factors are all present, or presupposed, different kinds of speech event will relate them in different ways, and when one is given primary focus, the corresponding function will be given prominence. The problem with Jakobson's formalist definition of the poetic function is that it is entirely to do with linguistic manipulation, and so relates message form only to code and to no other factor. But clearly if we are to consider the pragmatic effect of such manipulation, we need to relate the message form to the other factors as well – to addresser, addressee, context and contact. Thus, a message form might be a striking example of code manipulation, but fail to have any creative effect in a particular context. Similarly, a message form may be given particular focus in relation to the contact factor, simply to counter noise in the channel and ensure access to the message content. So what we need is some way of accounting for how message form relates to other factors in particular instances of communication.

One obvious way of doing this is shift perspective and consider how these speech event factors might serve as variables for the characterization of different speech acts as defined in Searle (1969). What Searle does is to give values to these variables as conditions that have to be satisfied for an expression to count as having a particular illocutionary force. What counts as a warning, for example, or a promise, or whatever, will depend in part on the wording (the message form) but in relation to who says it (addresser) to whom (addresser) and where, and in what circumstances of assumed shared knowledge (context). Similarly, effective reference, the successful performance of a propositional act, will also bring these factors into play. Now what one might propose is that instead of thinking of a focus on the message form in relation to code, as Jakobson does, and as arising as a non-conformity to a canonical encoding, which as such has no pragmatic, and so no creative significance, we might retain the notion of non-conformity, but in relation to the minimal requirements for speech act performance. In other words, we transfer the notion of canonical norm from sentence constituents to speech act conditions and suggest that attention is drawn to message form when the wording of a communication goes beyond what is needed to satisfy referential and illocutionary requirement.

To conform to a norm is, of course, to do what is customary and expected, in short to co-operate. This is a cue for Grice to make his entrance in the discussion. The maxims of his co-operative principle (Grice 1975) can be said to represent the canonical norm of communicative conventions that are presupposed as common knowledge. They can be said to regulate the minimal satisfaction of speech act conditions. This is not, of course, to say that these maxims are always adhered to and speech act conditions always minimally satisfied. The point is that the maxims represent a presupposed prototypical norm, a set of default values, and that any knowing non-adherence is marked and taken to imply some significance, an extra dimension of meaning not directly signalled by what is actually said. In other words, maxim violation creates implicatures. Now, as Grice himself points out, three of these maxims have to do with what is said, that is to say with message content: say as much as is required and no more (quantity), say what you believe to be true (quality), say what is relevant (relation). Here, the message form itself is not a determining factor. In the case of the fourth maxim (manner), however, it most decidedly is:

> ... under the category of MANNER, which I understand as relating not (like the previous categories) to what is said but rather to HOW what is said is said, I include the supermaxim – "Be perspicuous" – and various maxims such as:
> 1. Avoid obscurity of expression.
> 2. Avoid ambiguity.
> 3. Be brief (avoid unnecessary prolixity)
> 4. Be orderly. (Grice 1975: 46)

To co-operate by respecting these maxims of manner is to assign the message form an enabling function whereby it serves only to bring the other speech act factors into play in the achievement of propositional and illocutionary meaning. We need to notice, however, that these manner maxims (like all the others of the co-operative principle) are not absolute but relative to different speech act conditions, that is to say to what is required by conventional norms. As Grice makes clear, the manner maxim is only violated when the language produced is less perspicuous than is required by the kind of communication concerned. Some kinds will, as a matter of normal convention, require less perspicuity than others. If you violate the maxim by being abnormally obscure, ambiguous, prolix (for example, by being repetitive) or disorderly you focus on the form itself as significant and create an implicature. You are doing more with the language, so to speak, than immediately meets the eye, or the ear: ideationally, for example, to represent some novel take on conventional reality, interpersonally to impress, amuse, establish rapport and so on. You are, in short making the language distinctive so as to create a special effect – a perlocutionary effect, in speech act terms.

I would suggest then that "creativity in its poetic sense" cannot be equated with Jakobson's formalist concept of the poetic function as a "focus on the message for its own sake" but needs to be defined in pragmatic terms as a motivated violation of the manner maxim which focuses on the message form by disrupting normal expectations and so creates implicatures of one kind or another.

When we shift attention in this way from a focus on message form in relation only to the code, to its relation to the other factors in the speech event in actual and motivated usage, it becomes clear that this creativity both depends on, and subverts, the normal process of text production. As work in corpus linguistics has made apparent, this process involves the use of recurrent co-textual patterns, ready-made sequences, with text being assembled on what John Sinclair refers to as the "idiom principle": "The principle of idiom is that a language user has available to him or her a large number of semi-preconstructed phrases that constitute single choices, even though they might appear to be analysable into segments" (Sinclair 1991a: 110).

A focusing on the message form involves a de-construction of these semi-constructed patterns in some way, restoring the separate value of their constituent segments by applying what Sinclair refers to as the "open choice" principle. Thus creativity is in direct opposition to idiomaticity, a shift from the normal idiom principle to the abnormal open-choice principle. But if we are to think of creativity in the specific poetic sense, the shift has to be taken as deliberate and motivated. What becomes relevant here is the relationship between the message form and the factors of addresser and addressee. An addresser may mark a message form as abnormal with the intention of its being noticed so as to give rise to a particular implicature. But the addressee may fail to notice the abnormality, or interpret it as having a different implicature. Equally, of course, the marking may be inadvertent and the addressee assign a implicature where none is intended at all. It follows that creativity, in the poetic sense we are considering, cannot be directly inferred on the basis of textual evidence. In the case of the co-textual patterns that result from the application of the idiom principle, if a language user does not have these patterns available as single choices, he or she obviously cannot intentionally disrupt them. Familiarity with such patterns is acquired naturally by the native speakers of a language community and are used as markers of communal identity. It is that part of communicative competence that Hymes refers to as a knowledge of "whether (and to what degree) something is in fact done, actually performed, and what its doing entails" (Hymes 1972: 282). For non-members of the community, as users as well as learners of the language, the acquisition of such knowledge requires considerable exposure to these conventional norms of communal usage, and a readiness to conform to them, so such knowledge necessarily takes time to acquire, if it is acquired at all. Such language users resort to the open choice principle by necessity not choice and so their scope for creativity, in the poetic sense, is bound to be limited.

But this does not prevent them from being creative in a more general pragmatic sense, from appropriating and exploiting, in Halliday's phrase, the "meaning potential" of the language – but potential understood as something that goes beyond what has been hitherto conventionally encoded to include the unrealized resources of what I have called elsewhere "the virtual language" (Widdowson 2003: Ch. 5). Necessity is the mother of invention, and those who have only a limited knowledge of the established linguistic code, or of the patterns of attested native speaker usage, have perforce to make creative use of the resources at their disposal as best they can to express themselves. This kind of general pragmatic creativity is strikingly evident in the international use of English as a lingua franca which shows very clearly how effectively the meaning potential of the language can be realized in communicative interaction without being constrained to conform to native speaker norms (see, e.g., Seidlhofer and Widdowson 2007).

3 Applied linguistics, interdisciplinarity and disparate realities

In his preface to *The Oxford Handbook of Applied Linguistics*, its editor, Robert Kaplan notes in his preface that the diversity of topics included within the field has the consequence that "applied linguistics is a difficult notion to define" (Kaplan 2002: vii), and he makes it clear that it is not his purpose to provide a definition. Elusive of definition though it may be, however, there are two things that are generally said to characterize work that is undertaken in the name of applied linguistics. One is that it deals with problems in the "real world": "problems in the world in which language is implicated", as Cook puts it (Cook 2003: 5). The second is that it is, of its nature, interdisciplinary: it does not, in spite of its name, draw only on linguistics but on a much wider range of scholarly enquiry. The two features are taken to be related in that the second follows by implication from the first: to solve real-world problems you need to be interdisciplinary. This is made quite explicit in an editorial of the principal journal in the field: "It is perhaps uncontroversial to claim that applied linguistics, in becoming more interdisciplinary, is better prepared for the principled handling of a range of distinct types of real world issues, and more critically aware of its methodologies" (Bygate and Kramsch 2000: 2).

The claim here is that the more interdisciplinary applied linguistics is, the more capable it becomes of dealing with problems in the real world. This might be taken as uncontroversial, but that does not make it valid. And it seems to me that on closer inspection, it turns out to be a very questionable claim indeed, and that far from interdisciplinarity leading to a critical awareness of methodological issues, it actually distracts attention from them.

The belief in interdisciplinarity as the essential enabling feature of applied linguistics rests, I think, on rather shaky foundations. But a belief does not have to be valid to be effective as a basis for action, and I want to stress that in raising questions about this belief, I do not deny the value of the work that has been inspired by it. I recognize that much has been achieved in the field of applied linguistics through the publications and associations that bear its name.

One such association is the British Association of Applied Linguistics (BAAL). This serves an indispensable service in all kinds of ways, and has many an achievement to its credit. I would not want to question this. What I am concerned

---

Note: Revised version of a chapter in Bruthiaux, P., D. Atkinson, W. G. Eggington, W. Grabe & V. Ramanathan (eds.). 2005. *Directions in applied linguistics. Essays in Honor of Robert B. Kaplan*, 12–25. Multilingual Matters.

with, however, is how it defines what it stands for. As we might expect, interdisciplinarity figures prominently. As stated in its newsletter (Number 82, 2006) its aims "are to promote the study of language in use", and "to foster interdisciplinary collaboration" to that end. It has indeed incorporated the first of these aims in a slogan "Promoting understanding of language in use". This statement of aims prompts a number of questions. One might ask, for example, where the study of language learning and teaching comes in. This has perhaps been too exclusive a preoccupation of applied linguistics in the past, but that does not seem a good reason for now excluding it completely. One might argue, of course, that learning is a "kind" of language in use, but this surely smacks of casuistry. But leaving that aside, and returning to the main issue, one might ask what is distinctive about applied linguistics as described here. If its scope is to be confined to the study of language in use, then how does it differ from the discipline which defines its aims in the same terms, namely sociolinguistics? It is not a matter, it would seem, of collaborating with this discipline but of incorporating it. In which case, one wonders why there is a need for applied linguistics at all.

At this point we might invoke the first feature that is routinely said to characterize applied linguistics: its concern with real-world problems. But there is no mention of this in the BAAL Newsletter's statement of aims. Furthermore many sociolinguists would take the view that real-world problems fall within their purview as well, that their responsibility is not only to promote an understanding of language in use, but to intervene in linguistic affairs by correcting attitudes or protecting language diversity (see Trudgill 2002; Nettle and Romaine 2000). Labov goes so far as to say that the essential purpose of linguistic enquiry is to produce theories that can be used to "resolve questions about the real world", and he indicates what kinds of question he has in mind:

> A sober look at the world around us shows that matters of importance are matters of fact. There are some very large matters of fact: the origin of the universe, the direction of continental drift, the evolution of the human species. There are also specific matters of fact: the innocence or guilt of a particular individual. These are the questions to answer if we would achieve our fullest potential as thinking beings. (Labov 1988: 182)

Some of what Labov refers to as matters of fact, the origin of the universe, for example, can be seen as so remote from language as to be outside the scope of applied linguistics, no matter how comprehensive its conception. Others, like guilt and innocence, are not matters of fact of the same kind at all, and this brings up a crucial issue which I shall return to later. But the point to be made at present is that sociolinguistics would appear to be already engaged in what BAAL defines as the field of applied linguistics, and is indeed even assuming the problem solving role which BAAL's statement of aims actually makes no mention of at all.

For Labov, how problematic matters in the real world might be resolved is the prime motivation for his enquiry. There is no such motivation evident in the BAAL statement. Hence there is no indication of how dealing with "real world problems" might require the fostering of interdisciplinary collaboration. Here, one might suggest, there is too much concern with interdisciplinarity, not enough with the real world. Elsewhere, there are conceptions of applied linguistics which take adequate account of neither. An example here would be recent pronouncements about the necessary relevance of corpus descriptions to the design of language curricula. Thus Sinclair proposes a number of precepts for language teachers which derive directly and unilaterally from linguistic findings: "The precepts centre on data, and arise from observations about the nature of language. They are not concerned with psychological or pedagogical approaches to language teaching" (Sinclair 1997: 30).

The precepts are directed at resolving questions in the real world of language classrooms, but no account is taken of this reality, nor of the other disciplines which might conceivably bear on these questions. Paradoxically, these precepts invoke the concept of reality: the first enjoins teachers to "present real examples only" (ibid.). The reality invoked here, however, is that of native speaker users, not that of learners of the language in the contexts of classrooms. But it is this latter reality that pedagogy has to be concerned with: the problem to be addressed is not how one goes about describing the ways in which people actually use their own language, but how learners can be induced to learn a language which is not their own.

The confusion of two realities that is exemplified here brings us back to the two defining features of applied linguistics that I mentioned at the beginning, and to their relationship. The "real world" problems that applied linguistics purports to deal with arise from a direct experience of language in everyday life. Their reality is what I shall call that of the practical domain. It is the reality as lived and apprehended by what Niedzielski and Preston (2003) refer to as the "folk".[1] The other reality is that which is abstracted by the expertise of people initiated into the particular principles and procedures of enquiry which define a

---

[1] I intend this term in the sense of Niedzielski & Preston. They use it to refer to people without a specialist knowledge of the phenomena they experience. As they put it:

> We use folk to refer to those who are not trained professionals in the area under investigation (although we would not for one moment deny the fact that professional linguists themselves are a folk group, with their own rich set of beliefs). We definitely do not use

discipline. The realities of domain and discipline do not, of course, correspond (there would be no point in the discipline if they did), and where there is a conflict, it is generally the disciplinary expertise that is taken to represent the truth of the matter, and the ideas of the folk, based on direct experience, to be mistaken.

And often, of course they are. Developments in the disciplines of the "hard" physical sciences have demonstrated just how wrong the folk can be. The sun does not go round the world every day, as they might fondly imagine. What can be transmitted in sight and sound is not restricted by the natural physiological limitations of the organs of eye and ear. Things can be temporally present, and spatially absent at the same time. And so on. Although the folk may sense that there is a world beyond what they directly experience: "strange sights, things invisible to see" as John Donne has it, it is a mysterious one beyond human control. Puck, in Shakespeare's *A Midsummer Night's Dream*, may miraculously "put a girdle round the earth in forty minutes", but he had magical powers quite beyond human reach. Nowadays, the earth is girdled round a million times in seconds by means of electronic technology, and there's nothing miraculous about that. So expertise in the physical sciences, borne out by technological application, reveals the limitations of folk belief based on experience, and it is easy to dismiss this folk belief as the quaint vestige of unfounded superstition, remote from the real world of hard fact, and to be dispelled wherever possible.

And this is how such belief does tend to be dismissed when it comes to matters of language. As Niedzielski & Preston put it:

> Folk linguistics has not fared well in the history of the science, and linguists have generally taken as "us" versus "them" position. From a scientific perspective, folk beliefs about language are, at best, innocent misunderstandings of language (perhaps only minor impediments to introductory linguistic instruction) or, at worst, the bases of prejudice, leading to the continuation, reformulation, rationalization, justification, and even development of a variety of social injustices.   (Niedzielski and Preston 2003: 1)

The common assumption is that accounts of language provided by disciplinary enquiry will necessarily, as with the "hard" physical sciences, go beyond appearances and reveal some underlying essential reality that the folk have

---

> folk to refer to rustic, ignorant, uneducated, backward, primitive, minority, isolated, marginalized, or lower status groups or individuals.   (Niedzielski and Preston 2003: xviii)

The term is then a relative one and people who are expert in one particular discipline will be the folk in regard to another.

hitherto failed to appreciate. Where folk ideas are out of step, they are misconceived. One difficulty with this assumption of privileged access to the truth is that linguistic accounts of language are not infrequently out of step with each other. Structuralist accounts of a taxonomic kind are, according to generativists, misconceived, and generativist accounts in their turn are, according to functionalists, misconceived as well. Corpus linguists tell us that any grammar not based on the observation of actually occurring language behaviour is a misrepresentation. The authors of the recent Cambridge Grammar of English (Huddleston and Pullum 2002) claim that they have come up with a correct description of some aspects of English that all preceding grammarians got wrong. Other linguists tell us that there are no rules of grammar at all, so that presumably any attempt to describe them at all is futile.

By what criteria are we supposed to decide which of these alternative versions of linguistic reality is to be taken as authoritative, as revealing where the folk is in error? For disciplinary enquiry seems on the face of it to be just as prone to misunderstanding and prejudice as the unenlightened beliefs it is supposed to dispel. Perhaps the difference lies in the fact that the discipline is indeed disciplined, in that its theories and findings are under strict conceptual control, intellectually rigorous and rationally well-founded, quite unlike the rather random intuitive notions of the folk. But this does not always seem to be the case either.

Linguists, for example, will routinely assert that, contrary to popular belief, all languages are equal. This may be a morally laudable position to take, but it is not one for which any empirical substantiation, rigorous or otherwise, is provided, and it is difficult to see how it could be. It is a matter of faith, not a matter of fact. Indeed, as a matter of fact, the folk position would seem to be more tenable: all languages are certainly not equal in terms of their perceived relative complexity, or their status in particular communities. Again, sociolinguistics will routinely argue that language variation and change are natural social processes, and that it is futile to impede them, as some folk not infrequently do by complaining about linguistic abuse and deploring the decline in standards. But this argument is only applied in support of linguistic diversity, and when precisely the same process of adaptation to changing social circumstances leads to a diminishing of diversity and an increasing "homogenization", as with the case of the global spread of English, the argument apparently no longer applies (see again Nettle and Romaine 2000; Trudgill 2002 and the discussion in Widdowson and Seidlhofer 2003). Homogenisation is, one might note, an odd concept to invoke, for it suggests that variation and change are not necessary and natural linguistic processes after all, but cease when homogenisation sets in. The argument now is that when the survival of declining languages is at stake, it is no longer futile or foolish to intervene to prevent change. The goal posts seem to have been shifted.

To say this is not at all to deny the *cause* of linguistic diversity, but to question the basis on which the *case* for it is presented. For this rests ultimately on moral belief and not on the consistent application of a principle of disciplinary enquiry. In short, the basis is one of prejudice – positive, benevolent, laudable, but prejudice all the same.

So though their proponents might wish to suggest otherwise, disciplines that deal with language are changeable, unstable, not always internally consistent. They are indeed very like language itself, and it is not surprising to find that the factors and forces that Thomas Kuhn identifies as responsible for shifts in disciplinary paradigms (Kuhn 1962) should parallel those adduced by sociolinguistics to account for language variation and change. In spite of the imprimatur of academic authority that the disciplines bear, whatever truth they reveal is always provisional and partial, and the imprimatur often has the effect of preventing us from noticing this.

Linguistics, like all disciplines devise ideal models of one kind or another, abstract constructs that give selective prominence to certain features of the experienced world and leave others out of the reckoning. It deals essentially in simplified constructs, versions of reality, from different perspectives and positions, which cannot of their nature capture what language actually is for the folk who experience it. This is very obviously the case with formalist models, of course, and they have been much criticized over recent years on that account, but it is also the case, less obviously, with linguistic descriptions which claim a closer involvement with how language actually functions in use. Thus, as we have noted, corpus linguistics claims to describe the actual facts of real language, but what is presented is an analysis of the language usage which folk produce in the pragmatic process of social interaction, but this is not at all the same as the process itself. The concordance is an analytic construct and as such is no closer than constituent analysis to what the folk actually experience as language (for further discussion see Widdowson 2000, 2003). Of course the concordance gets closer to what goes on in the real world in the sense that it deals with the data of actually occurring behaviour. As Labov says: "It seems natural enough that the basic data for any form of general linguistics would be the language as it is used by native speakers communicating with each other in everyday life" (Labov 1972: 184). But taking language use as data does not, of course, mean that the description based on it represents the experience of the native speakers using it.

Different areas and eras of the discipline of linguistics, then, present us with different kinds of abstraction, all of them at a remove from the actual domains of use from which they are abstracted. Perceptions shift as to what is of central importance about the nature of language, acted upon by a range of influences – socio-political attitudes, commercial interests, technological developments and so on. And as perceptions shift, so the perspectives of other disciplines will be seen as relevant as potential collaborative partners, and various kinds of interdisciplinary "hyphenated linguistics" will emerge in consequence (Spolsky 1998). Psychology has in the past been the preferred partner, and in the generative era, linguistics was taken to be a branch of cognitive psychology, language being seen essentially something in the mind (e.g. Chomsky 1972). Latterly sociology has been seen as the more relevant discipline for linguistics to collaborate with, language being seen as essentially a mode of social action (e.g. Fairclough 1992). But there are three points about interdisciplinary collaboration that we need to note.

The first is that the collaboration tends to be unilateral and to result in a hybrid that is not always recognized as a legitimate issue by both parties. The appropriation of ideas from another discipline will involve some readjustment whereby they are recontextualized to fit a conceptual scheme which is bound to be different in some respects from the one they originally belonged to. Interdisciplinarity sounds like something that is intellectually liberating, but it also has its reductive side. For it is not simply a matter of coupling two disciplines together, with each retaining its own identity and integrity, but of one discipline assuming a dominant role and drawing from the other whatever can be conveniently accommodated within its scheme of things. As a consequence, of course, the adaptation will always be open to the charge of distortion. Thus, for example, Bernstein suggests that Labov's sociolinguistics is sociologically flawed (Bernstein 1990), and Bernstein's own excursion into linguistics has in its turn been subject to criticism on similar grounds of disciplinary naivite (Stubbs 1980, 1983). Such criticism might sound captious, based on too purist and protectionist an attitude. But it is, after all, the purpose of disciplines to establish particular modes of abstraction and to define what is proper to their enquiry and what is not. They have no *raison d'etre* otherwise. In this respect it seems entirely reasonable for scholars to defend them from abuse. At the same time it will not do for scholars to be too protective of their patch, for this would be to deny the possibility of any change at all.

An interesting illustration of this occurred some 10 years ago, when the name of the French philosopher Jacques Derrida was put forward for an honorary doctorate at Oxford. In a letter in *The Times* newspaper (9.5.1992) a number of senior academics express their objections. The tone to begin with is relatively measured:

> M Derrida describes himself as philosopher, and his writings do indeed bear some of the marks of writings in that discipline. Their influence, however, has been to a striking degree almost entirely in fields outside philosophy – in departments of film studies, for example, or of French and English literature.
>
> In the eyes of philosophers, and certainly among those working in leading departments of philosophy throughout the world, M Derrida's work does not meet accepted standards of clarity and rigour.

In the eyes of the philosophers, then, (or those at Oxford at any rate) Derrida's work is only philosophical in pretence, for it has compromised the proper principles of that discipline by seeking to link it with others, including some of very doubtful character (film studies, for example). The Oxonians feel the "standards of clarity and rigour" in their custody are under threat, and the tone of the letter becomes increasingly agitated and acerbic. Reference is made to Derrida's "antics", his "tricks and gimmicks similar to those of the Dadaists or of the concrete poets" and to his "semi-intelligible attacks upon the values of reason, truth and scholarship". The attitude of the philosophers is far from philosophical in an idiomatic sense: they bristle in defence of their discipline.

The first point about interdisciplinary collaboration, then, is that it tends to be one-sided, with the consequence that the resulting hybrid is often seen as compromising the integrity of the donor discipline. A second point closely follows it: quite simply, if ideas are successfully absorbed, then their interdisciplinary nature disappears. If sociological or psychological concepts get integrated into linguistics, then you get a different perspective on language, and a different kind of linguistics. Interdisciplinarity is a notion that commands universal commendation, "a consummation devoutly to be wished", in that it seems to provide for the possibility of seeing things more comprehensively from a diversity of perspectives. This is an appealing idea, but it is also largely an illusion. For it is simply not possible to see things from two different perspectives at the same time. You can, of course, shift from one perspective to another at different times and this can often prove enlightening, if only to show how incomplete and partial different representations of reality can be. But the requirement for disciplinary consistency and coherence must set limits on how much diversity you can accommodate, and how comprehensive your vision can be. The fact of the matter is that if you want to see things steadily, you cannot see them whole.

And you cannot see them as they really are. We come to the third point about interdisciplinary collaboration: it necessarily takes place at a level of abstraction at a remove from what the folk experience in the practical domains of the real world. When we are concerned with linguistics, hyphenated or not, what is abstracted from this reality has to be referred back to it to provide empirical substantiation. This reality is transformed into language data that is drawn upon selectively to serve as evidence for theoretical or descriptive statement. Thus the enquiry remains at the level of ideal abstraction: it does not seek to represent language as experienced by the folk. Indeed, as suggested earlier, if it did, it would have no point and serve no purpose.

Now if we consider the claim that applied linguistics is an interdisciplinary area of enquiry, we come across two obvious difficulties. The first is that, unlike linguistics, there is no host discipline, so to speak, to be modified by ideas from other disciplines, no given perspective to be adjusted. If one takes linguistics as the host, then applied linguistics ceases to be distinctive because it simply becomes a hyphenated version. The only reason for indulging in interdisciplinarity would appear to be that it provides a way of meeting the second criterial feature of applied linguistics, namely that of engaging with real-world problems. But then we come up against the second difficulty: interdisciplinary enquiry does not of its nature deal with such problems.

We have the contradiction, then, that the interdisciplinarity that is invoked to deal with language problems in the "real world" actually prevents any engagement with this reality. For this involves not the linking of ideas across the same plane of abstraction, but the mediating of a relationship between two quite different planes of reality: that of the abstract discipline and that of the actual domain where the folk experience of language is to be found. The essential issue for applied linguistics is whether, how, and how far the ideas and findings that have been refined out of actual data by idealisation and analysis can be referred back reflexively to the domains of folk experience whence they came and made relevant in practice. You can indulge in interdisciplinary collaboration to your heart's content without ever getting involved in this issue.

Mediating between disciplinary expertise and folk experience is, of course, a tricky thing to do, and given the authority accorded to experts and the low esteem in which folk ideas are held, it is not something that everybody would think worth doing anyway. It is much easier to assume that solutions to problems can be unilaterally provided. A case in point would be the precepts proposed for language teaching discussed earlier: what teachers themselves might think, or what the particular circumstances of different pedagogic domains might be, are not taken into account. No mediation here. Nor is there much sign of it in a great deal of the research that has been undertaken into second language acquisition research (SLA). Just as corpus linguists have tended to suppose that their procedures of analysis can yield an intrinsically real language that has pedagogic validity whatever the local circumstances might be, so SLA researchers have tended to suppose that there is an intrinsically real language learning process that can be identified, as soon as they get their theories sorted out, which can at last provide a universally reliable basis for course design and methodology. In both cases, the assumption is that hitherto the folk, in this case teachers, with only their own wit and experience to depend upon, have got things wrong. What Sinclair says about language expresses the SLA assumption about language learning as well: "We are teaching English in ignorance of a vast amount of basic fact. This is not our fault, but it should not inhibit the absorption of new material" (Sinclair 1985: 252).

This talk about fact takes us back to the remarks of Labov cited earlier. He too talks about matters of fact but in reference not to those of linguistic analysis but to "the world around us", and distinguishes between "very large" ones and those which are "specific". It is of interest to note that all of the large ones that he mentions are all matters which are dealt with by the "hard" scientific disciplines: the origin of the universe by astrophysics, the direction of continental drift by geology, the evolution of the human species by genetics. These disciplines operate at a level of abstraction which is a long way removed from immediate experience and can claim to reveal an empirically well founded factuality inaccessible to folk awareness and quite remote from their "real world". What the folk might think is quite irrelevant to how these disciplines conduct their enquiries, and conversely, their findings might be quite irrelevant to the folk's way of thinking. What Labov refers to as "specific matters of fact" are altogether different. The example he gives is "the innocence or guilt of a particular individual". But this is not something like continental drift that can be objectively established. What we have here is a matter not of fact but of belief: what counts as guilt or innocence is a figment of a particular set of sociocultural conventions. You can only treat such matters as factual by subscribing to such conventions, and accepting the values they embody. Clearly, facts of this kind (if they can indeed be so called) cannot be established without reference to what the folk think, and different communities of folk will think about these things in very different ways. They belong not to scientific disciplines but to social domains.

It is these "facts" that applied linguistics has to somehow deal with if it is to engage with problems in "real world": relative values, varying, and often opposing, beliefs and attitudes that constitute different ways of thinking and ways of life. This, of course, is a difficult thing to do, and it is very tempting to simplify matters. One way of doing this is to just ignore the diversity of local domains, as with the kind of unilateral imposition of disciplinary ideas and findings we considered earlier. Another way is to assign preferential status to one set of domain values and assume that all others can, and should, be brought into line. The complex variety of the "real world" is in this case simplified and made more manageable not by idealisation but ideology. Such a strategy has its attractions. There are ways of thinking and living that on the face seem self-evidently more enlightened and more moral than others, and it is surely only right and proper that these should be promoted. And so we get applied linguistics committed to a good cause. One obvious difficulty about this is that whether a cause is good or not is not self-evident at all. Often its turns out to be weighted with self interest and to be rather better for its promoters than for its putative beneficiaries.

And even if one discounts ulterior motives, the goodness of a cause may not be realisable in socio-cultural contexts other than that in which it originated. The point made earlier about the difficulties of transferring ideas across disciplines applies also to the transference of values across domains. Pennycook, among others, has advocated a critical applied linguistics, one that has a mission and is committed to a particular socio-political ideology: applied linguistics, as he calls it, "with an attitude" (Pennycook 2001). But having a preconceived attitude is not likely to make you open to an understanding of other values, and commitment is likely to preclude a critical appraisal of your own position. Some of the work that goes under the name of critical discourse analysis is a good illustration of this: texts are assigned interpretations from a particular ideological point of view and no consideration is given to how other readers, with other pretextual assumptions, might understand them (for further discussion see Widdowson 1998 and 2004).

Applied linguistics is said to deal with problems to do with language that crop up in "real world" domains. But these are infinitely many and diverse. The diversity is reduced by the abstractions of disciplinary enquiry, thereby putting itself at a remove from folk experience, and no amount of interdisciplinarity can close that gap. The diversity can also be reduced by paying selective attention to certain domains and the socio-cultural values associated with them, and then extrapolating to others, but this too, of course, involves the disregard of reality as experienced by the local folk. So on this account it would seem that the claim that applied linguistics engages in the investigation of real-world problems by means of interdisciplinary collaboration is questionable, to say the least.

What goes on under the name of applied linguistics is acknowledged to be highly diverse, which is seen to be positive. But it can also be seen, rather less positively, as a rather motley assortment of activities. The term seems to be used as a convenient designation for any discussion about observed language data from any source, and from any disciplinary perspective. There is no agreed set of principles and procedures that one would normally expect of an area of enquiry, and which would provide some measure of consistency and coherence to such activities. Indeed it has been suggested that any such agreement would be undesirable in that it would make applied linguistics too academic and too restrictive in scope (see Rampton 1997).[2] Any attempt to give explicit consideration to how the field might be defined tends to be dismissed as unnecessary agonising: let us not worry about what we are doing, is the common cry, but let us just get on with it, whatever it might be. The diversity of the field, especially if it can be associated with interdisciplinarity, is, in this view, its most commendable feature. If it is diffuse in consequence, then that, apparently is a price worth paying.

But it does not follow that if the scope of enquiry in applied linguistics is to range over a diversity of language phenomena that it should be correspondingly diffuse as a *mode* of enquiry. On the contrary, it would generally be the case that the reason why a field of enquiry can deal with diversity is precisely because there is some consensus about how this is to be done. The diversity is reduced by the very consistency of the methodology used to deal with it. One can readily accept that the problems concerning language in the "real world" that applied linguistics should seek to address are many and diverse, but that is all the more reason why there should be some degree of uniformity of approach, some set of agreed principles about how to proceed. Otherwise, "applied linguistics" is simply a term without substance, a label we find it expedient to attach, like a flag of convenience, to almost any activity that concerns itself with language.

It seems to me that really the only way of establishing what is distinctive about applied linguistics is to recognize that as a mode of enquiry it has conditions of accountability to meet which are very different from those of disciplinary study. All disciplines are necessarily concerned with reality as actually experienced since this provides the data which has to be empirically adduced as substantiating evidence for the underlying abstractions that are drawn from them. And so it is that in linguistics, however hyphenated, there has to be what Firth referred to a "renewal of connection" with language as it actually occurs in the real world (See Palmer 1978:19). But the connection is only selectively renewed with those aspects of language that can serve as relevant evidence. Applied linguistics cannot be selective in this way. If it claims to engage with language problems in the real world, it cannot just reduce these to data to substantiate some theory or other. Its procedures must somehow work in reverse: instead of looking at how actual language experience can be used to substantiate abstraction, it must look at how abstraction can be used to take a different fix on actuality. We renew connection with folk realities, not so as to use them

---

[2] Rampton's paper prompted a lively exchange of views about the nature of applied linguistics, which is reprinted in Seidlhofer (2003).

as data, but to see them in alternative terms, to reformulate what is problematic about them in the light of a detached disciplinary perspective.

But to do this, we need to be quite clear about what kind of "truth" or "factuality" disciplinary expertise can, and cannot, provide us with. And here we encounter the paradox that folk experience in the domains of the "real world" can only be described in terms which in some degree misrepresent the experience. The paradox is nicely expressed in a passage from Bruce Chatwin's *The Songlines*:

> Kidder, expanding on his theme, said that sacred knowledge was the cultural property of the Aboriginal people. All such knowledge which had got into the hands of the white man has been acquired either by fraud or by force. It was now going to be de-programmed. "Knowledge is knowledge," I said. "It's not that easy to dispose of."
>
> He did not agree.
>
> To "de-programme" sacred knowledge, he said, meant examining archives for unpublished material on Aboriginals; you then returned the relevant pages to the rightful "owners". It meant transferring copyright from the author of a book to the people it described, returning photographs to the photographed (or their descendents); recording tapes to the recorded, and so forth.
>
> I heard him out, gasping in disbelief.
>
> "And who," I asked, "will decide who these 'owners' are?"
>
> "We have ways of researching that kind of information."
>
> "Your ways or their ways?"
>
> He did not reply. (Chatwin 1987: 43)

The de-programming of knowledge that is expertly abstracted cannot possibly recover knowledge in its pristine unrecorded state as originally, or Aboriginally, conceived as sacred by the folk. The photographs and tapes necessarily misrepresent it: in returning the record, you obviously do not thereby restore the experience recorded. And the folk are not consulted about how the records are to be returned, any more than they are consulted when the records were made in the first place. The knowledge that Kidder wants to return to its owners cannot be returned because they do not own it. It is a construct of ethnographic enquiry. This does not render it invalid, of course. On the contrary, it is because such an enquiry is at a remove from the immediacy of folk experience that it can reveal aspects of it from an outsider perspective.

There is a confusion here, then, between two kinds of knowledge, two kinds of reality: that of disciplinary expertise and that of domain experience. Each has its own legitimacy, and each can draw support from the other: expertise uses experience as data to substantiate its abstractions, and experience can be reformulated in reference to the expertise. But the crucial point is that if these reformulations are to be effective they cannot simply be unilaterally imposed but must also take local "real world" conditions of relevance into account. Hence the need to mediate across these two realities without giving undue primacy to either.

The two realities correspond, of course, to the two features which, as I said at the beginning, are generally taken to be distinctive of applied linguistics: interdisciplinarity and a concern with problems in the real world. Although we are told (in the editorial cited earlier) that it is uncontroversially the case that interdisciplinarity serves as a preparation for the handling of real-world issues, there is no indication as to how it is supposed to do this. I have argued that interdisciplinarity, itself a very tenuous concept, cannot actually provide such a service since it operates on a level of abstraction remote from the actualities as experienced by the folk. If we are to engage with real-world issues we need to develop a methodological approach which mediates between these two orders of reality of discipline and domain.

One might argue, of course, that in practice this is what a vast amount of work in applied linguistics does anyway, inspired and not inhibited by the wider transcendental vision suggested by manifesto statements. In this case, there is no need to press for more explicitness in the specification of methodological principles. Good work will continue to be done, and whether you call it applied linguistics or something else does not matter much. What, after all, is in a name?

There is, no doubt, something to be said for this *laissez faire* view. But if, every now and then, and on reflection, one feels the need to be rather more specific about what applied linguistics is all about, then one might be led to the conclusion that if our field is to have any distinctive character, it must surely rest on the claim that it is a particular mode of enquiry which is really not only not essentially interdisciplinary, but not essentially disciplinary at all, because it does not deal with abstractions per se, and what data can be adduced as evidence for them. Rather it takes an approach which is the reverse of this in that it explores how the problems that folk experience with language in real-world domains might be clarified, reformulated, made more amenable to solution by reference to the abstract representations of language that linguistics (hyphenated and otherwise) has to offer.

4 On the applicability of empirical findings

We live in an age where everything gets wrapped and packaged for the convenience of the consumer. And knowledge is no exception. In the general area of language study there has been a proliferation of packages of scholarship in recent years in the form of handbooks. There is a handbook of discourse analysis, a handbook of pragmatics, a handbook of linguistics, sociolinguistics, corpus linguistics and so on. Their proliferation indicates that these handbooks are profitable from a publishing point of view, though, as I have suggested elsewhere (Widdowson 2011) their academic justification is less easy to determine.

I have always thought of handbooks as small things like guide-books and this accords with the definition given in the Oxford English Dictionary: "A small book or treatise, such as may conveniently be held in the hand ... for guidance in any art, occupation or study". But these handbooks of linguistics are not small. They are weighty tomes that cannot be held in the hand for long without risk of injury – it is not so much that they are books that you cannot put down, you can hardly pick them up. It is not clear either how far they serve the purpose of guide-books: they are not maps that give directions but rather miscellaneous compendia of diverse essays by various authors, and readers are left to find their way through them as best they can. Be that as it may, these so-called handbooks seem to have become recognized as the authorized packages of scholarship in linguistics, sociolinguistics, historical linguistics and so on. And, of course in applied linguistics. Here too we have a handbook. In fact we have no less than three: the Oxford one (Kaplan 2002), the Blackwell one (Davies and Elder 2004) and the Routledge one (Simpson 2011). These handbooks have few if any contributors in common and vary considerably in coverage, so the question arises as to which, if any, we can depend upon as giving authoritative account of the field. To review these volumes would be a dauntless task, which I do not propose to attempt, but even a cursory glance at their contents pages makes it clear how very diverse the enquiries are that are given the cover term "applied linguistics".[1] One might see such diversity as a reflection of intellectual dynamism in the field, but it is difficult to see how

---

[1] The extent of the diversity becomes even more apparent with the publication of encyclopedias of applied linguistics, of which there are now two. A concise one published by Elsevier (Berns 2009) and a distinctly non-concise one published in 10 volumes by Wiley (Chapelle 2012).

Note: Published in *European Journal of Applied Linguistics* 1 (1). 4–21. 2013. An earlier version of this paper was presented at the annual conference of the Spanish association of applied linguistics (AESLA) in Salamanca, May 2011. The conference had the title "Empiricism and Analytical Tools for Applied Linguistics in the 21st Century."

https://doi.org/10.1515/9783110619669-007

these different compendia of apparently disparate collection of topics can constitute applied linguistics as a distinctive "art, occupation or study".

The editors of the Blackwell handbook do, it is true, seek to impose some thematic pattern on the disparity of topics but the attempt is not very convincing. In his review of the book, Willis Edmondson, a scholar who is sadly no longer with us, describes it as "a mixed bag, less than cogently assembled" (Edmondson 2005: 396). As for the Oxford handbook, its editor makes no attempt to provide any thematic coherence at all. "Applied linguistics is a difficult notion to define", he tells us in his preface, and "it should not be assumed that this volume will provide a definitive definition of the field". Instead it "offers a snapshot of some of the subfields of applied linguistics" (Kaplan 2002: vii). Taking snapshots suggests a rather haphazard kind of procedure, especially since it is not made clear how a subfield can be identified without identifying the field it is a subfield of.

One can, of course, take the view, and many people do, that there is no point in trying to resolve uncertainty about what applied linguistics actually is. Indeed it is sometimes said that the uncertainty is a positive advantage in that it allows for a wide range of occupational activity unhindered by the constraints of definition – applied linguistics is simply the label that people who chose to call themselves applied linguists attach to what they do.

At all events, we can agree with Kaplan that a definition of our field is elusive, whether we think this matters or not. There are, however, two things that are generally said to characterize work that is undertaken in its name. One is that it deals with problems in the "real world": "problems in the world in which language is implicated", as Cook puts it (Cook 2003: 5). The second is that it is, of its nature, interdisciplinary: it does not, in spite of its name, draw only on linguistics but on a much wider range of scholarly enquiry. The two features are taken to be related in that the second follows by implication from the first: that interdisciplinarity makes applied linguistics "better prepared for the principled handling of a range of distinct types of real world issues, and more critically aware of its methodologies" (Bygate and Kramsch 2000: 2).

This claim that being interdisciplinary necessarily makes applied linguistics more capable in principle of dealing with real-world issues leads to an understandable tendency to engage in abstract theorizing rather than with the practicalities of the real-world issues themselves. This perhaps helps to explain the diversity of offerings to be found in the handbooks and their tendency to focus attention on the various areas of disciplinary enquiry that might, in principle, serve as preparation for the handling of real-world problems rather than on particular problems that demonstrably require this disciplinary service. What I want to do in this short paper is to shift the focus of attention and begin with real-world problems and consider how far a disciplinary/interdisciplinary perspective has in practice been effective in handling them. The problems I am concerned with have to do with language learning and teaching, and particularly the learning and teaching of English.

I am aware that this is not the most fashionable area to talk about, and many scholars have been at pains to point out that the scope of applied linguistics goes well beyond language teaching and engages with sociocultural and sociopolitical issues of much wider import, with the implication that this extended scope has necessarily led to the development of more theoretically sophisticated methodologies of enquiry. In a promotional blurb for the most recent Handbook of Applied Linguistics – the Routledge one – James Lantolf writes: "(...) the field has come a long way since its early focus on the teaching and learning of languages beyond the first". This would seem to suggest that this early focus, and no doubt the methodologies of enquiry that went with it, are things of the outdated past which applied linguistics has grown out of. But in much of the work that goes on under the name of applied linguistics the focus is still on the real-world problems of foreign or second language teaching and learning and, as I hope to show in what follows, the issues that this gives rise to are still with us. So it would seem reasonable to suggest that it is just as relevant in this domain of practical activity, as in any other, that applied linguistics should be "critically aware of its methodologies".

And these methodologies involve giving empirical substantiation to theoretical ideas. The generally accepted definition of applied linguistics proposed by Christopher Brumfit (another scholar who is sadly no longer with us) goes as follows: "(...) the theoretical and empirical investigation of real-world problems in which language is a central issue" (Brumfit 1997: 86). The theoretical *and* empirical investigation of real-world problems. The question arises as what kind of relationship this conjunction *and* might signify and what kind of empirical findings are relevant to the investigation of the problems of language pedagogy?

There are two areas of study that have claimed to produce empirical findings directly relevant to the central pedagogic issue of how a foreign or second language should be effectively designed as an instructional construct, as a subject to be taught. One of these is second language acquisition research, SLA, and the other the description of second language usage. The focus of attention of each of these is on different aspects of the language subject: SLA on *how* language is to be presented to activate the learning *process*, usage description on *what* language is to be presented as the *objective* to be achieved. The real-world problem for language teaching is how these two aspects of process and objective can be related and reconciled. The applied linguistic question is how far these two areas of enquiry, which deal with these aspects separately, can give guidance as to how this problem might be addressed.

Perhaps the first thing we need to note is the very different disciplinary bearings these two areas of study take. Both are empirical in that both adduce actually occurring language data as evidence, but as evidence of two different things: of how a second or foreign language is learned on the one hand, and how a first language is used by its native speakers on the other. As far as disciplinary affiliations are concerned, the first, concerned as it is with the learning process, would seem to be essentially informed by psycholinguistic principles. The second, concerned as it is with actual usage, with principles of linguistic description. The obvious question that arises is how, and how far, these different principles of enquiry, and the different kinds of empirical evidence they yield, can be related to provide a "principled handling" of the "real world issues" of language pedagogy.

But this question seems rarely to be raised. On the contrary, these two lines of enquiry would seem to have gone their separate theoretical and empirical ways, apparently in disregard of the other. Since both make the applied linguistic claim that they are relevant to the practical problems of language pedagogy, the assumption must presumably be that somehow or other they eventually come together and complement each other in interdisciplinary convergence at the site of the real-world problem itself, in the language classroom. But when they are brought together in pedagogic reality, they do not converge at all: on the contrary, they conflict. And they always have.

A historical perspective is relevant here. Forty years ago, in 1972, there appeared two publications which can be said to have really got these two lines of enquiry going. One was Wilkins' "Linguistic and situational content of the common core in a unit/credit system" (Wilkins 1972) and the other Selinker's "Interlanguage" (Selinker 1972).

The Wilkins publication was a Council of Europe pamphlet which recorded its deliberations about foreign language learning objectives and how syllabus content might be specified to meet them. Its conclusions were that the emphasis had to be shifted from linguistic form to communicative function essentially on the grounds that what learners needed to learn was what native speakers actually did with their language in natural contexts of use. Significantly, Hymes' highly influential paper on communicative competence, though first presented in 1966, was also published in 1972 (Pride and Holmes 1972) and this was taken as a theoretical endorsement for these practical proposals for revising the language subject. It was communicative and not just linguistic competence that learners had to acquire. But for the Council of Europe this was not taken to mean the general ability to make communicative use of linguistic resources: the focus was on communicative use, but this had to be specifically use that conformed to what native speakers did with their language. It was *their* communicative competence that was the learning objective. And it was this way of thinking that informed the subsequent production of Threshold Level specifications.

These are specifications for syllabus content and represent features of competence that learners are to eventually acquire, but without regard to what methodology might be employed in the process of getting learners to acquire it. Methodological considerations are excluded on the grounds that these must be a matter for local decision. The assumption here is that the specification of syllabus content has no necessary implications for how this might be empirically substantiated in the teaching/ learning process: the objective, *what* is to be learned, is one thing and the process, *how* it is to be learned, another. The two aspects of the subject are taken to be separate and how they might be effectively related in the classroom is a problem left for teachers to resolve.

It is the second aspect of the language subject, the learning process that is, of course, the concern of the second line of enquiry, SLA, represented by the other 1972 publication that I referred to: Selinker's "Interlanguage". This too is pursued as an independent operation. Attention here is focused not on what *native speaker users* do when they communicate but on what *non-native learners* do in the process of acquiring the formal properties of the language code. The norm of reference remains native-speaker competence, but linguistic competence, with the term "interlanguage" being used to refer to the interim stage learners reach on their way to acquiring it. Since the learners' interlanguage does not correspond with the user language that is specified in the syllabus, there is clearly a disparity between what teachers teach and what learners learn, between the objective and process of learning.

This disparity between the process and objective of learning has always been one of the most intractable of pedagogic problems. And I would argue that far from helping to resolve it, the two lines of disciplinary enquiry make it more problematic because when they meet in the language classroom, which is where their applied linguistic credentials have to be empirically validated, they create a contradiction. Far from helping to solve the real-world pedagogic problem, as they claim to do, they actually exacerbate it.

But all this, it might be objected, is ancient history: it is about what was going on 40 years ago in 1972. But the point is that it is still going on now. The description of native speaker usage that provides the input for Threshold Level specifications is largely impressionistic and subjective, mainly based on the first person data of native speaker intuition. In subsequent years, of course, the development of electronic technology has provided detailed third person data on the basis of which actually observed usage could be objectively recorded and analysed with a high degree of precision. With the Threshold Level, and the teaching materials derived from it, language course content was represented essentially in terms of communicative functions and they were given linguistic form by reference to how it was thought they were normally expressed. The form-function correlations were in other words subjectively contrived.

Corpus analysis now provides factual data in abundance, but we need to note that it is textual data and as such it can only be adduced as empirical evidence of what linguistic forms people produce but not of how these forms function pragmatically. We cannot tell what people might have meant *by* what they said, even less what people might now mean by saying the same thing, because to do this we would need take contextual information into account which the corpus does not provide. The term "corpus" has in a way a certain aptness, etymologically related as it is to the term "corpse" for that in a sense is what a corpus is: an inanimate body of language, textual remains of expired discourse.

Corpus linguists like to claim that the data they deal with is authentic and so should replace the invented examples that have hitherto been used as content in language courses. But although corpora do indeed record real text, they cannot re-animate the reality of the discourse that gave rise to it. These textually attested forms can only serve as examples of communicative functions if contexts are provided whereby these functions are realized. Such contexts are not provided by a corpus and even if they were they obviously could not be replicated in classrooms. So although the language forms can be said to be real in that they have been really produced, the contexts that would animate them to make them communicatively functional have to be invented (for a more detailed discussion of these points, see Widdowson 2003). The obvious consequence of this is that the forms have to be adjusted in some way to make them suited to classroom contexts thereby reducing their authenticity as textual data. So it seems clear that although corpus linguistics is an enormous advance on the specifications of the Threshold Level in that it is an empirical description of the form that actually attested native speaker usage takes, it does nothing to solve the problem of how to reconcile the disparity between the objective and the process of learning that I have been referring to. If anything it makes matters worse.

This authenticity doctrine is the most recent version of the traditional view that what is taught and learned in classroom should replicate the use of native speakers, without regard to the methodological question of how this user data is to feed into the learning process. It is this learning process, of course, that is the exclusive concern of our second "applied linguistic" line of work and this continues in its own separate way. In the 40 years since 1972 there has been a vast proliferation of papers and books reporting SLA research, enough to fill a library (for a survey, see Ellis 2008). It is by far the most productive area of what is called applied linguistics, and the most influential – for countless students, especially, it would seem, in the United States, it *is* applied linguistics. How does it measure up to what are claimed to be the two defining features of the field.

As far as interdisciplinarity is concerned, it has essentially been psycholinguistic in orientation and some of its proponents have shown considerable resistance to interdisciplinary influence, especially to sociolinguistics (see for example Block 2003; Firth and Wagner 1998, 2007; Lafford 2007). There have been, however, signs of an increasing awareness of the relevance for SLA of the linguistic description of actual usage, particularly of the relationship between acquisition processes and the corpus-based description of formulaic language. In a recent issue of *The Annual Review of Applied Linguistics*, for example, N. Ellis remarks: "There is a strong consensus that research on formulaic language, phraseology, and constructions is in dire need of triangulation across research in L1 acquisition, L2 acquisition, corpus linguistics, usage-based linguistics, and psycholinguistics" (Ellis 2012: 29). The relevant applied linguistic question that we are concerned with here, however, is not how interdisciplinarity might enhance research in L1 and L2 acquisition but on how such research, enhanced or not, actually serves as a preparation for handling the real-world problems of pedagogy.

As far as the handling of such problems is concerned, the claim still seems to be that SLA findings point to underlying learning processes that can and should give guidance to teachers. These findings, according to one influential school of SLA thought, are said to reveal that the acquisition of the grammatical features of a second language, whatever the language, follows a certain cognitive course, to some extent predetermined, and moves from one interlanguage stage to another. This natural acquisition process necessarily controls the learnability of these features and therefore, the reasoning goes, provides a reliable indication of the order in which these features should be pedagogically presented. This would prevent teachers wasting their time trying to teach something that learners are not naturally disposed to learn. Findings so far are perhaps not so secure as to provide a reliable blue-print for pedagogy, but researchers seem to be confident that they are getting there.

Some researchers, indeed, seem to feel they have got there already. With regard to the kind of classroom activities which most effectively induce the learning process, they have concluded that research has now provided clear support for a task-based approach to language teaching (TBLT) to replace all the other misconceived and unsatisfactory approaches that have prevailed so far. As I have argued elsewhere, however (e.g. Widdowson 2003), what are said to be the distinctive features of a task are so vaguely and ambiguously defined as to be interpreted as applicable to almost any classroom activity, and are in stark contrast to the detailed and specific precision of the research findings upon which they are said to be based. Rather than seeking to describe different stages of interlanguage, recent research has tended to focus on what has been identified as three essential aspects of acquisition. These, still defined exclusively in reference to native speaker competence, are complexity, accuracy and fluency (CAF) (see, for example, Housen and Kuizen 2009).

How the empirical findings of research into these three aspects actually inform the design of tasks, however, remains unclear. In the "key precepts" proposed in Ellis (2009) for the specification of task design, there is no mention of these three essential aspects at all. Elsewhere, Ellis is at pains to say that SLA research provides no "blueprint" for task design, but simply points to issues that need to be taken into account (Ellis 2003). This seems reasonable enough, but one needs to ask just what these issues are, for there is still the claim that there is, and should be, some correspondence between tasks which are constructed for SLA research and tasks as classroom activities, a correspondence, in other words between the findings of research and the experience of pedagogic reality. We are told by another researcher that: "It is expecting too much to imagine that research will show task-based instruction is a more effective way of classroom teaching than any other methodology" (Foster 2009: 250).

This is disarmingly frank. But if this is expecting too much, what *should* we expect SLA research to show us which has relevance to classroom teaching? For if it claims to be applied linguistics it surely has to show us something empirically substantiated that can be pedagogically acted upon. And anyway, if too much is being expected of the research, it is the researchers themselves who have created the expectation: it is researchers, not teachers, who suppose that their research shows that a corresponding task-based instruction is the most effective way of classroom teaching. This is the way of teaching that is promoted and any other methodology is mentioned only to be dismissed. There is no doubt that the advocacy of task-based teaching is based on the authority of SLA research and assumed to be endorsed by its findings. Empirical evidence for the effectiveness of task-based teaching in actual classrooms is in rather short supply.

SLA researchers generally take the same view of current language pedagogy as the corpus linguists I referred to earlier, namely that teachers are teaching the wrong thing in the wrong way because they are uninformed. From the corpus linguists point of view they are uninformed about authentic language, and from the SLA point of view they are uninformed about authentic language learning. Teachers have a problem because what they are doing is wrong on two counts and they need to get real.[2]

The difficulty is that teachers are being enjoined to be real in two contradictory ways. Let us suppose that they follow the corpus linguistic injunction. Here too we find precepts for pedagogy to follow. One of them is expressed by the late John Sinclair as follows: "Present real examples only" (Sinclair 1997: 30). Now John Sinclair was a thinker of remarkable originality, and I have nothing but admiration for his work in corpus linguistics, but this precept has to do with practical pedagogy, so in proposing it, he is assuming the role not of linguist, but of applied linguist. And as an applied linguistic proposal, this precept, as I have argued elsewhere (e.g. Widdowson 2003: Ch. 8) does nothing to resolve a pedagogic problem but actually creates one.

What is it, to begin with, that makes an example real? The fact that it comes out of a corpus, might be one answer, for "The language of the corpus", McCarthy tells us, "is, above all, real" (McCarthy 2001: 128). But as I have already suggested, this reality is only very partial. A corpus is, above all, a collection of texts which have been extracted from the contexts in which they originally and naturally occurred and isolated from the purposes which motivated their production in the first place. It is obvious, therefore, that these texts only represent the reality of language as experienced by its users to a very limited extent. And we should note that this extent is even more limited when analysis takes place and corpus findings are displayed in concordance lines. Language does not naturally occur in concordance lines. What you get out of corpus is a textual *samples*. When samples are sorted by analysis and displayed they become *examples* of certain co-textual regularities. But to the extent that context is absent, these are not examples of real language use.

The obvious point is that while samples are *actual*, examples are *abstract*: they do not occur but are a function of inference. We make something into an example by noting that it represents a typicality of one sort or another, that it is a token of a type. A sample is a selection of data, and can be said to intrinsically real as data, but an example can only be made real or realized when it is identified as evidence of something by some kind of analysis. Now with regard to the learning process, the central problem in language pedagogy is how to effectively induce learners to infer examples from samples of language data. As

---

[2] It is convenient for SLA researchers and "real" language advocates to take it as self-evident that teachers get things wrong, because they could make no claim to pedagogic relevance otherwise. But no actual empirical evidence is ever given in support of this belief. If anything, Swan (2012: 90–114) among others has claimed, on the circumstantial evidence of large numbers of successful learners, teachers seem, in some respects at least, to have got things right.

teachers know well enough, if they are to present real examples in the classroom, then they will have to create conditions which enable the learners to realize them as examples. Otherwise no learning takes place.

So this precept, "Present real examples only", like the other precepts that are proposed in Sinclair (1997), takes no account whatever of the learning process. As with Threshold Level specifications, they derive directly from a description of native speaker usage. This Sinclair himself makes quite explicit: "The precepts center on data, and arise from observations about the nature of language. They are not concerned with psychological or pedagogical approaches to language teaching" (Sinclair 1997: 30). So here we have a precept for teaching that is quite explicitly not concerned with pedagogy. It is based on the assumption that the language used for learning must necessarily be the language of the native speaker user and that where the language presented to the learner does not correspond with the facts of actually attested usage, it is pedagogically defective.

This assumption has given rise to a number of studies comparing the language in textbooks unfavourably with "real" language. To take one example, in Römer (2004) a corpus of English language teaching texts is compiled and analysed so as to "(...) help us to answer two crucial questions related to language teaching: 'Do we teach our pupils authentic English, i.e. do we confront them with the same type of English they are likely to be confronted with in natural communicative situations?' and 'What can we do to improve EFL teaching materials?' " (Römer 2004: 151–152).

The obvious implication here is that the second question follows logically from the first, that is to say that if we do not teach the authentic English of native speaker usage, teaching will necessarily be improved if we do so. We need to note also that authentic English is equated with what occurs in "natural communicative situations". This assumes that the pedagogic objective has to be the replication of native-speaker usage on the grounds that the only communicative situations that are natural are those involving native-speakers, and that it is only such situations that learners will ever be confronted with.

The same assumption would seem to lie behind the upsurge of interest in formulaic language in SLA which was referred to earlier. As Alison Wray puts it: "(...) we have an increasing body of evidence that instructed L2 learners have an impoverished stock of formulaic expressions" (Wray 2012: 236). This, it has been assumed, necessarily results in equally impoverished communication and has led to proposals, along Römer lines, that it needs to be remedied by increasing the stock of formulaic expressions in teaching materials (Martinez and Schmitt 2012; Millar 2011; Meunier 2012). This of course takes it for granted that in learning English the only possible objective is to conform as closely as possible to native speaker norms, and that failure to do so makes learners communicatively deficient. This completely disregards the fact that English is also used in "natural communicative situations" on a global scale by non-native speakers and that it is these lingua franca situations that learners are most likely to be confronted with. And there is "an increasing body of evidence" here that an impoverished stock of native speaker formulaic expressions does not, in empirical fact, result in communicative deficiency (see Seidlhofer 2011).

With regard to the learning process, Wray poses the interesting question as to why, if formulaic expressions are so communicatively effective, learners do not learn them more readily: "(...) why learners do not feel more empowered to harvest L2 input in larger chunks in pursuit of painless routes to effective communication" (Wray 2012: 236). This seems to me to be just the kind of relevant pedagogic question we need to ask: it brings into focus the very issue of the disparity between the objective and process of language learning that I have been talking about. One answer might be that though these chunks might be called "authentic" in that they are samples of attested native speaker usage, the authentication of these linguistic forms as pragmatic expressions depends on contextual conditions that classrooms do not naturally provide. So it is far from self-evident that learning larger chunks will provide learners with "painless routes to effective communication". The general point to be made is that the forms of the language, which is all a corpus can record, cannot capture the authenticity of their pragmatic use in "natural communicative situations" and that these forms have somehow to be authenticated in the very different situations of classrooms and in a way that will activate learning.

It seems clear that the precept "Present real examples only" takes no account of the pedagogic reality of classrooms. How such a global precept can be put into local practice, how such "real" language can be actually taught in a classroom so that learners can engage with it, and learn from it, is not considered to be relevant. So much for the handling of real-world problems. The precept is explicitly not concerned with psychology either, so it is presumably meant to be applied in complete disregard of all the psycholinguistic research into learning that SLA has been so busy with over the past 40 years. So much for interdisciplinarity.

It is of interest to note that in spite of this declared unconcern for psychology or pedagogy, this precept is paradoxically elsewhere justified on psychological and pedagogic grounds: "(...) it should not ever be necessary for students to 'unlearn' anything they have been taught. They cannot be taught everything at once, and because our knowledge of the textual detail of language has been so vague, they have been taught half-truths, generalities which apply only in some circumstances" (Sinclair 1991: 499–500). From a psychological and pedagogic perspective, this makes no sense at all. If there is one thing on which SLA researchers and practising teachers agree, it is that the acquisition of competence is not cumulative but adaptive: learners proceed not by adding items of linguistic knowledge, but by a process of continual revision and reconstruction. In other words, learning is necessarily a process of recurrent unlearning and relearning, whereby encoding rules are modified, extended, re-aligned or abandoned altogether to accommodate new language data. The whole learning process is a matter of continual cognitive adaptation as the learner passes through different transitional stages, each of which is an adapted version of the one preceding. Learning can only proceed by unlearning. Even if you presented real language only, as input, its reality would not survive, for it would be converted into data for learning and subjected to different degrees of noticing. And actually the more real or authentic the input, the more difficult is the conversion likely to be.

So here we have two lines of "applied linguistic" enquiry, each generating its own momentum and going its own separate way, each claiming to engage with the real-world problems of language pedagogy, more specifically to the teaching of English as a foreign or other language. Let me be clear that I am not here seeking to question the validity of these enquiries as such. I am not against corpus linguistics or second language acquisition research. Both provide empirical findings of great interest within their own disciplinary areas of descriptive linguistics on the one hand, psycholinguistics on the other. The difficulty is that when these findings are then taken out of their separate disciplinary contexts and transferred to the practical domain of language pedagogy they are in conflict.

As I have argued elsewhere, disciplines of their nature deal with theoretical abstractions and cannot directly match up with actualities in the practical domain: they represent different orders of reality. The challenge for applied linguistics is to find ways of relating the two. From an applied linguistic perspective, different disciplines need to get their act together in this practical domain, and as I have tried to show, it is this that these two areas of enquiry emphatically fail to do. Each seeks to apply its empirical findings directly and unilaterally to language pedagogy. They are in effect to refer to a distinction I have made elsewhere (Widdowson 1980, 2000), exercises in linguistics applied rather than in applied linguistics.[3]

---

[3] In the Blackwell Handbook referred to earlier (Davies and Elder 2004), "linguistics applied" and "applied linguistics" are indeed distinguished but only as labels attached to two separate sections of the book. But, confusingly, the title of book indicates that, at the same time, applied linguistics somehow subsumes both.

To return to the quotation cited earlier, although what goes under the name of applied linguistics may be "becoming more inter-disciplinary" in some areas of enquiry – in SLA, for example, as was noted earlier – this may provide intellectual satisfaction, and even lend greater validity to their particular lines of "theoretical and empirical investigation". But it does not follow that they will therefore be better prepared "for the principled handling" of pedagogic problems. From an applied linguistic perspective the only point in being interdisciplinary is that the problem you are supposed to be dealing with requires you to be. This cannot just be taken on trust but needs to be empirically demonstrated. Rather than start with the assumption that interdisciplinarity is necessarily a good thing it would surely make better sense to first focus attention on the real-world issues and *then* consider which disciplines, or combination of disciplines are relevant. It is this condition of relevance that is crucial and this can only be demonstrated at the site of the real-world problem itself. And as far as being principled is concerned, there is in applied linguistics no virtue in interdisciplinarity in principle if it is pointless in practice. Unless you focus attention on the problem first, it is indeed difficult to see how you would know which disciplines you need to call on and combine as relevant to handling it. Otherwise you are in danger of defining problems unilaterally to suit your own preconceived disciplinary or interdisciplinary ideas rather than engaging with the problems as they are actually experienced in the practical domain by people in the real world – interdisciplinarity applied rather than applied interdisciplinarity.

What about the empirical side of things? Both SLA and corpus analysis come up with empirical findings. But as I noted earlier they are empirical in very different ways. SLA findings are 2nd person data elicited from language learners and can be adduced as evidence of the learning process. Corpus findings are 3rd person data observed in language use and can be adduced as evidence of what native language users actually produce. But in neither case can it be assumed that these empirical findings are of direct relevance for the pedagogic design of the language subject. Just as there is no virtue in just being interdisciplinary so there is no virtue in just being empirical either. Being empirical is part of the methodology of disciplinary enquiry whereby data are adduced as evidence in support of theoretical constructs of one kind or another. They cannot be adduced as evidence of anything else. Empirical findings are necessarily partial and relative: they are a function of analysis at the disciplinary level and cannot represent the reality that is actually experienced in the practical domain where real-world problems have their being. Although they cannot be directly applied, however, such findings can, of course, be used to raise awareness, to clarify and analyse these problems, reformulate them so that they are more amenable to solution. And it is precisely in the exploration of how they can be used, how and how far they can be made relevant to issues in the practical domain that is, in my view, the real business of applied linguistics.

As I pointed out at the beginning of this paper, "applied linguistics" is an ill-defined term attached to a vast and varied area of occupational activity. According to the journal *Applied Linguistics* the field has to do with "research into language with relevance to real world problems". It is not easy to think of any research into language where you cannot, with some ingenuity, discover some *potential* relevance to real-world problems and this allows just about any research into language from any disciplinary perspective to qualify as applied linguistics – any research for example, in corpus linguistics, cognitive linguistics, discourse analysis, pragmatics, post-modern philosophy, complexity theory, all of which do indeed make an appearance in the handbooks of applied linguistics I referred to earlier.[4] But the claim for applied linguistics is that it is not just potentially but *actually* relevant, that it is able to handle real-world issues that real people, like language teachers and learners, have to cope with and being interdisciplinary is pointless unless its relevance to this purpose can be demonstrated. To return to the Brumfit definition: "the theoretical and empirical investigation of real world problems". So the investigation is into *problems*: problems are what you start with and the investigation can only be validated by its effectiveness in dealing with them.

That, it seems to me, is the crucial defining condition that applied linguistics has to meet. Other kinds of theoretical and empirical investigation, within and across disciplines, have their own conditions of validity to meet. But if the term applied linguistics is to be anything but a conveniently vague catch-all term, an expedient label, then the validity condition it has to meet is that of relevance – not a presupposed *potential* relevance but relevance that is empirically substantiated in domains of practice. The domain that I have been particularly concerned with in this paper is that of language pedagogy, but although the field may have moved on to focus attention on other domains, the challenge for applied linguistics, and for this new journal that bears its name, remains the same: to demonstrate that, whatever its disciplinary or interdisciplinary source of inspiration or frame of reference, as far as its *terms* of reference are concerned, it really is prepared, in both senses of that word, to engage directly with problematic issues in the real world.

---

4 For example, conversation analysis, corpus linguistics, discourse, lexis, phonetics and phonology and pragmatics all appear as areas of applied linguistics in separate sections of the Wiley Encyclopedia referred to earlier (Chapelle 2012).

Section 3: **The analysis and interpretation of language use**

Preamble

The papers in this section are all concerned with how language is used pragmatically in the making of meaning. Central to this theme is the conceptual distinction expounded in Section 1 between text and discourse (see also Widdowson 2004). The point is made in a number of places that texts, spoken or written, are the linguistic traces of communicative intent and though they can be assigned semantic meaning as encodings by analysis, pragmatic meaning can only be inferred by interpretation which is dependent on the extralinguistic factors of context and pretext. The meaning of language in use is therefore indeterminate, crucially dependent on variable local conditions of production and reception. Some of these conditions can be defined in social terms, but ultimately interpretation is an individual matter. The very act of communication involves coming to terms with the necessary tension between the social need to co-operate and the individual need to protect personal space from intrusion. This way of thinking about communication, represented by the conceptual bearings described in Section 1, raises questions about what aspects of language use are accounted for in the text analysis of corpus linguistics and more generally how far analysis can provide evidence of intended meaning, or provide guidance as to how a given text is to be interpreted.

This question about the relationship between text analysis and discourse interpretation comes up whatever and however language is put to communicative use. So it is as pertinent for the study of literature as it is for any other language use. It is this, as is pointed out in the Introduction, that should logically lead to the disciplinary convergence of linguistics and literary criticism, traditionally seen as quite different areas of study. It is this too that warrants the prominence of literary texts in these papers. A Conrad novel and a Shakespeare play can exemplify with particular clarity this indeterminate relationship between analysis and interpretation, as is demonstrated in two of the papers in this section.

And in the last paper. This can be read as simply frivolous entertainment making mock of strait-laced Shakespearean scholarship. But as I point out in the Introduction, this kind of writing can serve a serious critical purpose. And so, I would claim, it does here. The vastly different productions of Shakespeare on stage and screen are all varied discourses derived from the same text. The lines that are assigned to different characters in the script do not determine how the characters are realized, or what prominence they have in play. Inventive directors, particularly those with all the cinematic tricks of the trade at their disposal, can radically diminish or increase the relative prominence of characters no matter how the lines are distributed in the script. But it is not only directors of Shakespeare that impose individual interpretations on texts. We all do it with all texts.

5 The pretext of interpretation

I will begin by stating the obvious and then go on to consider implications which are perhaps not so obvious. When people want to relate to others for one reason or another – to communicate with them, persuade them, co-operate with them, inform or instruct them, impress or oppress them or whatever – then they make use of language as a convenient means for doing so. They draw on the linguistic resources at their disposal to produce texts of one kind or another – articles, reports, manifestoes, public notices, cooking recipes, letters and lectures – like this one. I am producing text as I speak so as to relate to you. Texts are then a convenient means for mediating between people. But how does this mediation work?

Texts are composed of linguistic signs in combination, so what do these signs signify, and what significance can we attach to them?

It is a common assumption, taken as self-evident in much work on critical discourse analysis, CDA, that significance can be assigned to texts by means of an analysis of their linguistic features. I want to argue against this assumption and to suggest that it is not only misconceived, but that it distracts attention from what I think are the essential issues about the use of language in communication. No amount of analysis, I shall argue, no matter how precisely it is carried out, can reveal the significance of texts, and indeed the more precise the analysis, the less revealing it will tend to be.

Texts are produced, as visual marks in writing or sounds in speech, by a first person writer or speaker, P1 for short, and received and processed by second person readers or listeners, P2 for short. I am a P1 producing text now, of course, as I speak to you P2s, and you are, I hope, processing it. The claim of critical discourse analysis is that the linguistic features of a text are indicative of the ideological position of the P1, but that these indications are not apparent to ordinary second person readers/listeners, the P2, who, lacking the analytic skill to identify them, fail to realize their significance: thus the ideology is subtly insinuated into the readers' minds. The task of CDA, indeed the cause that it embraces, is to expose such covert and subversive intentions by close textual analysis so as to make the reader aware and wary of the persuasive power of texts and the deception that is being practised on them. The cause is, of course, a worthy one. How language is used to persuasive effect by those in power, whether for political or commercial purposes, is

Note: First published as a chapter in Dontcheva-Navratilova, O. & R. Povolná (eds.). 2012. *Discourse interpretation: Approaches and applications.* Cambridge Scholars. Originally presented as a plenary address at the 4th Brno Conference on Linguistic Studies, September 2010.

something that warrants serious and critical investigation. My argument, though, is that the procedures of CDA, or at least those that are widely followed, are unhelpful to this investigation because they are based on a misconception about the nature of text and a confusion between analysis and interpretation.

What then is a text? It is a linguistic object, a manifestation of language that can be anything from a one word public notice to a scholarly monograph, from a tweet to a treatise. Texts can be analysed in isolation, and their lexical and grammatical features described, nowadays with the aid of computers to a high degree of precision. But though they can be analysed in isolation by linguists, they are never produced or received in isolation by language users. When we produce or process a text, in speech or writing, we are prompted by some reason or other: P1s do not just produce texts unprompted out of the blue and P2s do not just pick up texts at random. There is, in short, always some preconceived purpose in producing or processing a text, a pretextual purpose. In fact, users do not really experience language as texts, any more than they experience language as sentences. Writers do not write texts and readers do not read them, they write and read notes, notices, letters, articles, reports, monographs, poems, novels and so on. Texts are simply the linguistic trace of a pragmatic process whereby the writer, the producer, the first person or P1 uses language indexically to make a contextual connection and act upon a P2 for some communicative purpose or other. It is this pragmatic process of meaning realization that I refer to as discourse. Language users enact discourses by means of texts, and in doing so, two other factors are crucially implicated: context, the extra-linguistic reality that linguistic features point to, and pretext, the intended purpose of P1 that motivates the communication in the first place.

All this sounds, and indeed is, somewhat abstract, so let me give you an example. Here is a piece of text – an old text, but not any old text. It is one of the most cited and celebrated in history: the opening of the *American Declaration of Independence*: "We hold these truths to be self-evident, that all men are created equal, that they are endowed by their Creator with certain unalienable Rights, that among these are Life, Liberty and the pursuit of Happiness".

"*We hold these truths to be self-evident*". But who does the pronoun "we" refer to? If we – you and me – now look at the language of this text and consider the phrase "all men" we can assign it a semantic meaning without difficulty since we know the denotation of each constituent word. But what the phrase is intended to *refer* to in this text crucially depends on who the pronoun "we" refers to and this is a very different matter – a pragmatic and not a semantic matter. Is the reference meant to override the denotation of "men" and include women as well? Given the context of the time, probably not. But what of the denotation of "all"? All men. *All* men? "We" in the text refers to Thomas Jefferson and the other founding fathers who drafted this document. They were, of course, slave owners, and they certainly did not hold it as a self-evident truth that slaves were divinely endowed with an unalienable right to life, liberty and the pursuit of happiness. On the contrary for them it was a self-evident truth that slaves were not endowed with this right. And there were other men, too, who are referentially excluded – the indigenous people of the continent, who, later in the document are referred to "the inhabitants of our frontiers, the merciless Indian Savages". The self-evident truth that all men are created equal does not apply to them: no unalienable rights for aliens such as these, for they are beyond the pale, outside the frontiers imposed upon them, within which alone such rights are recognized. So it is very clear that what the phrase "all men are created equal" means semantically is not at all the same as what the authors of this text meant *by* the phrase. What it is intended to mean is not all men, but all men of a certain kind – white men, men like Jefferson in fact. The first person "we" and the third person "all men" are in effect co-referential.

So the historical context here determines the scope of reference intended by the writers of this text. But we can relate this text to a different context and so change the referential scope to include all human beings, slaves, indigenous people, men as well as women. And this indeed is what generally happens when these words are cited these days, and used to express the principle of universal human rights. The phrase "all men" is now taken to mean all human beings, without exception, across all frontiers, which is not at all what the original writers of the text intended by it. The central point is that reference is contextually local and cannot be directly inferred from the text.

But it is not only that the text is now related to a different context. It also serves a different purpose, and here pretext comes into play. This text is part of a proclamation, a declaration of independence and is simultaneously directed at two kinds of P2 recipient: like-minded fellow American colonials on the one hand, and the British colonizers on the other. So the declaration is at one and the same time designed to be the expression of common aspiration and also an act of defiance directed at the colonial power. And if it had the desired effect on the readers for whom it was intended that was really all that mattered. In other words, the writing of the text was motivated by a pretextual purpose to bring about a certain effect on certain readers who could be counted on to recognize and ratify this purpose. They would not subject it to close reading, certainly not to linguistic analysis. For them it would not be a text as such at all, but a declaration, an act of defiance, a call to arms in a political cause and they would regulate their attention to the text accordingly. And as with context, we can of course, relate this text to a different pretext, as when it is cited, as it frequently is, as a declaration of the democratic principle of universal human rights, whoever the humans may be. And this, we should note, is in effect directly contrary to the pretextual purpose of the signatories to the *Declaration of Independence* which was essentially to invoke the principle as a convenient tactic to assert the exclusive rights of their own community.

So what the writers of this text do is to make expedient pragmatic use of the semantics of English to suit their ideological purposes. In so doing, they follow a natural communicative practice which is as common now as it was then. Fast forward 250 years to the present day and we still find the same thing. As Chomsky observes: "When Western states and intellectuals use the term 'international community', they are referring to themselves (...). Those who do not support the actions of wealth and power are not part of the 'global community', just as 'terrorism' conventionally means 'terrorism directed against us and our friends' " (Chomsky 2001). So like the term *all men* the term *international* is used pragmatically to mean what it suits its users to mean, in defiance of its semantic denotation. This, to change the context rather abruptly from the real world to the realm of fantasy, is also what Humpty Dumpty does – a character in Lewis Carroll's *Alice Through the Looking Glass*. He uses the word "glory" and tells Alice that it means "a nice knock-down argument". Alice objects that this is not what the word means, and here is his reply: " 'When I use a word,' Humpty Dumpty said in rather a scornful tone, 'it means just what I choose it to mean – neither more nor less.' 'The question is,' said Alice, 'whether you CAN make words mean so many different things.' 'The question is', said Humpty Dumpty, 'which is to be master – that's all'".

Obviously we cannot master words to the extent that Humpty Dumpty claims we can. Using language as it suits us cannot extend to assigning to words any arbitrary meaning we choose. There has to be some convention in invention, some semantic common ground; otherwise texts could not mediate between P1 and P2 in the communication process at all. Without such consensus about encoded meaning, there can be no convergence. But the question is not, as Alice has it, whether we can make words mean so many different things. Clearly we can. But to what extent and in what circumstances? How far does what words mean semantically constrain what we can mean by them? We can make words mean many different things pragmatically, but the question is what are the contextual and pretextual conditions that enable us to do so.

What I am saying, then (and it is obvious enough), is that texts do not vary but their interpretation very definitely does. In other words, texts are fixed and determinate linguistic objects but they give rise to variable discourses. To return to the *Declaration of Independence*. This must be one of the most cited texts ever written, and each time it is cited, it is the same text. But the point is that though the text remains the same, its significance does not because the contexts and pretexts it relates to change depending on when it is cited, by whom, for what purpose. So although we can analyse the text linguistically in terms of its lexis and grammar, describe the meaning that is semantically encoded in its sentences, this will not tell us what discourse it is a trace of. Nor what discourse its readers derive from it.

For of course the discourse that the first person writer, the P1, intended to textualize may well not correspond closely, or even at all, with the discourse that the second person reader, the P2 derives from the text. What writers have in mind may not at all transfer to the minds of their readers. The novelist Doris Lessing has interesting things to say about this in the preface she wrote for the reprint of her novel *The Golden Notebook*:

> Ten years after I wrote it I can get, in one week, three letters about it .... One letter is entirely about the sex war, about man's inhumanity to woman, and woman's inhumanity to man, and the writer has produced pages and pages all about nothing else, for she – but not always a she – can't see anything else in the book. The second is about politics, probably from an old Red like myself, and he or she writes many pages about politics, and never mentions any other theme.
>
> These two letters used, when the book was, as it were, young, to be the most common.
>
> The third letter, once rare but now catching up on the others, is written by a man or woman who can see nothing in it but the theme of mental illness.
>
> But it is the same book.
>
> And naturally these incidents bring up again questions of what people see when they read a book, and why one person sees one pattern and nothing at all of another pattern, how odd it is to have, as author, such a clear picture of a book, that is seen so differently by its readers.

Doris Lessing is of course talking about a literary text and literary texts, not being so tied to contextual constraints, are particularly prone to variable interpretation – they are indeed designed to be, and this is essentially *their* pretextual purpose, as Lessing herself recognizes. She goes on to make what she calls "a most fundamental point": "Which is that the book is alive and potent and fructifying and able to promote thought and discussion only when its plan and shape and intention are not understood, because that moment of seeing the shape and plan and intention is also the moment when there isn't anything more to be got out of it" (Lessing 1972: xix–xx). In other words (in my words), if the meaning of a text were to be fixed, no discourse could be derived from it and it would in effect cease to function as a text.

Although Doris Lessing is talking about novels, what she says applies to all texts, not just literary ones. But whereas it does not matter how variably a literary text might be interpreted, how other kinds of text are interpreted could matter a great deal. An obvious example is how differing interpretations of sacred scripture like the Bible or the Koran, have given rise to centuries of sectarian conflict. But a text does not have to be religious to be interpreted as the justification for dogmatic belief. Thus, in the current contentious debate in the United States about gun control, the National Rifle Association, NFA, routinely invokes another celebrated historical document, the 2nd Amendment, as endorsing the constitutional right of all citizens to carry firearms. The text of the Amendment runs as follows: "A well regulated militia being necessary to the security of a free state, the right of the people to keep and bear arms shall not be infringed".

The NFA obviously finds it convenient to cite the main clause of this text without reference to the dependent adverbial phrase that precedes it. But the grammatical connection between them signals that this phrase sets semantic conditions on how the main clause is to be understood: the bearing of arms is related to the need for a militia to ensure the security of the state, which was no doubt a necessary precaution in the early uncertain years of independence. The definite article in "the people" indicates reference to potential members of the militia previously mentioned. It obviously follows that as the need for a militia disappears, so does the need to bear arms or to enshrine this need as a right. And of course the term "arms" would also have historically restricted reference to such contemporary weapons as muskets and flintlock pistols. What the NRA does is to isolate the second part of the Amendment from the first, and then interpret it as meaning that everybody has the unconditional right to carry an arsenal of arms like assault rifles and machine pistols for their own personal security.

All texts, then, are subject to variable interpretation and they would not function as texts otherwise. They always presuppose some context and some pretext, and it is only because these are presupposed that texts exist at all, and only by reference to these factors that they can be interpreted. As I have said, they are never produced, or received in isolation, and so to isolate them as linguistic objects for analysis is necessarily to misrepresent them. So really it makes no sense to ask what a text means. It does not in itself mean anything. What we have to ask is what do writers mean *by* their texts and what do texts mean *to* their readers.

Now of course writers will always rely on readers' shared linguistic knowledge to serve as a common semantic base and so the linguistic features of the text will give indications of writer intentions and some of these will be easy enough to identify. As I have already said, there will always be some consensus about what writers are talking about and it is this that leads to the illusion that there is meaning in the text itself, but to say that a text means such and such is really only shorthand for saying that we can infer what the writer meant by it. Some intentions are clearly signalled and easy to identify. Others however, are not. And anyway, we do not normally read a text with a view to discovering what the writer meant by it. Our main concern is what it means to us. So in reading a text, we do not subject every linguistic feature to analytic scrutiny to try to find out just what the writer might have intended by using it – we would not do much reading if we did. We focus selectively on some features and disregard others, regulating our attention according to what our own pretextual purpose is in reading the text in the first place – what we are reading it *for*.

So the pragmatic significance of a text, either as intended by its producer or interpreted by its recipient, is not inscribed in the text itself, and cannot be assigned to its linguistic features. Text, we might say, mediates between discourses but the mediation is unreliable and indeterminate. It follows that this significance is always a matter of interpretation and cannot be inferred from linguistic analysis. And this interpretation is always bound to be partial, subject to variable extra-linguistic contextual and pretextual conditions. This is why the texts of the *Declaration of Independence* and Doris Lessing's novel *The Golden Notebook* can be understood in so many different ways.

We use language as the means for signalling our communicative intentions. It is not the only means we have, but for most purposes it is the most convenient and effective. We have something in mind we want to refer to, and this reference is only made in order to perform a communicative or illocutionary act of one kind or another – to inform, describe, advise, warn, apologize and so on. But the textualization of reference and force is itself only the means to an end: to achieve an effect. So it is that in the *Declaration of Independence* reference to life, liberty and the pursuit of happiness has the force of a declaration, but its essential purpose is to achieve an effect – to express defiance and inspire patriotic feelings. And all texts, great and small, spoken and written – speeches, reports, theses, food labels, emails, tweets – all are designed by P1s with the intention of having an effect on P2s of making them act or think in a certain way. If we did not have this primary purpose, there would be little point in producing texts at all.

The idea that texts are necessarily subject to variable and indeterminate interpretation is of course unsettling. It undermines our sense of security. We are so dependent on language as a means of communal interaction and the expression of socio-cultural values that it is disturbing to think that it is of its nature an unreliable means of communication, its meanings relative, unstable and approximate. It is therefore not surprising that the idea persists that pragmatic meaning can be pinned down, that the interpretation of discourse significance can be directly inferred from text analysis. Such belief would seem to inform much of the research that goes under the name of Critical Discourse Analysis, which is particularly concerned with effect, how language is used in the exercise of ideological persuasion. The basic assumption here is that a writer's covert intention to impose a partisan representation of reality can be revealed by a close scrutiny of the linguistic features of texts they produce, and that readers, who typically do not process texts in this analytic fashion, are therefore not likely to notice what ideas, beliefs, values are being subtly conveyed and so are vulnerable to a persuasive effect they are unaware of.

Every text, of course, consists of some combination of selected words and structures available in the language code. The question is, what significance can we, or should we, attach to this selection. The tendency of much critical discourse analysis is to suppose that every selection can be charged with ideological significance. Let us consider an example from one of its most prominent exponents.

In his influential book *Discourse and Social Change*, Norman Fairclough sets out to analyse a particular newspaper headline to demonstrate how it expresses ideological values that the unwary reader would fail to notice. This is the headline: "*Gorbachev Rolls Back the Red Army*". Fairclough comments: "We might well see here a different ideological investment from other ways of signifying the same event, for example 'The Soviet Army Reduces its Armed Forces', or 'The Soviet Army Gives up 5 Divisions'". We might well see this different ideological investment, but equally we might well not. As with the "we" in the *Declaration of Independence*, it all depends on who this "we" refers to. In presuming to represent all readers, Fairclough seems to assume that the change in ideological investment will be self-evident from his examples and so sees no need for any explanation as to how this is actually signalled by these textual alternatives: readers will see this for themselves once their attention is drawn to it. But we as readers might well feel the need for explanation and so seek to find one for ourselves. So how might we proceed in this case?

Fairclough notes that the original "signifies a process of a particular individual acting physically (note the metaphor) upon an entity". So we might infer that the point being made is that in the original the event is represented as brought about by a physical action on the part of Gorbachev, whereas in the alternatives, the agency is represented as an impersonal institution, the soviet army, now promoted to subject position where its agency is supposedly given prominence. So what significance are we to read into this? Institutions themselves cannot act as agents: there has to be some person or persons to make decisions and this is disguised in the alternative headlines which represent the army as an agency in its own right, an independent force over which Gorbachev has no control. Not only has he lost his agency status, and is no longer in control of his army, but he has disappeared from the scene altogether. He has become superfluous. So as far as "ideological investment" is concerned, we might well see these two ways of signifying the same event as highly significant in that they represent radically different power relations between Gorbachev and the soviet army. We might well see this. But equally we might not. I have no idea whether Fairclough himself would agree with this interpretation.

And we have so far only considered one or two linguistic features. Fairclough himself points to other features we need to take note of:

> "Gorbachev" is topic or theme of the clause, as the first part of a clause usually is: the article is about him and his doings. On the other hand, if the clause were made into the passive, that would make "the Red Army" the theme: "The Red Army is Rolled Back (by Gorbachev)". Another possibility offered by the passive is the deletion of the (bracketed) agent, because the agent is unknown, already known, judged irrelevant, or perhaps in order to leave agency and hence responsibility vague. (Fairclough 1992: 75–76)

The theme of a clause is, of course, a formal feature and is not necessarily to be interpreted as having the function of topic, so we cannot infer from the wording of the headline that the following article is about Gorbachev and his doings. The passivization and especially the omission of agency might perhaps be interpreted as a way of leaving responsibility vague and so changing "ideological investment". Perhaps, but, equally, perhaps not.

And what of other linguistic features? What change in "ideological investment" would be signalled, for example, by a change of terms of reference, from *the Soviet Army* to *Soviet Forces*, for example, or *Red Army* to *Soviet Army* – are the terms marked with different connotations, with the *Soviet Army* a more neutral or objective term, the *Red Army* suggestive of menace, perhaps, or heroism? Or what if *Gorbachev* is replaced by *Mikhail Gorbachev*, or *Soviet President*, or *Soviet Leader*? Would this indicate that his action is more or less individual or institutional? And what of the verb phrase? What if we were to replace *reduce* with *cut*, *rolls back* with *cuts back*, or *reduce* with *make reductions*? So we can think of all kinds of other ways of signifying this event:

Mikhail Gorbachev Rolls Back Soviet Forces
Mikhail Gorbachev Cuts Back Soviet Army
Soviet Army Cut Back by Gorbachev

> *Soviet Forces Reduced by Gorbachev*
> *Soviets Reduce Red Army*
> *Armed Forces Reduced by Soviets*
> *Reductions Made in Red Army*
> *Gorbachev Makes Reductions in Soviet Forces*

And so on through a whole range of permutations, to each one of which we could no doubt assign a different "ideological investment" if we were ingenious enough.

But the obvious point is that I would not normally indulge in such ingenuity. When I come across a headline, it is in a newspaper and I read it as a headline and regulate the attention I pay to it accordingly. I do not analyse it as a text in isolation to try to discover what possible ideological significance might be assigned to it. It is pointless to try, for the possibilities, as we have seen, are endless. And this is always going to be the case whenever texts are dissociated from the contexts and pretexts that they are related to in the natural pragmatic process of making meaning.

What users of language pay attention to when they interpret texts and what linguists do when they use texts as data for analysis are two very different things. Interpretation is subject to contextual and pretextual conditions and analysis is not. This is particularly clear in the case of ambiguity. Take the famous example: *Visiting aunts can be boring*. This is ambiguous, as linguists point out, because the surface sequence of forms fuses two distinct structures: To visit aunts can be boring/Aunts who visit can be boring. But it is the sentence in isolation that is semantically ambiguous. But what if this sequence were to be used pragmatically as part of a text? Let us suppose, for example that it occurs in a letter to a friend: *Aunt Anna came round to see us again and spent a lot of time telling us in tedious detail about her holiday in Brighton. Visiting aunts can be boring.*

The ambiguity disappears. The recipient of the letter is not going to notice it. Linguists may notice these things, but only by assuming a non-reader role. My favourite example of this was pointed out to me by a colleague many years ago about an expression that occurred in a news item about stormy weather on the East coast of England. The text went something like this: *Severe storms hit the East coast yesterday with winds reaching hurricane force. Off the coast of Lowestoft, five people were lost in a rowing boat.*

The second sentence here is ambiguous: it could mean that the boat was lost with five people in it, but it could also mean that five (presumably very small people) were lost inside the boat. Well, yes, it *could* also mean this but that is not what it is likely to mean to the readers of the report, primed as they are by the context and assuming that the writer's pretextual purpose was to provide information rather than play with words to make a joke. The point is, of course, that the semantic ambiguity that is assigned to the sentence by analysis is pragmatically over-ridden. The context and pretext do not provide the conditions for activating it.

The problem with a good deal of critical discourse analysis is that how semantic meaning is encoded in linguistic forms is confused with how these forms are pragmatically interpreted. Hence ambiguity would not only be noticed but assigned significance as expressing some underlying attitude, some ideological point of view. This confusion is apparent in the following statement by Michael Stubbs: "Much text analysis, especially within critical linguistics, starts with the Hallidayan assumption that all linguistic usage encodes representations of the world. It is always possible to talk about the same thing in different ways, and the systematic usage of different syntactic patterns encodes different points of view" (Stubbs 1996: 130).

What Stubbs is referring to here is Halliday's assumption that the grammatical features of a language are what they are because they reflect the social functions that they have evolved to serve. But this is an assumption about the language code and its historical development, not about its current usage. One can accept that, historically, linguistic forms are functionally motivated in that they have semantically encoded representations of the world. But as we have seen semantic encodings do not get directly projected in actual usage. How language functions pragmatically here and now is a very different thing from how the functioning of language in the past has become semantically encoded. What the user of a particular syntactic pattern means *by* using it is not at all the same as what meaning a particular syntactic pattern encodes. And we do not understand what is meant by a particular syntactic pattern, or what it means to us, by just decoding it.

Critical linguists (or some of them, at any rate) do, however, seem to understand texts in this way and so to fall prey to what I have referred to elsewhere as the functional fallacy (Widdowson 2004). This is the assumption that *semantic signification* is directly projected as *pragmatic significance* in language use, and that therefore what somebody really means by a text can be recovered from the text itself if one is perceptive enough to read the signs. It is further assumed that readers generally lack this perception and so need to be told what texts really mean and what texts ought to mean to them. Fortunately, critical linguists are on hand to provide an expert exegesis by analysis to put readers right.

But, as I have argued, and I hope demonstrated, texts never contain meaning. A collection of papers by the late John Sinclair, distinguished linguist and pioneer in corpus analysis, bears the title *Trust the Text* (Sinclair 2004), and if one is concerned, as he was, to describe the language that people actually produce, or more strictly what they have produced, in the discourse process, this is an entirely valid piece of advice. But the trust is misplaced if one is concerned with the discourse process itself, the pragmatic use of linguistic resources to make meaning. Here, the last thing you do is to trust the text to tell you what is going on. Trust the text by all means if you are concerned only with text analysis. But if you are concerned with discourse interpretation – Distrust the Text.

For discourse meaning is never discovered in text but always to some degree invented. Significance is never simply signed but always *as*signed and this can only be done by taking context and pretext into account. And of course, the significance that critical discourse analysts assign to texts is no exception. These analysts too have their pretextual purposes. Although they may claim that they can reveal what texts really mean, what they actually do is to provide a commentary on what certain texts mean to them, and they focus on whatever linguistic features suit their purpose. To their credit, they acknowledge their pretext, and state quite explicitly that they are in the business of discourse analysis for ideological reasons – this, for them, is what makes discourse analysis critical. As van Dijk puts it: "Critical Discourse Analysis (CDA) is a type of discourse analytical research that primarily studies the way social power abuse, dominance, and inequality are enacted, reproduced, and resisted by text and talk in the social and political context. With such dissident research, critical discourse analysts take explicit position, and thus want to understand, expose, and ultimately resist social inequality" (van Dijk 2005: 352).

This is, as I said earlier in this talk, a worthy cause, and one I would myself wish to endorse. But the problem with this activist agenda is that being critical in this sense necessarily invalidates the claims that are made for the analysis. For this pretext, like any pretext, is bound to result in a partial and prejudiced interpretation which has no more claim to being real or revealing or significant than any other. Like the readers of Doris Lessing's novel and the members of the National Rifle Association, critical discourse analysts will read into the text whatever meanings suit their own pretextual views of the world. So long as we recognize this, and read the work of critical discourse analysis as what it actually is, namely exercises in critical discourse *interpretation,* no harm is done. On the contrary, their very partiality yields thought-provoking interpretations that can provide us with insights into possible ways of reading meaning into texts we would not otherwise have been aware of. The problem is that these interpretations are presented as having a special authority because they are supposedly based on expert linguistic *analysis* and should therefore take precedence over any other interpretations based on different pretexts. But as I have argued, expertise in linguistic analysis provides no privileged authority to determine what writers or speakers mean by texts or what they should mean to readers and listeners. Text analysis, always necessarily selective, will support whatever partial interpretation fits the pretext of the analyst. Distrust the text, and distrust the text analysts if they are pretending to be authorities on interpretation.

"The question is", said Alice, "whether you CAN make words mean so many different things". Well, Alice, Yes we can. And this phrase itself provides some proof of it – "Yes we can", used by Barack Obama as text in association with a certain context, and a certain pretext can be assigned particular significance. And as with the phrase in the *Declaration of Independence* "all men are created equal" the significance will vary. In the context of the US Presidential campaign in 2008, and for the people who the pronoun "we" was intended to refer to, "Yes we can" had the effect of a clarion call for change. But of course for others of different pretextual persuasion, and who did not take the "we" as referring to them, the text would have a very different effect. And what the phrase means to people now, even those who found it inspiring at the time, is again likely to be different. Again it is obvious that the significance is not in the text itself but a function of how it relates to variable contextual and pretextual conditions.

Can we make words mean many different things? Yes, we can, but what is of interest is not *that* we do it, but *how* we do it. And in investigating how we do it we can be led to understand how communication really works, how it actually depends on meanings not being semantically fixed, how the creative process of making meaning pragmatically crucially depends on the essential indeterminacy of language. This, I think, is what Doris Lessing is getting at in making what she calls "the most fundamental point". If an understanding of a text is taken as fixed, "there isn't anything more to be got out of it". She is referring to a novel: a literary text. And with literary texts understanding is particularly elusive since such texts do not key into context and pretext in conventional ways. All the more reason, one might suppose, to allow for variable interpretation.

But, to turn to educational matters, what allowance for variable interpretation is made in how literature is generally taught in schools and universities? The customary approach to literature teaching is to tell students what texts really mean rather than to get them to explore what these texts might mean to *them*. Indeed, students are not generally expected to engage with literary texts directly but rather to accept the authorized interpretations which teachers and literary critics provide. If they do that, it is possible for them to succeed in their literary studies without really studying literature as such at all. For, as Doris Lessing indicates, literary texts are designed to elude the assignment of definitive meanings, so to deny scope for individual interpretations is to misrepresent the very nature of literature. This would suggest that what literature teaching should do is to get students to engage with literary texts and explore and explain how they relate to their own contextual and pretextual realities and so give rise to variable interpretation. Distrust the text, and, again, distrust those who claim to have privileged access to its meaning. And I think it is one of the main aims of language education to encourage that distrust.

But it is not only literature teaching that represents meanings as text contained. When dealing with conventional non-literary texts, students are also often led to believe that meaning is in the text itself, there to be discovered, but in this case discovery is thought to depend mainly on their degree of linguistic rather than literary competence. Take the kind of comprehension exercise, for example where students are presented with a text in isolation and required to answer questions about what it means, without being cued into any context or pretext that would normally accompany any text, and without any pretextual purpose of their own. As I have said, nobody normally is called upon just to read a text in isolation, out of the blue. There is always a pretext and this pretext, as I have suggested, naturally regulates how much attention you pay to the text – you do not process all of it, every linguistic detail. But this is what these students are being asked to do – to find meaning in a text that is not actually there to be found. No wonder they find it difficult. They can no doubt do some decoding of its linguistic features, but, as we have seen this is a process of semantic analysis and not pragmatic interpretation. So the misunderstanding about the nature of text and the pragmatics of interpretation that I have been discussing is not confined to critical discourse analysis but seems to be prevalent in literary studies and language education generally.

Distrust the text. Let me be clear that I do not mean by this that we should *disregard* the text. We obviously cannot do that because in many cases this is the only trace we have of the discourse process. People make text out of common semantic resources so text provides us with essential *data*. The question is what *evidence* do these data provide of this discourse process of pragmatic meaning making and to answer that question we have to take into account the conditioning factors of context and pretext. So, to return to Alice once more, the question is not whether but *how* words can mean so many different things. Language is of its nature indeterminate, or it would not otherwise function pragmatically at all, so its meaning is always variable and always conditional. This, critically, is what critical discourse analysis actually reveals in spite of its assumption to the contrary. And this, I think, is the essential understanding we need to promote in language and literary education.

But now I must bring this talk to a close. My own pretextual purpose, as will be obvious, has been to provoke you to think about the nature of text and how it gets interpreted. And this of course necessarily applies to the text I have been producing here today. As I have been producing it, you have been processing it – regulating your attention quite naturally according to your own pretexts, deriving no doubt different discourses from it. I do not know whether my intentions match up with your interpretations. Indeed, since all communication is partial and approximate, I shall never know how far what I have meant *by* my text corresponds with what it has meant *to you*.

6 Interpersonal positioning and genre conventions

What are *you* doing here? This is a question one might ask when you come across someone where you don't expect them to be. What am *I* doing here? Well I was invited to give a talk at this conference, I might reply. But what am I *doing* here as I stand in front of you giving the talk? I, as a first person, P1 am producing a form of words by using the resources of the English language, making a text in English that I am addressing to you, the collective audience, P2. Actually I have already made my text, in written form, and I am now reproducing it as spoken text. So how have I made this text? What is it that determines how I design it, what wordings I use?

There are two crucial considerations. First, I, P1, have something in my head I want to say, some message or other, some observation or opinion or an argument, in a word I have some meaning that I intend to express. But a P1 not only *expresses* the self but *addresses* the other, the P2, and so also needs to design text to make his/her intended meaning accessible. It is not enough to make my text express what I mean to say, I must also bear in mind what it might mean *to you*. How a text is designed in other words, depends very much on what P1 assumes to be shared not only with regard to the language the text is made of, but, more crucially perhaps, with regard to the context of world knowledge, attitudes, social beliefs and values and so on. P1 and P2 are each at the centre of their own life space their identity of self which is in some degree socially delimited but which also represent individual contextual worlds which can never completely converge. These spaces may sometimes correspond very closely, of course, and where they do, very little text may be needed for P1's meaning to get interpreted as intended. But even when contextual correspondence is close, as it might be, for example, when the interaction is between partners, or between sons and lovers, this does not guarantee that communication will always be without a hitch. There will always be times when one party will sigh and say, to use the words of the title of a celebrated book by Deborah Tannen, "You Just Don't Understand" (Tannen 1990). There will always be occasions in any communication when intentions are misunderstood and meanings need to be negotiated.

Note: Published in Hopkinson, C., R.Tomaskova & G. Zapletalova (eds.). 2012. *The interpersonal language function.* Universitas Ostraviensis. Originally presented as a plenary address at a conference on the interpersonal function of language, University of Ostrava, November 2012.

https://doi.org/10.1515/9783110619669-010

And when *positions* need to be negotiated too. Here we come to my title and the main theme of my talk. What am I doing here? Producing a text and designing it so that it expresses what I want to say but in such a way, I hope, that it will enable you to access my meaning –that you will understand what I am getting at. But that is not all I am doing here. Getting my meaning across is not my only intention – indeed it is not my main intention. I do not only want you to *access* the meaning I am textualizing, I want you to *accept* it, to recognize its truth or validity so that it has an effect on the way you think. The design of my text has designs upon you: it is motivated by a pre-conceived, a pre-textual purpose. What I am doing at this moment is enacting a discourse through the mediation of my text in order to have an effect upon you. This in Speech Act Theory is called a perlocutionary effect, and it has tended to be left rather in the background in the mainstream pragmatics literature, where more attention is paid to illocutionary force. But I would like to bring it centre stage.

It is not only my present talk that is motivated by a perlocutionary purpose. *All* discourse is. The production of any text, as small as a single word, or as big as a book; be it a public notice, recipe, instruction manual, or philosophical treatise – all are motivated by the pre-textual purpose of achieving an effect Otherwise why would anybody bother to produce a text at all? Even when a P1 makes a text with no particular P2 recipient in mind – writes an entry in a diary, or composes a poem, for example, there is an intention to produce some effect, even if it is only a reflexive one on self. In enacting a discourse of any kind, P1 will always involve the intention of acting upon P2.

So what am I doing here? I am trying to act upon you, not only to make my ideas accessible to you, but also to get you to ratify or share them. These ideas represent my position, my own personal take on the nature of communication, my own conceptual space, and my attempt to get you to share it is a kind of intrusion into your position, your own conceptual space, your territory of self. On this occasion, I am also in a privileged position to do this in that I can take advantage of the conventions of the genre of lecture or plenary address which gives me license to intrude. If you conform to these social conventions, as I am assuming you will be polite enough to do, you will sit there and pay attention to what I have to say, or at least pretend to, and will not start conversations among yourself, or get up and leave the room. Like the wedding guest in Coleridge's *Rime of the Ancient Mariner* you "cannot choose but hear". You can choose not to listen, of course and retire to the private space in your own head, or even doze off, and so reduce my talk to background noise. So although I have the advantage that I am conventionally allowed a long turn uninterrupted by your active participation, I have to find ways to engage your attention and to persuade you to accept my intrusion into your conceptual space.

As I say, since what I am doing here is delivering a plenary address, I am able to assert my position without interruption – you may resist in your mind, even mutter dissent, but you have no P1 turn in this discourse. I have the floor: it is my space. Where discourse takes the form of overt interaction, of course, the case is very different. Here the P1 role is interchanged as different participants take the floor and their positions are overtly negotiated, with each seeking to have whatever effect on the other suits their perlocutionary intention – tactically conceding ground here, tactfully encroaching there as expedient to their purpose.

Interactive encounters may not be equal, of course, and although there may be an interchange of turns, the turn taking may be controlled by genre convention, as in interrogations or interviews, for example. Here the positions of the participants are predetermined and there is little scope for negotiation on the part of the party being interrogated or interviewed. Similarly, the positions of the participants may, to some degree at least, be defined in advance by social status or institutional role, as in the case of the interactions between private soldier and officer, boss and the subordinate, or between teacher and pupil. In such unequal encounters where one party has the power to impose a position on the other, we have cases of what we might call impositioning, although even here, with a little ingenuity, the disadvantaged party can usually find some room for manoeuvre.

The general point I want to make is that all discourse, spoken or written, involves interpersonal positioning, with each participant seeking to have an effect on the other. For there to be any communication at all, there has to be some positional convergence, some give and take. In other words, communication depends on co-operation. In my attempt to communicate my thoughts to you now, I count on your co-operation in allowing them access to your conceptual space, and I might resort to all kinds of rhetorical tactic to make you disposed to co-operate – I have ways of making you listen. So I might, for example, try to impress you with my scholarly authority to make you think that what I have to say is bound to be enlightening, no matter whether it fits in with what you think or not, so you had better pay attention. This is what writers of academic articles seek to do when they sprinkle their texts with references with the sole purpose of displaying their scholarly credentials. Conversely, I might be deferential and suggest that what I have to say is nothing very new but rather common knowledge, or received wisdom, so our positions are congruent and not in conflict. So I might make frequent use of expressions like *of course, as we all know* and so on.

Communication depends on co-operation. And it is this (of course, as we all know), that leads Grice to propose the Co-operative Principle (Grice 1975).

This, with its constituent maxims, is perhaps the most cited reference in the whole literature on pragmatics, and also perhaps the least understood. So let us examine what Grice actually says about it. He calls it "a rough general principle which participants will be expected (*ceteris paribus*) to observe". *Ceteris paribus*, notice – all other things being equal. But, as I shall argue presently, all other things are not equal – there are other things that run counter to this general principle. But for the moment, let us see how Grice formulates it: "Make your conversational contribution such as is required, at the stage at which it occurs, by the accepted purpose or direction of the talk exchange in which you are involved" (Grice 1975: 45).

The obvious question that arises here is who decides, or what determines, "the accepted purpose or direction of the talk"? There are certain accepted social conventions that define different genres which participants will be expected to observe. This present plenary address is a case in point, as I observed earlier. You and I know what kind of communicative event a plenary address is and you will assume that I will conform to the format and follow Grice's maxims accordingly, and try to be as informative, truthful, clear and relevant to its accepted purpose as possible. If the genre and purpose were to be different – if I was giving a sermon, for example, or a funeral oration, or a political speech – then what would be acceptable and required as informative, truthful, clear and relevant would be different. Different genre conventions set different conditions for how the maxims of the co-operative principle are to be appropriately observed.

These conventions map out shared social space, common and communal cultural territory which both parties can occupy, and no negotiation is called for. So when the accepted purpose of a communication is established by the social conventions of genre, co-operation is a matter of conforming to them, and it is clearly in the interests of the participants to conform. This, of course, is why in the teaching of English for specific purposes, so much attention is paid to instructing students in how to conform to the conventions of genre. It is the generic conventions that make the purposes specific.

But genre, like role and status, is a social construct, and like all social constructs it influences but does not determine behaviour. As with the unequal encounters I referred to earlier, the conventions of genre always leave room for individual maneouvre. Although P1 and P2 may accept the conventional generic purpose of the communication they are engaged in, they also have individual purposes of their own. They do not simply enact social roles but as individuals seek to act upon each other in ways I have already talked about. And they do this not by keeping to the maxims of the co-operative principle but by flouting them. People do not always, perhaps do not usually, keep to the maxims, they do not always tell the truth or keep to the point, they may not say what they mean in the most economical or accessible way. Why not? Because they want to express themselves more forcibly, because they want to impress, or avoid offence. In short because they want to act upon each other to achieve an effect. The flouting of maxims, in other words, is a positioning tactic. P1 does it to express an individual position in relation to what is being said, to make it more imposing or more accessible or more acceptable to P2. So what flouting does is to assert P1's personal space and/or facilitate P1's intrusion into the space of P2.

Co-operation is a communicative imperative. Unless you co-operate in some degree, you cannot communicate at all. But since co-operation must involve some convergence of space, there is always another imperative involved which has to be taken into account: what I have called the territorial imperative – the natural urge to assert one's own personal space and protect it against intrusion. The enactment of any discourse involves the tactical reconciliation of these two imperatives as each participant negotiates position on line.

What I am calling the territorial imperative does not only affect how people relate to each other when they use language. It is an instinctive aspect of all human behaviour, as indeed it is of the behaviour of other living beings: all birds and beasts, "all creatures great and small" from ants to antelopes, map out and protect their own territorial space and human beings are no exception. The difference with humans is that this instinctive sense of space is explicitly institutionalized by social convention and custom and their territory assigned to them on the basis of such factors as role and status. This socio-psychological space of self is often socio-culturally symbolized by the delimitation of physical space. Thus, for example, it may be taken for granted that the higher the institutional seniority of a person, the bigger the space entitlement so that whereas the chief executive of a company has sole occupancy of a very spacious office, the lowly underlings get crammed together in a small one. The emperors of China closed off the vast area of the Forbidden City as their personal space, into which nobody outside was allowed to intrude.

So what counts as the physical manifestation of personal space is socio-culturally defined. For example, how close you get to the person you are talking is regulated by social convention and this may well differ across communities. What is a customary, comfortable spatial positioning for one participant may for the other be uncomfortably close and intrusive, or may be too far away for any co-operation to be engaged. Protection of personal space is enshrined, so to speak, in socio-cultural conventions, and so long as both participants in communication share a familiarity with the conventions, and a willingness to conform to them, all is well. Problems arise when, for one reason or another, they do not. But what if circumstances are such that you cannot keep your distance as conventionally required. Consider, for example, how people behave in a lift. If you are alone in the lift, you can claim the whole space as your own, and you can stand right in the middle. If somebody else gets in, you make room and move away, perhaps into a corner, and if more people arrive, they all shift position to keep their distance. You would find it odd if when alone in a lift, a stranger were to come in and stand right next to you – you would take this as an intrusion and feel uncomfortable, perhaps threatened with harassment. Not if this were a friend, of course, for friends are, almost by definition, people you are willing to share space with. But what happens, one might ask, when the lift is crowded and when there is quite literally no room for manoeuvre? In this case, you keep your distance and so protect your self-space by avoiding eye contact. What I am suggesting is that all discourse entails positioning with each participant acting upon the other, each protecting and projecting the position of self and that this necessarily involves somehow reconciling the naturally opposing demands of the co-operative and territorial imperatives.

Now this phenomenon that I call positioning has not, of course, gone unnoticed or undescribed. It is, for example, what Brown & Levinson's Politeness Theory is centrally concerned with (Brown and Levinson 1987). So is positioning just another term for politeness? I think not. Politeness is a theory about face or self-esteem and how participants in an interaction use language to preserve or undermine it. But the question is: what is politeness *for*, what pragmatic purpose does it serve? People do not position themselves just to be polite for politeness sake. If I, as a P1, take care not to offend by respecting your self-esteem, or seek to undermine it, it is because I think that it will further my territorial intentions or make you amenable to co-operation. Politeness, positive or negative, is a positioning tactic, a means to an end. To put the point epigrammatically: people save face to make space. So as I conceive it, politeness is just one way in which positioning is socially enacted.

Positioning is of course a realization of the general interpersonal function of language, and so relates to another notion that has been much discussed in more recent years under the name of metadiscourse. We can, I think, credit Ken Hyland with making a major contribution to this discussion, indeed perhaps initiating it. "The term 'metadiscourse' ", he says, "has emerged to help re-establish the importance of interpersonal aspects of language following a period when linguists were almost exclusively concerned with the ways language is used to convey information" (Hyland 2005: 14).

The term may be new, but the importance of the interpersonal aspects of language it refers to has already long been established. I do not know which period of linguistics, or which linguists Hyland has in mind here. Linguists, even of the most formalist persuasion have always been concerned with modality, that is to say with how interpersonal aspects of language are linguistically encoded. And linguists working in the fields of discourse analysis and pragmatics have always been concerned with how interpersonal aspects are pragmatically realized in contexts of use. What is new is the way these aspects are conceptualized as constituting metadiscourse. This has proved somewhat problematic, as is evident from the following comment: "Despite considerable interest in metadiscourse by teachers and applied linguists, however, it has failed to achieve its explanatory potential due to a lack of theoretical rigour and empirical confusion" (Hyland and Tse 2004: 156).

My own view is that it is in the very concept itself that there is confusion and lack of theoretical rigour. The term "metadiscourse" is used to refer to what I have been referring to as positioning – the various ways in which P1 expresses the position of self and addresses the position of P2. But this is represented as a pragmatic process which is distinct from discourse itself. The basic idea is that in communication there are two kinds or levels of meaning: the propositional and the metadiscoursal. Since the term "metadiscourse" literally means "discourse about discourse" this inevitably represents discourse as constituted only of propositional content, separated from its interpersonal expression. But as I see it, and as I have been arguing, in the pragmatic use of language there is no separable propositional content. It may be convenient for linguistic analysts to pretend that there is, but in actuality there is not. Everything that P1 talks about is interpersonally motivated. The positional and the propositional merge into one. So there is no metadiscourse apart from discourse. There is only discourse. It seems to me that to suggest otherwise is to misrepresent how language actually functions in communication. And I would argue that this misrepresentation comes about because of a conceptual confusion in the use of the very term "function" itself.

Much of the literature on metadiscourse draws inspiration from Michael Halliday's systemic/functional approach to linguistic description. As Hyland says: "Because metadiscourse analysis involves taking a functional approach to texts, writers in this area have tended to look to the Systemic Functional theory of language for insights and theoretical support" (Hyland 2005: 26).

The basic idea of Halliday's theory of language is that what is encoded in language is functionally motivated. There are two essential things that people need language for: to talk about third person things out there and to talk to each other. So we can identify two main functions: the ideational on the one hand, whereby P1 can connect with P3, and the interpersonal on the other, whereby P1 can connect with P2 – or as Halliday himself puts it "to understand the environment (ideational) and to act on the others in it (interpersonal)"

(Halliday 1994: xiii). The encodings of a language are informed by these so-called meta-functions and so provide the potential resource for discharging them. So in Halliday's grammar, the ideational function is provided for by transitivity systems, and the interpersonal by the mood systems. In the metadiscourse literature, the propositional level of meaning seems to be equated with the ideational and the metadiscoursal with the interpersonal. So if Halliday can distinguish them and show how they are separately accounted for in his grammatical description, this would surely justify a similar treatment in the description of discourse (or metadiscourse). No, I would argue (and have argued elsewhere), it does not (Widdowson 2004). And here is where the confusion lies.

Halliday distinguishes these functions so as to provide a rationale for linguistic analysis. They are separated only in order to establish different formal systems which can be used to analyse clauses into their different systemic components, with each reflecting its functional origin. Such an analysis can display what semantic resources are available, what Halliday calls the "meaning potential" that the encoded language provides. But how people draw on these resources, how they realize this semantic potential in various and unpredictable pragmatic ways, is an entirely different matter. Linguistic analysis is one thing, and communicative use another. They simply do not match up.

This becomes particularly apparent, it seems to me, when we consider the third "metafunction" that Halliday proposes: the textual. Whereas the other two obviously have to do with basic human survival and social needs, this one has no such function. This is how Halliday puts it: "Combined with these is a third metafunctional component, the 'textual', which breathes relevance into the other two" (Halliday 1994: xiii).

This textual metafunction is then said to be linguistically encoded in the theme systems of the grammar. One can, of course, understand why, for analytic purposes, it might be convenient to deal with certain formal features of the language in separate encoded theme systems and one can understand too why, since this is meant to be a functional grammar, a metafunction has to be provided to correspond with it. But in reality, in the actuality of language use, there is no separate textual function. Halliday says that it "breathes relevance into the other two" but it is rather that without the other two, it has no functional relevance at all. It exists only to realize these other functions. I only produce a text if I have some purpose in doing so, and, as I have argued, I, as P1, design it in such a way that expresses my position on the propositional content and acts upon the position of my P2.

Now this is not at all to question the validity of these functionally informed systems of grammar for linguistic description. If you want to treat texts as products, dissociated from the contexts and purposes which motivated their productions, if you want to treat them as linguistic objects consisting of clauses and sentences then you can apply these systems to analyse them into their separate components to your heart's content. But if you want to treat texts *pragmatically* as what language users produce so as to engage others in a discourse process, then such analysis will not get you very far. For in actual language use, there are no such separate components, no distinct levels of ideational, interpersonal or textual functions. There is no such thing as metadiscourse as a separate interpersonal level of pragmatic meaning. There is only discourse and discourse *is* positioning, the process whereby people draw on linguistic resources to design texts as suited to their interpersonal purposes. And achieving these purposes, I have argued, will always be a matter of reconciling the cooperative and territorial imperatives.

This negotiation of position is, of course, not an unconditional free for all. As I indicated earlier, individual participants in an interaction are bound to some extent to conform to social custom. The "purpose and direction of the talk exchange" as Grice puts it, will always in some degree be established by sociocultural convention. When people use language, they do so by keying into a kind of discourse or genre they assume to be mutually familiar – they have a chat, make an enquiry, conduct an interview, write a reference, or a report, or an article, deliver a sermon, or, as I am doing now, give a plenary address. And all of these speech events are the socio-cultural constructs that establish the conventional purpose and direction of talk in each case. These constructs are, of course, very likely to vary across different communities – what it is normal to talk about, and how it is talked about, in a chat, or an interview, or a sermon or whatever will differ from community to community. These generic conventions or norms of communicative behaviour effectively stake out the spaces of shared social territory and set the limits within which individuals are expected to co-operate. So at a social level, the common ground for interpersonal positioning is already in place at the onset of the discourse the participants are to engage in.

But people are not just social agents enacting assigned roles, they are individuals and find, as I say, room for manoeuvre at an individual level of interpersonal positioning. There are, it is true, genres or kinds of discourse where the room for individual manoeuver is very limited. In encounters where inequality is institutionalized, as in interrogations or cross examinations at court, for example. Here only one participant is in control of the direction of talk and allowed the initiative to negotiate position. And there are other discourse types where the purpose and direction of talk is prescribed as a fixed routine, as in call centre enquiries, where employees are instructed to keep strictly to a formulaic sequence of utterances. In these cases of what we might call unilateral impositioning, the requirement to conform at the social level holds sway and the level of individual positioning is hardly engaged, if it is engaged at all.

What I am proposing, then, is that there are indeed two levels of discourse, but they are not the levels of propositional or ideational meaning on the one hand and metadiscoursal or interpersonal on the other. The two levels, as I see it, are both levels of interpersonal positioning. One is conventional and social and sets the recognized purpose and direction of the discourse and these participants subscribe to as a precondition of communication. At this level, they recognize that they are involved in a particular speech event – having an informal chat, conducting an interview, delivering a speech, or writing an academic article or whatever – and as social agents, so to speak, they co-operatively regulate their behaviour accordingly to conform to conventional expectation. But, as I have said, people are not just social agents. They are individuals, and they will naturally negotiate the relationship between self and other as individuals. At this individual level, interpersonal positioning is immediate, tactical and largely unpredictable.

On some communicative occasions, as I have indicated, it is the first, the conventional level that dominates and allows little scope for initiative at the individual level- where taking such initiative would be seen as inappropriate, where it would run counter to expectation and have the effect of disrupting the communication. Sometimes, of course, this is just the effect that individuals might want to create – to deliberately withdraw co-operation by breaking free from the territory delimited by social convention and assert their own. There are also cases of personality disorders, like autism, where participants are so enclosed within their own life space that they have problems engaging at the social level of interpersonality at all.

I am suggesting then that we think of discourse as interpersonal positioning that operates on two levels. One is the social level, where it is conventionally circumscribed, and where the relationship between the co-operative and territorial imperatives is mapped out in advance. The other is the individual level, which is a matter of participants negotiating their positions on line, reconciling the demands of the two imperatives as they go along, exercising whatever room for manoeuvre they can find. In normal circumstances, the two levels are interdependent. People do not act independently in disregard of any social convention: all individuals have in some degree been socialized into certain ways of communicating. Nor do people usually just exemplify social conventions: they act upon them in different individual ways, perhaps transferring features from other socio-cultural sources. And these variations on the individual level can, of course, get adopted and conventionalized in the wider community and bring about changes at the social level. An unfamiliar nonconformist way of conducting an interview or writing a financial report – or giving a lecture – may take on a certain popularity or prestige, get imitated and become conventionalized as common practice. This is how change happens in any community.

It is these social conventions that are described under the name of genre. A good deal of research has been done on specifying, to use Grice's words, the "purpose and direction" that are accepted, and expected as appropriate to a particular use of language by a particular community of its users. Thus, to take a well- worked example, the genre of the academic research article is typified as a certain way of organizing ideas – that is to say of staking out, and mapping out, conceptual territory (Swales 1990). This way is authorized by the scholarly community concerned and members of that community are expected to conform to it. So, of course, are those who are aspiring to be members, which is why genre figures so prominently in courses of English for academic purposes. The assumption is that you cannot achieve the purpose unless you follow the right directions as laid out by the genre. And this, it seems, also involves not only getting the discourse right by following the conventions of conceptual organization but also getting the textualization of the discourse right by using the approved linguistic devices, thereby conforming not only to a particular authorized mode of thinking but also to a particular authorized mode of expression. Here conformity to genre conventions would leave little room for interpersonal positioning at the individual level.

But where, I think we need to ask, does this scholarly authority come from and how valid is its jurisdiction? The communicative conventions of a genre are adopted by a particular community. The two concepts are inter-related. As Hyland puts it: "In fact, genre and community determine each other's domain, each helping to form and being formed by the other. Together they provide a descriptive and explanatory framework of how meanings are socially constructed, considering the forces outside the individual which help guide purposes, establish relationships and ultimately shape writing" (Hyland 2005: 138).

Agreed that there are indeed forces outside the individual at the social level, but there are also forces *within* the individual that regulate discourse. What I have been arguing is that meanings are not actually socially constructed in this pre-determined way but are individually constructed on line within the constraints of the social conventions of the genre. Genres are indeed determined by communities and provide the necessary framework for communication: they are necessary for an explanation of the interpersonal function of discourse.

But though *necessary* they are not *sufficient*, because they leave the individual level out of account and of course it is only at this individual level that discourse actually happens at all. Genres are conceptual abstractions that only become apparent when they get realized as actual behaviour, and they naturally get realized at this immediate individual level in all kinds of variable ways. Hyland says that "[g]enres are not (...) overbearing structures which impose uniformity on users" (Hyland 2005: 88). But genres of their nature cannot impose uniformity: no social construct can. There is always bound to be variation in the way social constructs are realized by individual users. Where it is required that genre structures should be closely conformed to, however, then they can indeed become overbearing in that they set limits on individual initiative.

It is communities that determine genre conventions, and conformity to them is a condition of community membership. So it is that we all get socialized into the conventionally accepted patterns of lingua-cultural behaviour in the communities we are born into. These are the primary communities which we inevitably become members of in the process of upbringing. But there are other kinds of community that are not at all like that, where membership does not just happen to you: you have to consciously learn new ways of thinking and behaving to qualify for membership. These are secondary communities that represent professions and academic disciplines, discourse communities (Swales 1990) or communities of practice (Wenger 1998). It is communities of this kind that determine the generic conventions of legal documents, technical reports, and, of course, academic research articles.

So if you want to be accepted as a member of this kind of community, you have to learn to conform to its generic conventions. Now as far as academic communities are concerned, these conventions are enshrined in the editorial policy of so-called learned journals. The editors and editorial boards, as well-established members of this community, are, of course, custodians of these conventions. No matter how innovative the research paper you submit for publication might be, if it does not conform closely enough to these conventions it is likely to be rejected. Well, you might say, that is fair enough – that is how academic standards are maintained. This is to assume that academic standards and generic conventions are essentially the same thing.

But are they? How far do these conventions actually delimit a discipline or practice? Is it the case, for example, that you cannot do research in medicine or physics or economics without conforming to these conventions, that you are not really doing medicine or physics or economics unless you do? These are critical questions which, as Barbara Seidlhofer has pointed out, have far-reaching implications (Seidlhofer 2012).

Although genre is a concept that has to do with discourse in general, whatever language is used to textualize it, writers on academic genres have, generally speaking, been concerned with how these are given particular expression in one language. Their descriptions are mainly of the generic conventions that are followed in academic publications written in English. This, in a way, is only to be expected since most academic publications in the world are indeed in English. But it also raises the question of how far these discourse conventions are to be equated with their particular textual expression, and how far they can be said to represent members of academic communities working in other languages.

The learned journals which maintain these generic conventions are, as Seidlhofer notes, overwhelmingly Anglophone-centric and represent ways of communicating that are sanctioned as appropriate in the English speaker's world. What this means is that, to a considerable extent at least, the authority for determining generic conventions resides in those members of the secondary academic community who happen also to be members of the primary community of English speakers. But what of all the members of this academic community who happen not to be English speakers – all the physicists, biologists, economists whose modes of thinking and expression are informed by a different lingua-cultural upbringing? As Hyland points out: "Discourse communities (...) are often hybrid, characterized by varied values and discourses and by individuals with diverse experiences, interests and influences" (Hyland 2005: 149).

Secondary discourse communities are indeed hybrid and diverse: their values and discourses are informed by different primary cultures, they use different languages in doing their professional and academic work. If such communities determine genres, then one would suppose that their members might have some say in how they are defined, that some allowance would be made for "varied values" and "diverse experiences".

But as far as English is concerned this seems not to be the case: if they want to get published they have to meet genre specifications that have been prescribed for them. And these do not only relate to discourse features like the ordering of content or the structure of argument but also to how these are given textual expression. Journal editors, and indeed those who write about genre or teach courses in English for academic purposes, do not seem to make this distinction. For them, adherence to generic conventions usually also means conforming to standard English and established patterns of native speaker usage. There is little or no tolerance here for the expression of "varied values" or "diverse experiences, interests and influences".

It is just this variation and diversity in modes of thought and expression that characterize the work of members of a discourse community other than those who belong to the primary community of English speakers and which represent academic standards for them. So I would argue that academic standards can be maintained by a discourse community without conforming to currently prescribed generic conventions. Disciplinary fields of enquiry are continuously in flux, paradigms come and go, one way of thinking makes way for another, different ways of conducting and presenting research emerge. And as academic discourses vary and change, academic standards vary and change accordingly. If generic conventions are to correspond with these academic standards, they too have to be subject to the same continual reappraisal and revision.

So, to conclude, what have I been doing here? I have been expressing my own particular position on the nature of discourse and trying to get you to co-operate by sharing my conceptual space. I have sought to persuade you into my way of thinking: that discourse is essentially a matter of interpersonal positioning which takes place at the individual level, within the limits of the social level of genre. As far as genres are concerned, I have taken up the same position, shared the same space, as other scholars by agreeing that they represent the necessary social framework within which individuals have to operate and without which they would have problems communicating at all. In this respect, generic conventions provide enabling conditions for communication within the discourse communities that subscribe to them. But I have tried to get you to share my view that, if, as in the case of English, these conventions are imposed by a particular sub-group within these communities and disallow the expression of "varied values" and "diverse experiences, interests and influences" then they become disabling constraints on variation at the individual level. And since it is variation at this individual level that is the driving force for change, genres then become inflexible and lose their relevance for the discourse communities they are supposed to serve.

In reference to the title of this paper, what I have done is not only discuss interpersonal positioning but actually exemplified it in my own performance. But as I have argued, the effect a text actually has on those who read or listen to it may be very different from that which its producer intended. So how far what I have said has had the desired effect of positioning the reader or listener on my side, I, of course, really have no idea.

7 "So the meaning escapes". On literature and the representation of linguistic realities

Metaphors of a Magnifico

Twenty men crossing a bridge,
Into a village,
Are twenty men crossing twenty bridges,
Into twenty villages,
Or one man
Crossing a single bridge into a village.

This is old song
That will not declare itself . . .

Twenty men crossing a bridge,
Into a village,
Are
Twenty men crossing a bridge
Into a village.

That will not declare itself
Yet is certain as meaning . . .

The boots of the men clump
On the boards of the bridge.
The first white wall of the village
Rises through fruit trees.
Of what was I thinking?

So the meaning escapes.
The first white wall of the village . . .
The fruit trees . . .

In this poem by Wallace Stevens, an event is conceptually represented in three ways, as having three kinds of reality and I want to suggest that these can be seen as corresponding to different ways of conceiving of language. The first reality is one that is directly accessible to third person observation and in this respect is certain as meaning. Concept equals percept. Twenty men one bridge, one village. This, I want to suggest, is the way language is conceived of in corpus linguistics. There they are, men, bridge, village: attested facts of actual occurrence. A second way of conceiving of the event is to see the twenty men as simply one man multiplied so that generalizing from the single instance we can

---

Note: Originally published in 2003. *The Canadian Modern Language Review* 60 (1). 89–97.

https://doi.org/10.1515/9783110619669-011

take it as a replication of twenty, or a hundred and twenty, or any number of men. This, one might suggest, is the way language is conceived of in generative linguistics: no matter how many men there are, they are equivalent in that it is the same bridge they cross, and the same village they see.

But what of the third conception? Each man is also an individual with his own particular experience of the event, and so not just one of a number, nor an exemplary member of the group, and from this point of view there are twenty different perceptions: twenty bridges and twenty villages. This last conception is highly problematic, of course, and it is not surprising that it has on the whole received little scholarly attention. It is much more straightforward to simply record the observable facts or assume that men as the plural of man is just a plurality. And so long as you are only concerned with the noise of their boots on the boards of the bridge, this seems adequate enough. But what when the first white wall of the village rises through fruit-trees? This only happens through individual perception. So the meaning escapes ...

But individual experience has its own reality. And while it may be convenient to rule it out of account on the grounds that it is empirically and conceptually elusive, it will not do to pretend it is not there. Quite apart from anything else, it needs to be acknowledged as a corrective to any claims that might be made about the comprehensiveness of linguistic descriptions. Although we might talk loosely about the linguistics of *parole*, the accounting for the data of actually performed language, we need to recognize that whatever reality is captured, it is not that of individual *actes de parole*. Thus, in corpus descriptions, for example, what is distinctive about these as particular acts of intended meaning necessarily disappears in patterns of collective regularity. And, of course, the variability of individual *interpretations* of texts does not figure in corpus accounts at all. Indeed what is quantified is the reality of production, not reception: there is no measure of the frequency and range of the realization of these texts in actual acts of reading. Though such accounts provide us with a great deal of factual information about texts that have been written, they tell us nothing about the individual motivations that inspired their production, nor of how often they are read or by whom, nor the different discourses that individual readers derive from them. I am not suggesting that corpus analysis should deal with these things – indeed it is hard to see how they could – nor am I saying that its findings are invalid because they do not. I would only point out that their absence must set limits on any absolute claim to be capturing the nature of real language. The reality of the bridge and the village as perceived by each man is missing.

What corpus linguistics provides us with, in fact, is a social construct. Unlike that of Saussure's *langue*, it is behavioural rather than cognitive, a generalized *parole,* but a social construct all the same: patterns of production that represent the collective usage of language communities. There is another area of current linguistics which is concerned with the analysis of actually occurring texts, namely critical discourse analysis. Here too attention is directed to their social features but in this case not simply in order to record their actual textual occurrence but to discover their significance as discourse. Again, it is the communal features of language that are in focus with its individual features factored out. However, whereas corpus analysis is not concerned with what is intended by texts, or how they are interpreted, critical discourse analysis very definitely is. What is of interest now is how texts are expressive of a particular discourse community and its ideology.

The procedure is to look for textual features which are thought to be symptomatic of the ideological position of a particular discourse community. Anything which is idiosyncratic is edited out of consideration. If there are features in a text which cannot be accounted for within the definition of a particular discourse, they tend to be seen as an encroachment of another discourse. The possibility that they may be particular to the individual appears not to be considered. The assumption seems to be that individuals simply act out social roles, and think along the lines determined by their ideological allegiances. They are thus conceived of essentially as representative members of certain discourse communities, as tokens of a type of social construct. Fairclough defines them as institutionally and discursively constructed subjects (Fairclough 1995). This seems to me to be of the same order of abstraction as ideal speaker-listeners in homogenous speech communities. In both cases, the actual reality of the individual is overlooked: the assumption is that one man's perception can stand as representing that of the group and there is only one bridge and one village.

Now of course one can ascribe social roles to individuals and part of their individuality can obviously be associated with this group identity. At one level of generality, we can talk in terms of discourses and genres, and up to a point individuals do conform to social conventions. But only up to a point. The interesting question is up to *what* point? You do not account for what a writer means by a text, or what a text means to a reader by simply identifying its common generic or discursive factors.

The alternative to a general and generic typifying of text is not, as is sometimes suggested, a free-for-all relativization whereby any text can mean anything the individual chooses it to mean. Since individuals are also inevitably social beings, socialized into their communities by the very language they use, they are bound to converge on shared meaning to some degree. As Pennycook points out, quoting Stuart Hall, there are "preferred meanings" and people will "interpret texts in line with, in negotiation with, or in opposition to such preferred readings" (Pennycook 2001: 111). This is obviously true, and such readings clearly provide the basis for the default interpretation of texts. The point I would want to make, however, is that socially formed and informed though they may be, it is individuals who do the lining up, the negotiating, the opposing. They are not just assuming a communal role. They are individual persons, not social persona. As George Steiner puts it:

> No two historical epochs, no two social classes, no two localities use words and syntax to signify exactly the same things, to send identical signals of valuation and inference. Neither do two human beings (...).
> Each communicatory gesture has a private residue. The "personal lexicon" in every one of us inevitably qualifies the definitions, connotations, semantic moves current in public discourse. The concept of a normal or standard idiom is a statistically-based fiction ... The language of a community, however, uniform its social contour, is an inexhaustibly multiple aggregate of speech-atoms, of finally irreducible personal meanings.
> (Steiner 1975: 47)

What both corpus and critical linguistics do, in their different ways, is to focus attention on the social contours of public discourse and disregard the private residue of personal meanings. With corpus analysis this poses no problem. The residue of personal meanings is automatically factored out in the quantification of textual regularities. With critical linguistics, however, things are not so simple. Since it is crucially concerned with the discourse significance of text, it is faced with the problem of identifying which textual features are significant of social contours, and which can be ignored as simply the private residue. Of course, you can reject Steiner's view and say that there is no private residue at all, that every feature of every text carries a social significance, an ideological charge. To demonstrate this would involve a very complex operation indeed, and to my knowledge no procedures have ever been proposed for carrying it out. In practice, Steiner's distinction is presupposed: the analyst fixes on those textual features which seem to be socially significant and just ignores the rest, thereby, of course, imposing a partial interpretation on the text.

And this is what we all do. For of course the conduct of our everyday social lives depends in some degree on our disregarding this private residue. One may accept Steiner's point that no two human beings ever send the same signals, never mean exactly the same thing, but to all social intents and purposes, they have to make believe that they do. For people are also social actors, and as such they have to conspire to co-operate, to a degree at least, by ignoring linguistic particulars and adjusting to a level of common and approximate understanding if they want to engage in public discourse at all.

But to say that people's behaviour, linguistic or otherwise, is socially *informed*, is not to say that it is socially *determined*. When all is said and done, the irreducible "private residue" remains. The cultural commonalities of value and belief that people subscribe to are crucial to their well being since they provide for their security, but precisely because they are common they are bound to leave out of account what is distinctive of individual identity. Communities are constructed out of simplified categories, oppositions and polarities which are sanctioned by social prejudice and political expediency: protestants vs catholics, Marxists vs liberals, good guys vs bad guys, insiders and outsiders, them and us.

The normal business of social life requires a measure of conformity and consistency of behaviour, distinctions and decisions have to be fairly clear-cut and reliable. So it is that what is counted as valid or valued is socially constructed, and is accordingly reflected in our language and the ways it is customarily used. But there is always a kind of individual anarchy lurking just below the surface of this social order. Here good and bad, love and hate, right and wrong, here and there, past and present, fair and foul, and so many other neatly coded oppositions continue to have an inchoate co-existence in individual experience. Every individual is a complex of contradictions.

In reading literature we can inhabit plural identities, invest ourselves in other kinds of being, indulge vicariously and irresponsibly in thoughts and feelings normally kept in check, co-exist in contradictions which would normally need to be resolved. It is this individual and essentially asocial complexity which is represented as an alternative order in literature. In his inaugural lecture as Professor of Poetry at Oxford, Seamus Heaney says that what he calls "the impulse of poetry" is to "place a counter-reality in the scales, a reality which is admittedly only imagined but nevertheless has weight because it is imagined within the gravitational pull of the actual. This redress of poetry comes from its being a revelation of potential that is denied or constantly threatened by circumstances" (Heaney 1990).

"*Poetry*", he says later in the lecture, "gives voice and retaliatory presence to suppressed life".

I believe that the counter reality is that of the private residue of individual experience. The reality of the twenty different bridges, the twenty different villages.

This is what is necessarily edited out of our lives for social convenience: all those controversial, contradictory elements of the individual which have perforce to be suppressed for us to co-operate effectively in our communities. These individual elements are necessarily left out of account in linguistic descriptions which focus attention on the commonalities of social behaviour and belief.

Heaney refers to a potential, and this I take to mean the capability of the individual to create counter-realities by the exploitation of linguistic resources, both those which are encoded and those which are latent in the language. Poetry, he says, is the revelation of this potential. How far it can be revealed in linguistic description is an open question. At all events, we should at least acknowledge the existence of this individual capability and the necessary limitations of a linguistics that does not take it into account. In applied linguistics we are concerned with the relationship between theoretical and descriptive constructs of language, all abstract in one way or another, and the way language is actually experienced by people – by people, not persona, not social actors or discursively constructed social subjects, but people as individuals. Unless we can somehow engage with their reality, our own work in applied linguistics is bound to be limited too.

But the issue of individual reality is not only central to the problems that applied linguistics needs to confront, but is directly relevant to other and wider concerns in the world we live in, which we cannot morally ignore in the cosy enclosures of academic enquiry. I have said that linguists of the corporeal or critical kind find it is convenient to think of people as a collectivity, of the individual simply as one of a number, or exemplary member of a group. One man or twenty men there is only one bridge and one village. But linguists are not the only people who have an interest in reducing individuals to manageable categories. Business people and politicians alike find it expedient to reduce individuals to discursive constructs and treat people as tokens of a type: consumers, communists, fascists, terrorists. Thus categorized, their individuality disappears and they are easier to deal with. And political discourse will always strive for a kind of ideological cloning by invoking a common cause. We have seen this clearly enough over recent years, during which time callous destruction and the denial of human rights on a massive scale have been perpetrated in the name of the democratic values of the so-called civilized world. Contradiction, hypocrisy, injustice, these do not matter: you wave your flag and, like a wand, it transforms everything you do to good, and everything opposing you to evil. To dissent is to side with the enemy.

Now more than ever, it seems to me, is it important to assert the significance of non-conformist, dissident, individual realities of the kind that poetry and literature in general give expression to. Twenty men crossing a bridge into a village. Who are these men, their boots clumping on the bridge, marching into the village? Of what were *you* thinking as the reader of this poem? An invading army, perhaps? That is certainly one possibility: the reality of the third person observer. But it is not the only one. There is also the first person reality of just one man, one individual crossing the bridge, and his unique perception of . . . .

The first white wall of the village . . .
The fruit trees . . .

8 Critical practices: On representation and the interpretation of text

What I want to do in this chapter is to consider what it means to be critical in response to a text. The term *critical* itself is associated with what would appear to be two rather different approaches to textual interpretation: literary criticism on the one hand, and critical linguistics on the other. In the former, the critical response is typically related to *appreciation:* the apprehension of aesthetic effect in texts identified as literary. In the latter, it is related to *analysis* and the uncovering of covert ideological intent in texts in general. There is no reason, however, why literary appreciation should not be consistent with linguistic analysis, and it is precisely the bringing of these two into close and meaningful conjunction that defines the purpose of stylistics. This is what I sought to show in my book *Stylistics and the Teaching of Literature* (Widdowson 1975). In that book I try to demonstrate how literature can be conceived of as discourse, and how one might infer literary effects from linguistic features and so provide a textual warrant for interpretation. What I was engaged in resembled the practical criticism of literary tradition in its general aesthetic purpose (see Cox and Dyson 1963, 1965), but brought more precise linguistic analysis to bear in the process.

The book was, in this sense, an excursion into critical discourse analysis. Not, of course, as that term is currently understood, for critical discourse analysis (henceforth CDA) is the practice of revealing the underlying ideological bias and exposing the covert exercise of power in all texts. It is committed to a quite explicit political cause. As Caldas-Coulthard and Coulthard put it: "Critical Discourse Analysis IS essentially political in intent with its practitioners acting upon the world in order to transform it and thereby help create a world where people are not discriminated against because of sex, creed, age or social class" (Caldas-Coulthard and Coulthard 1996: xi).

This is quite an agenda, and certainly well beyond the modest aims of my own efforts at critical analysis. I had no such commitment to a cause: my purpose was not to expose, but to explain; not to discover devious intent, but to try to work out what it was in texts that gave rise to certain interpretations. Furthermore, I restricted my attention to literary texts. My practical criticism was a far cry from critical practice as defined by CDA. All of which might be said to reveal a certain liberal naivete on my part, or worse, a connivance in the concealment of truth. I was not being critical in the currently accepted sense.

Note: Originally a chapter in Sarangi, S. & M. Coulthard (eds.). 2000. *Discourse and social life*, 155–170. London: Longman.

Indeed, from a CDA point view, I was probably not really doing discourse analysis at all, for from that perspective discourse can only be seen as a set of socially constructed values in which ideology is inevitably implicated. Not only that, but it would seem that the title of my book is a misnomer: I was not really doing stylistics either, since apparently "(...) no analysis can be anything other than ideologically committed. Stylistic analysis is a political activity" (Carter and Simpson 1989: 8).

My work on stylistics was further invalidated, it would seem, by its exclusive concentration on literary texts, and, to make matters worse, by being predicated on the assumption that there is such a thing as literature at all. The orthodox CDA position is that there is no basis for distinguishing a literary text from any other, and therefore there is no such thing as literary criticism: all criticism is linguistic (Fowler 1986). Such an idea is not (as one might suppose) restricted to linguists:

> My own view is that it is most useful to see "literature" as a name which people give from time to time for different reasons to certain kinds of writing within a whole field of what Michel Foucault has called "discursive practices", and that if anything is to be an object of study it is this whole field of practices rather than just those sometimes obscurely labelled "literature".
> Eagleton (1983: 205)

So it would seem that CDA has so defined the field that any discourse analysis which does not conform to its tenets does not really count as critical practice. In this sense, CDA seems to have staked a claim to the whole field of enquiry: it *is* critical discourse analysis, and there is no other, just as, in some people's minds, SLA *is* second language acquisition. In a way, there is no cause for complaint about that. A field will always tend be defined in the terms of its most vigorous development, which is all the more reason for questioning the equation, and this is what I propose to do in this chapter. I shall argue that CDA (in some of its manifestations at least), in seeking to extend its scope of analysis, actually ends up by being reductionist, and far from incorporating literary criticism into a more comprehensive concept of critical practice, it actually applies literary critical procedures in quite inappropriate and uncritical ways.

We may begin by noting that, historically, CDA originated in literary criticism, as Fowler makes clear when speaking of its pioneering days: "... our education and working context made us familiar with the hermeneutic side of literary criticism, and we, like the literary critics, were working on the interpretation of discourse" (Fowler 1996: 4).

It is therefore not surprising to find striking resemblances between the two enterprises. Both assume that there is significance in texts below the level of appearances, and seek to prise it out of the linguistic texture. Both draw on the concept of genre and have an eye for intertextual echoes and allusions. Both assume a privileged authority to provide an exegesis and reveal to unenlightened readers covert meanings which would otherwise escape their notice. The difference lies, Fowler tells us, in the toolkit they were using. The critical linguists had instruments to hand which enabled them to make more precise statements about the language; but they also, of course, were applying these for the interpretation of all discourse, whether recognised as literary or not, on the assumption that there was no real difference between them. The question is: How valid is such an assumption?

As we have seen, it is perfectly valid as far as Eagleton is concerned. So-called "literature" is simply a discursive practice like any other: just a label that people stick on certain kinds of writing for some obscure reason or other, signifying nothing. It is a name, not a concept, and what's in a name? There is, nevertheless, a curious contradiction here. The use of the *term* "literature" is itself a discursive practice and it is precisely the purpose of critical analysis to infer what its use might signify. The point repeatedly made by sociolinguists, and not only those of critical linguistic persuasion, is that there is good deal in a name: that the way things are labelled marks sociopolitical values. They are not just randomly attached. So if people identify something as distinctive, then it *is* distinctive. If, for example, they say that what they speak is a distinct language, then that defines it as a language and there is no point in the linguist insisting that it is a dialect. By the same token, if people say that certain texts are literary, that defines them as such, no matter what literary theorists might say; and to identify texts as literary is to adopt a certain attitude to them and a certain way of reading them. So which way?

Let us enquire into the question by considering two texts. They are alike in that they are both in English and have a common topic: the death of a woman. They are comparable in length, both about 80 words, and in each case the text is vertically rather than horizontally aligned – that is to say, it does not extend over the whole page but is confined in a column of print.

Text A
Annabella, film actress,
died on September 18
aged 87, she was born on
July 14, 1900

Even from earliest childhood
Annabella had a passion for
cinema. As a child playing in
the garden of her family home
near Paris, the chicken shed

out in the yard became her
imaginary studio where, lost
in a world of imagination, she
would act out scenes from the
films she had watched, taking
upon herself the roles of director,
cameraman and leading
lady all at once.
       (From *The Times* 23. 9. 96)

Text B
She dwelt among the untrodden ways
Beside the springs of Dove,
A Maid whom there were none to praise
And very few to love.

A violet by a mossy stone
Half hidden from the eye!
– Fair as a star, when only one
Is shining in the sky.

She lived unknown, and few could know
When Lucy ceased to be;
But she is in her grave, and, oh,
The difference to me!
   (From William Wordsworth. *Collected Poems*)

We readily identify these texts as different in genre: the first as a newspaper obituary, the second as a poem. One immediate consequence of this is that we disregard the vertical arrangement in Text A as a feature of no significance. We know that columns of print are conventionally used in newspapers to save on space, or to provide convenient blocks of text for easy reading when folded. In Text B, on the other hand, we recognise that we do not just have an expedient disposition of print, but a pattern of metrically regular lines which are intrinsic to the text itself. Identifying the first text as a conventional obituary also leads us to overlook other textual features. We recognise that its purpose is to provide information about a particular person and that the language is effective to the extent that it succeeds in doing that. In other words we use the language indexically as a set of referential directions, and ignore any textual features which are not referentially functional. So it is that while we take note of structural features, we attach no particular importance to their sequential realization. Consider the consequence of making *structural* changes to the heading of the text so that it reads:

Annabella, film actress,
was born on September 18
aged 87, she died on
July 14, 1900

The text now fails in its indexical function: it directs the reader to a referentially impossible world, but a non-structural *sequential* alteration has no such referential effect. The sequence, we might say, has no *con*sequence:

Film actress, Annabella
Was born on July 14, 1900,
Died on September 18 aged 87

Now consider where sequence involves structural change:

From earliest childhood
Annabella even had a passion
for cinema.

The shift of the word "even" completely alters the referential meaning and makes it pre-suppositionally dependent on some non existent context of shared knowledge. Not so with a sequential shift of the adverbial phrase:

Annabella had a passion for
the cinema even from earliest
childhood

Text A, then, can be sequentially reformulated in different versions which do not affect structure and so do not change its meaning in any substantial way. The differences do not matter and this suggests that there are features of conventional texts which readers edit out as of no pragmatic importance. What matters is that the texts should indexically refer, and this means that they should effectively refer readers to some context of situation that they can recognise in their world. Even structurally malformed texts can be pragmatically effective. It is unlikely, for example, that newspaper readers would be disturbed by the dangling participle in Text A: "As a child... the chicken shed". It is not the chicken shed that is playing in the garden. This is nonsense as grammatically signified; but it is nonsense that, pragmatically speaking, does not signify. None of the people to whom I have given the text to read (even abstracted from its normal appearance on the newspaper page) has noticed the structural non-sequitur.

It is a pragmatic truism that readers normally proceed on a least effort principle, and treat language in a fairly cavalier fashion: they pay attention to it only to the extent that it makes a satisfactory indexical connection for them.

Writers also, of course, design their texts accordingly, assuming, for their part, that the Gricean co-operative principle is in place (Grice 1975) and that readers will not perversely dissect their texts and analyse the grammatical entrails. They assume that they are writing for readers not analysts. They do not realise that they might have critical linguists to reckon with. But I anticipate. We have yet to consider Text B.

As I have already mentioned, in identifying this as a poem, we recognise that its actual textual shape is intended to be significant. It is a series of metrically regular lines, which are ordered in a rhyme scheme. There is here a patterned texture, a secondary arrangement of language which is not informed by the requirements of the language code itself. There is significance here in the textual design which is not simply a matter of what the linguistic elements signify. With Text A you can meddle with sequence without altering the referential functioning of the text. Meddling with Text B, however, is a very different matter, for in so doing you inevitably alter the second order textual design (for further discussion, see Widdowson 1986):

> She dwelt beside the Springs of Dove,
> Among the untrodden ways,
> A Maid whom there were none to praise,
> And very few to love.
>
> A Maid whom there were very few to love,
> And none to praise,
> Dwelt among the untrodden ways
> Beside the Springs of Dove.

So why then should it matter if the textual design gets changed? If it does not affect referential functioning in Text A, why should it do so here in Text B?

My answer would be that there is no referential functioning in Text B, and that the textual design in effect closes the text off from contextual connection. Thus although both texts are about women, their mode of existence is quite different. The description of Annabella in the obituary corresponds to a factual counterpart. She has independent existence quite apart from the text, and we could, if we chose, check up on the accuracy of the information we are given about her. The text is organised to achieve this referential purpose as effectively as possible. Thus Annabella is named at the start, and information about her is provided to establish her as the topic, and the pronoun *she* then functions anaphorically for subsequent reference in the normal co-operative way. But Lucy has no separate existence outside the poem: she is created in its very design. And so it is that her first appearance is not as a person at all but as a pronoun, a pro-person, and we are kept in the dark about who she is until the last verse, and even then all we get is a name. Her identity is traced only in the patterns of negative phrases: *untrodden, none, very few, only one, few, unknown, ceased to be*. The language itself *represents* who she is.

I suggest, then, that the secondary patterns of language in the poem close it off from context and, in so doing, set up conditions for representation rather than reference. It would follow that if you wanted to be referential, you would avoid such patterns. And here one might cite the example of William Whewell, author of a learned work (published in 1819) entitled *Elementary Treatise on Mechanics* (quoted in Butler and Fowler 1971: Text 23). In it Whewell wrote the sentence: *There is no force, however great, can stretch a cord, however fine, into a horizontal line that is accurately straight*. It was pointed out that he had thereby produced inadvertent verse. When it was pointed out that this secondary patterning would be distracting, Whewell restored normal referential conditions by deleting the offending sentence in the next edition of his book. Where such patterning is apparent, the reader will, I argue, read the text as representation rather than reference.

So, if we were to modify Text A in only quite minor ways to provide it with such patterning by changing the way the text is disposed on the page and giving metrical regularity to the lines of print, it would, even though its propositional content remains essentially the same, no longer be read as a conventional obituary, but as a poem, and Annabella would accordingly, like Lucy, be closed off within it, and take on a different existence.

> Even from her earliest childhood
> Annabella had a passion
> For the cinema and she
> As a child and playing in
> The garden of the family home,
> The chicken shed out in the yard
> Became her studio and there,
> Lost in her imagined world,
> She acted out the scenes from films
> She had watched, while taking on
> In turn the different roles herself
> of film director, cameraman
> And leading lady all at once.

I would not claim much merit for this as a specimen of verbal art. It may not be adjudged to be a very good poem, but it is read as a poem nevertheless, and so understood quite differently from the way the original Text A is understood. You do not treat it indexically by using it as a set of directions for engaging some existing reality. In the reading of normal conventional texts your attention is directed *away* from the text and you take note of its linguistic features to the extent that they are referentially effective. But in reading a poem, your attention is directed *into* the text, and you seek significance in the very textual pattern. So, to take just one example, in the Annabella obituary, it does not matter in what sequence the noun phrases *director, cameraman, leading lady* occur. In the Annabella poem, it does: you read significance into the sequence. And it matters too that the last of them has a line all to itself.

The literary texts we have been concerned with so far take a poetic form, and here, of course, the secondary patterning and its enclosing effect are particularly apparent. But I believe that enclosure is a defining feature of all literature. So I would argue still (as I have argued with stubborn persistence ever since Widdowson 1975) that if you read something as literature, you recognise that it does not have any direct referential connection with your concerns. The text is essentially parenthetical and unpractical, and you are relieved of any obligation to take it seriously. It would not matter if you did not read it at all. Literature is an optional extra. It represents an alternative reality in parallel, which co-exists with that of the everyday world, *corresponds* with it in some degree, but does not *combine* with it. You do not have to act upon it, or incorporate it into the continuity of your social life, or make it coherent with conventional modes of thought. You do not have to worry about whether your interpretation corresponds with the author's communicative intention. You assume that the very existence of the text implies intentionality, some claim to significance, but you are free to assign whatever significance suits you. There is no possibility of checking out whether your understanding matches what the author meant, and no penalties for getting it wrong. In this respect, the literary text is in limbo: there is authorship but no ownership. As the French poet Paul Valery observed: "There is no true meaning for a text. No author's authority. Whatever he may have wanted to say, he has written what he has written" (quoted in Butler and Fowler 1971: Text 542).

In literature, the text does not mediate between first and second person parties. It floats free in a state of vacant possession for readers to appropriate and inhabit. The reader engages *with* the text but cannot participate in interaction with the writer *through* the text. *Interpretation*, therefore, is not concerned with what the writer meant by the text, but what the text means, or might mean, to the reader. One might indeed hazard the proposition that what defines a literary text is that it is essentially vacuous, in the sense that it creates a vacuum for the reader to fill. Here, for example, is the beginning of Hemingway's story *The Short but Happy Life of Francis Macomber:* "It was lunch time and they were all sitting under the double green fly of the dining tent pretending that nothing had happened".

Here a scene is textually set, with time and place location linguistically specified. The definite article signals shared contextual knowledge, but there is no shared contextual knowledge. The pronoun *they* presupposes that we know who the referents are, but we don't: the specification leads to no identification. They are pretending that nothing had happened, and this presupposes something *had* happened, a previous event to which this text refers, and that we are in the know. But we are not in the know, and there is no previous event. In short, the text creates the illusion of contextual space, a referential vacuum which the reader is drawn into to give imaginative substance to. It is this being drawn into a different contextual reality, being absorbed into a different order of things that is, I think, the essence of aesthetic experience. In this way, readers make the literary text their own.

Let me illustrate this by referring to another literary text. This is from R. K. Narayan's novel *The English Teacher*. Krishna, the hero, teaches at the Albert Mission College in the little town of Malgudi. He has a thick notebook in which he intends to write down the poetry he has ambitions to compose. Inspiration flags, however, and he has only ten pages or so to show for his pains. His wife, Susila, mocks him.

> The trouble is I have not enough subjects to write on,' I confessed. She drew herself up and asked: "Let me see if you can write about me".
> "A beautiful idea", I cried. "Let me see you". I sat up very attentively and looked at her keenly and fixedly like an artist or a photographer viewing his subject. I said: "Just move a little to your left please. Turn your head right. Look at me straight here. That's right ... Now I can write about you. Don't drop your lovely eyelashes so much. You make me forget my task. Ah, now, don't grin please. Very good, stay as you are and see how I write now, steady ..."

Krishna then writes down in his notebook the following lines:

> She was a phantom of delight
> When first she gleamed upon my sight,
> A lovely apparition sent
> To be a moment's ornament ...

and several more, thirty lines in all. His wife is most impressed.

> "I never knew you could write so well."
> "It is is a pity that you should have underrated me so long; but now you know better. Keep it up," I said. "And if possible don't look at the pages, say roughly between 150 and 200 in the Golden Treasury. Because someone called Wordsworth has written similar poems."

Of course his wife looks through these pages and discovers that the poem is word for word a copy of one by Wordsworth. *"Aren't you ashamed to copy?"* she asks, and Krishna replies: "No. Mine is entirely different. He had written about someone entirely different from my subject".

One reason why Krishna can make this claim is because the pronoun *she* that begins the poem is indeterminate. It refers to no person: it represents a persona, and so he can appropriate it to represent his wife. In conventional terms, third-person pronouns are used as tokens of more complete references. *She* encodes the semantic features of singular and female. That is a linguistic fact. In normal circumstances it can therefore be used to refer to some single female person who does not have to be explicitly identified because the addressee knows who it is. The pronoun is pro somebody. But who is *this* she? There is nobody around for the pronoun to be pro for. There is no indication of identity in the poem. *She* is used like a proper noun, as if referring to some specific and unique identity, a named person: Barbara was a phantom of delight... or Sally, or any other *she* who delights you. But the use of the pronoun as a proper noun is most improper, because it presupposes specific reference when there is none. So a referential vacuum is created and readers can fill it with whatever identity they choose And notice, in passing, that it is not only a matter of investing this pronoun with unique significance as a term of reference. Krishna pretends to be composing the poem from life, as if it were a verbal painting. His wife is sitting for her portrait. "Let me see if *you* can write about *me*", she says. "Let *me* see *you*", Krishna says. The poem is thus made specific to this interaction and the pronoun in it therefore acts also as a term of address. Part of Susila's pleasure in the poem is that she takes it not just as *referring* to her but as *addressed* to her:

> *You were a phantom of delight*
> *When first you gleamed upon my sight (...)*

She is a third-person pronoun which encodes singular and female so in the absence of anybody that it can refer to, the reader can invest it with any singular and female identity. This is a literary effect. So in a way Krishna is right. He makes the poem his own. The text may be Wordsworth's, but it is a poem only because its meaning can be individually invested by other people. In performing the poem, they appropriate it.

The general point, then, is that a literary text is different because it does not mediate between first-and second-person parties as other texts do. This means therefore that Grice's co-operative principle, the normal social contract between parties which enables them to converge on agreed meaning, is necessarily in abeyance. However, literature is not normal communication. We assume intentionality, but there is no way of assigning intentions. It makes no sense to ask whether the events are being presented as true, or according to normal expectations of economy or clarity of expression, or as relevant to what has been previously said or to the immediate context. We do not require of literature that it should be true, but only that it should carry conviction; we do not require of it that it should be relevant, but only that it should be consistent and coherent on its own terms and in its own terms. There is no point in trying to trace what is being referred to, because the point of literature is that it does not refer to actual worlds, but represents imaginary ones.

Literary texts are not bound by the co-operative conditions of conventional communication because they are disconnected from the social contexts in which those conventions operate. They are of their nature untrue, uninformative, irrelevant and obscure. The Gricean maxims of quality, quantity, relation and manner are consistently denied, and consequently literary texts give rise to complex and unresolvable implicatures on a vast scale. It is this which constitutes their aesthetic effect. Ordinarily, in the normal, non-literary business of communication, the text *does* of course mediate between parties in the general social process, and the co-operative principle *does* come into play. Authors assume first-person responsibility, mindful that they will be held accountable for the text, and that it can be referred back to them by the reader. Readers, for their part, co-operate by indexically interpreting the spirit rather than the letter of the text. To return for a moment to the Annabella obituary, as readers we would normally assume that the writer is not being deliberately untruthful and obscure, so we edit out of our reading any textual feature that might suggest otherwise. Thus the dangling participle referred to earlier is not fixed upon as evidence of obscurity, and we do not scrutinize the semantics of individual words for their truth value. Take the expression "Even from earliest childhood". *Earliest* childhood? From the moment of birth? When "mewling and puking in the nurse's arms"? In her pram? The fact is that we relate what is said in the first sentence of the text to what is said in the second and realize that, whatever he may have actually *said*, what the writer *meant* was not the earliest period of childhood, but the one at which children are capable of playing on their own in a garden. We take this as read. We do not accuse the writer of falsehood.

But critical linguists do not take such things as read. They operate by denying the co-operative principle. They take a fix on specific textual features and assign them significance. Here, for example, is Fairclough commenting on the newspaper headline "Quarry load-shedding problem":

> The grammatical form in which the headline is cast is that of nominalization: a process is expressed as a noun, as if it were an entity. One effect of this grammatical form is that

crucial aspects of the process are left unspecified: in particular we don't know who or what is shedding loads or causing loads to be shed – causality is unspecified.

(Fairclough 1989: 51)

What is left unspecified is crucial, according to Fairclough, because it "avoids attributing any responsibility". But significance is here assigned to the grammatical device of nominalisation *per se* in disregard of the fact that the use of this form is a matter of standard format, a convention for newspaper headlines, motivated by considerations of space and so on. It serves the same practical function, therefore, as the vertical alignment of text in columns, as in the Annabella obituary (and it is indeed this alignment which commonly requires headlines to be so compacted). If one is to be taken as significant, then by the same token presumably the other ought to be so as well. But readers would normally attach no significance to either.

Leaving all this aside, however, it should also be noted that although it is a semantic fact that nominalization leaves aspects of the process unspecified, it does not follow at all that its pragmatic *effect* is necessarily to conceal such specification. Effect is a matter of reader response, and although we might not know who or what is doing the shedding, the readers of *The Lancaster Guardian* (from which the headline was taken) probably do, in which case there is no concealment. There is also some textual evidence that they do know, for in the body of the text reference is made to the fact that the load-shedding lorries are "still causing problems". This text, therefore, has contextual and/ or intertextual connections: it apparently refers to something already familiar to the readers for whom the text is written, and/or something already mentioned in the newspaper, and if this is so, then there would seem to be no reason to read an ulterior motive into its use here. Nominalization is, after all, routinely used as a cohesive device, as is pronominalisation, in the interests of communicative economy: it serves not to establish reference but to maintain it, anaphorically, through second mention. Also, its use is essentially co-operative since, without it, texts would be clogged up with unnecessary information, and so its use for this purpose is considerate of the second-person reader. In short, referential *avoidance* is not the same as referential *evasion*.

The same point can be made about the critical analysis of the following text that is offered in Lee (1992): "The black township of Soweto which has been simmering with unrest since the riots on June 16 and the shooting of 174 Africans erupted again today".

Lee comments: "(...) the emotions of individuals and the actions they give rise to are transferred onto the place where they live. It is the 'township' that has been simmering and that now erupts, rather than the Sowetans experiencing anger and deciding to march" (Lee 1992: 93).

Here we are told the effect of predicating the verb *simmer* of a township is to deflect attention from the fact that it is its inhabitants who are simmering. But this ignores the entirely normal and productive metonymic process whereby a place is routinely taken to refer to people in it: *France declared war ... Britain claims fishing rights ... Moscow denies ... The White House is worried* and so on. Nobody, presumably, would suggest that in these cases there is any devious attempt to conceal human agency. It is also worth noting that on corpus evidence there is nothing particularly unusual about the collocation of the word *township* with *unrest* and *violence*. It would appear that, as with the other nominalisation we have considered, the expression *township unrest* would generally serve quite normally and cooperatively as a conventional device for referential avoidance (not evasion) in the interests of economical topic continuity.

These are just two examples, but they are typical of much CDA work of this kind.[1] The procedure is to fix on some particular linguistic feature, grammatical or lexical, and assign it ideological significance without regard to how it might be understood in the normal indexical process of reading. Indeed the analysis is designed to counteract this normality: critical analysts take up a deliberately non-co-operative position on the grounds that to co-operate is to collaborate in the hegemonic imposition of ideological values. Thus, the whole purpose of critical analysis of this kind is to isolate the text from the contextual conditions that would normally be associated with it. In other words, it treats texts (or, more usually, text fragments-see Stubbs 1996: 129) as if they were literary.

The point about literary texts, as I have indicated earlier, is that they are *designed* to be contextually detached, so that, free of the constraints of co-operation, readers are licensed to focus selectively on whatever textual features they might fancy, and infer significance from them. Hence, of their very nature, literary texts will give rise to divergent interpretations. That is what is distinctive about literature: that is what it is *for*, but other uses of language are based on the assumption that co-operation is in place. The basic contradiction in CDA

---

[1] *work of this kind*: an important proviso. I would not want to say that all critical analysis as currently practised is textually fixated in this way, nor that many of its practitioners are unaware of the limitations of an analysis that is. It might also be objected that in taking these particular comments out of context and subjecting them to critical appraisal, I am falling into the same trap of partial interpretation based on fragmentary evidence. There is the difference, however, that I am considering not the covert significance of textual features, but claims that are explicitly made; and the two examples I discuss here are not isolated instances but are representative of a very general tendency. For further exemplification and discussion see Widdowson (1996, 1998, 2004) and for other criticism along similar lines of this kind of analysis, see Hammersley (1996), Stubbs (1997) and O'Halloran (1999).

is that it detaches the text at the receiving end, by denying the normal process of co-operative reading, but keeps it firmly attached at the producing end by assuming it to be informed by ideological intent.

The fact is that textual data will always yield uncertain evidence. This is something that writers of literary texts exploit, and writers of conventional texts have to counter. Either way, the uncertainty can only be resolved by adopting a particular second-person position, and so it is that a quest for what the author intended by the text will always lead you back to your own interpretation. Your findings will effectively be inventions, and the further you need to quest, the more you will invent. This seems clear from the two examples I have considered here. The analysis is bent on uncovering what is going on behind the textual scenes and pays selective attention to particular details: a word here, a grammatical form there. There is little if any consideration of how these features act upon each other in the text, or upon contextual conditions outside it or, in general, how the text is actually processed as discourse. There appears to be no principled theoretical motivation for picking on particular features.

So on what basis are they selected? The only basis, as far as I can see, is the analyst's own second-person position as interpreter. Critical analysts may claim that they are assigning significance on behalf of other readers, but they can only do so by imposing their own position in disregard of the response of readers for whom the text was designed. They exploit the text for their own ideological purposes.

So what, in effect, critical linguists do is to read themselves into texts, just as Krishna reads himself into Wordsworth's poem. The crucial difference, of course, is that Krishna does not claim special validity for his reading as revealing the real significance of the poem, which other readers have failed to notice. Of course, if he were a literary critic, and not just an English teacher, he might be tempted to do so, for literary critics, like critical linguists, have a way of claiming privileged status for their partial interpretations, similarly based on a selective attention to text, and, as Fowler points out, using a limited toolkit to boot. It was, in fact, the purpose of Widdowson (1975) to demonstrate how, in a stylistics approach to literature, such partial interpretations might be referred to more specific linguistic evidence. This, however, was not in order to close down on interpretation and confirm any particular reading as "correct", as recovering the meaning that was "really" there, embedded in the text; on the contrary, my purpose was to show how reference to textual patterns revealed how the diversity of literary effects was necessarily a function of the essential indeterminacy of language. This is what, to my mind, made it critical. It is an odd irony that critical discourse analysis is the name that is now given to the use of linguistic insights (the better toolkit) for the assertion of the same kind of privileged partiality of interpretation that is characteristic of the kind of literary criticism that I was seeking to counteract with my stylistics.

I believe that literary criticism and critical linguistics depend, for their validity as areas of inquiry, on recognizing the nature of the texts they are dealing with and why they give rise to variable interpretation. Both are, to my mind, centrally concerned with how meanings are read into texts. What distinguishes the two activities is the *kind* of interpretative conditions that apply. As I suggested earlier, if people give the name "literature" to a certain kind of writing, then they will read it in a particular way, and this, I have proposed, essentially involves *recognising* that the text is contextually disconnected and so the co-operative principle is in abeyance. So, whereas both activities must be centrally concerned with how meaning is variously derived from text by a process of pragmatic inference, critical linguistics has to show how this is done when the co-operative principle is in place, literary criticism when it is not.

9 The novel features of text. Corpus analysis and stylistics

These are only hints and guesses,
Hints followed by guesses.
   (T. S. Eliot *The Dry Salvages*)

Stylistics claims to provide linguistic substantiation for the interpretation of literary texts. Since corpus analysis is *par excellence* a means of revealing textual features in precise detail, it seems reasonable to suppose that it must be relevant to the stylistic enterprise. One advantage of corpus analysis by computer is that it can be so comprehensive in its coverage of the textual facts: it can yield a quantitative account of the recurrence and co-occurrence of all the words in a text. It is, however, precisely because it provides such detailed information that it brings into particular prominence the criticism that Stanley Fish levelled at stylistics in general, long before corpora and computers came on the scene (Fish 1973). As Stubbs points out (Stubbs 2005), Fish charges stylistics of being circular and arbitrary in that it presupposes relevance in advance. The analysis either selects literary features that are deemed to be significant and then adduces linguistic features to substantiate their significance, or it selects linguistic features and then claims that they are of literary significance. In the pre-corpus period, stylistics is particularly vulnerable to the first charge: generally speaking, what directed the selection of linguistic features was some impressionistic sense of literary significance. It worked from the literature to the language. With corpus analysis, however, we have the possibility of working in the other direction. Now that we have the linguistic facts of texts available to us in such comprehensive detail, we are in a position to make inferences from them about their literary significance. We can at least be certain about the linguistic facts. The problem of relevance, however, remains, and indeed becomes more difficult precisely because we have so much linguistic information to deal with. How do we decide what to select as significant?

This problem is both explicitly addressed and exemplified in the article Stubbs (2005) already referred to where by methods of quantitative stylistics are applied to Conrad's well-known short novel "Heart of Darkness". This article is a fascinating exercise in corpus analysis which reveals textual facts which are likely to be unknown even to those readers who know the novel well.

Note: Originally a chapter in Gerbig, A & O. Mason (eds.). 2008. *Language, people, numbers. Corpus linguistics and society. A Festschrift for Michael Stubbs*, 293–304. Amsterdam & New York: Rodopi.

https://doi.org/10.1515/9783110619669-013

They certainly came as a revelation to me. But the article is of particular interest because the analysis raises more general issues about text interpretation – about linguistic facts and literary significance, about the limits of analysis, about the Fish dilemma. What I intend to do in this paper is to take up some of the points that Stubbs makes in his article in order to reflect on these wider issues.

The aim of his article is to apply a computer program to the text as corpus data and to demonstrate how the software can "identify textual features which are of literary significance, including features which critics seem not to have noticed" (Stubbs 2005: 6). As I have already observed, it is unlikely that the literary critic will have noticed many textual features of the kind that computer software will reveal, and one can acknowledge that the value of corpus analysis is that it can provide textual substantiation to impressionistic interpretation. And indeed this particular analysis provides convincing linguistic evidence to support what literary critics have identified as the motif of dark indeterminacy that runs thematically through the novel. Thus, for example, MS points out that the computer reveals a high incidence of words denoting perceptual unclarity: *darkness, mist, shadow, gloom* and so on, and of expressions of vagueness: *seem, some, something* and *like*. He notes that there is a repeated occurrence of adjectives with a negative prefix like *impossible, uneasy, unexpected, impenetrable* and so on.

Inspired by this kind of analysis, one finds oneself scrutinizing wordlist and concordance for other findings which might be revealing. Use of the Wordsmith Tools software (Scott 1997; Scott and Tribble 2006), enables me to note, for example, that though these negatively prefixed adjectives occur frequently, adjectives generally seem to be in short supply in the text. Only two (*sombre* and *black*) appear in the first 50 keywords (using BNC World as a reference corpus), and the most frequently occurring are simple, descriptively spare, monosyllabic (*long, great, black, white, old*). The description of river and forest is almost colourless (of the colours that one might expect to figure in such a description, *green* occurs only five times, *brown* only four). One might conclude that it is a rather featureless world that Marlow describes, a monochrome world in black and white, a kind of abstraction. All of these textual features can be said to substantiate the general impression that in Conrad's novel there is a pervasive presence of something essentially negative and indeterminate. The very texture of the style is, we might say, a representation of reality that can only be perceived, in the words of the apostle Paul, "through a glass darkly". The textual facts, then, can be adduced as evidence that "[t]his is a novel about the fallibility and distortions of human knowledge" (Stubbs 2005: 12).

But, of course, only some textual facts are adduced as evidence, and their selection has been prompted by an impressionistic literary presumption that this is indeed what the novel is about. We have yet to contend with Fish. For the computer software will also reveal a whole host of textual features that the literary critic, or anybody else for that matter, would also fail to notice but which do not seem to be noteworthy. MS recognizes that textual features, however selected, "still require a literary interpretation". But then it cannot be the case that "the software can identify textual features which are of literary significance". This is because literary significance can only be assigned to *Heart of Darkness* as a *novel*, not as a *text*.

In this article, MS almost always refers to *Heart of Darkness* as a book or a text, hardly ever as a novel. But for the literary critic, of course, as for the normal reader, that is what it is. It is not just a book. Even less is it a text: a text is something you analyse, not something you read. Stubbs, always admirably cautious in making claims for his analysis, acknowledges that "textual frequency is not the same as salience, and does not necessarily correspond to what readers notice and remember in a text" (Stubbs 2005: 11). But the point is that readers do not process texts qua texts at all, and what they notice and remember are not textual features as such but their discursive realization in newspaper articles, manuals, leaflets, letters. And novels. The corpus analyst necessarily deals with *Heart of Darkness* as a text, a linguistic object. But the literary critic deals with it as a novel, a discourse, a particular genre of verbal art. So they are naturally inclined to notice different things: features of the text on the one hand, aspects of the novel on the other.

To return now to the point made earlier about the two possible directions of enquiry in stylistics, it seems obvious that we need to identify literary features first. In the present case, we need to consider not which linguistic features can be analysed out of the text, but which features seem to be significant in realizing different aspects of the novel. To take one simple example: the title. As part of the text, it will be included in the data to be analysed. But as a title, an aspect of the novel, it has a distinctive literary function which its textual features realize. There are two things one might note about it. First it has no determiner (*Heart*, not *The Heart of Darkness*), and second it is ambiguous ("heart consisting of darkness", cf *heart of gold*, vs "at the heart, i.e. the centre of darkness"). What is the significance, if any, of these linguistic features? One might suggest that the theme of indeterminacy and uncertainty is already keyed in as a theme by the very title of the novel.

A text consists of words which combine with each other in various ways to form different kinds of linguistic pattern which the computer, of course, can identify. A novel consists of characters and events which combine in various ways to form narrative patterns which the computer cannot identify. But for the textual patterns to have literary significance, it has to be shown how they correspond or key in with the narrative patterns of the novel. Although, in reference to the point made earlier, Stubbs refers to *Heart of Darkness* as a book, he does begin by treating it as a novel in that before proceeding to the main business of analysing it as a text he provides an account of its narrative structure. This, he says, is "embedded in different frames" as follows:

1. *The book starts with an unnamed narrator on a boat on the Thames*
2. *Marlow becomes the narrator, and talks about the Thames in Roman times.*
3. *Marlow tells of his visit to a European city*
4. *Marlow tells the story which takes up most of the book . . . . . .*
5. *Marlow tells of his visit to Kurtz's fiancée back in the European city*
6. *[There is nothing corresponding to frame 2, but some vocabulary from frame 2 is repeated in frame 7]*
7. *The book ends with a paragraph from the unnamed narrator back on theThames.*

(Stubbs 2005: 8)

Whatever criteria are used for identifying these frames, they are apparently not textual. Indeed the only textual feature that is mentioned here, vocabulary, is explicitly excluded. For if it were a factor, then repetition of vocabulary would presumably give some textual grounds for putting frame 7 in correspondence with frame 2. Interestingly, later in his analysis, Stubbs does, however, suggest that this framework is marked by textual features, pointing out that the phrase "waterway leading to the uttermost ends of the earth" is repeated in the first and last frames. He also mentions that the phrase "the pose of a (. . .) Buddha" that occurs in the last frame is also a repetition, but in this case the first occurrence appears not in the first frame but the second, after Marlow has already assumed the role of the narrator. Such textual features, then, do not seem to be a reliable indication of the narrative structure.

I shall return to these verbal repetitions presently. For the moment, the point I want to make is that the framework that is proposed is an analysis of narrative – an aspect of the novel, not of the text. It can only be based therefore on a literary view on what is significant. For Stubbs, who does the narrating is one significant factor: when Marlow takes over the narration we shift into a different frame. If only this factor were to be considered, then the novel would consist only of frames 1 and 7 with Marlow's story in the middle. But a quite different factor is introduced to distinguish the frames in between, namely the shift in the setting of Marlow's story. This gives us frames 3 and 5 in the European city with Africa in between. So in fact we have two separate kinds of narrative framework, and the attempt to fuse them into one leads to the postulation of the non-existent frame 6, which imposes a symmetry on the novel that appears to have no warrant in textual structure. The question arises as to why these two aspects of the novel, narrator and setting, should be taken as the only significant determinants of narrative structure. One is led to wonder whether, if this is indeed the only structure that can be discerned, it is, perhaps, not in itself of much significance anyway. Certainly the analysis does not reveal what the significance might be: it concentrates on the content of frame 4, which covers a good 75% of the text, which, on this account, has no narrative structure worth mentioning at all.

In the case of the narrative framework, we have an aspect of the novel described without substantiation from textual features that a computer analysis might provide. But there are other kinds of narrative pattern that *are* shown to be textually realized, and here we return to the repeated phrases cited earlier. In his discussion of the way certain words are distributed in the text, Stubbs indicates a number of other instances of intra-textual repetition, where the words repeated are not necessarily frequent in the text at all. Thus, for example, he points out the description of the city that Marlow returns to is in several ways a lexical reprise of its first description, and again that the words *voice* and *idol* are used in reference to both Marlow and Kurtz. Such facts "start to say something about the structure of the whole text" (Stubbs 2005: 12). Just what that something might be is left to the reader to ponder on. And in my case, these observations provoked a good deal of pondering. Though it is not clear to me what such facts tell us about the structure of the text, they set in train all manner of speculative reflection about the possible literary significance of intra-textual repetition of this kind.

So, with Wordsmith Tools at the ready, I set off in quest of other instances of such repetition. Stubbs provides us with the example of recurring words that provide a textual link between the two descriptions of the city: "high houses", "narrow and deserted street", "doors ponderously ajar" in the first description, "a ponderous door", "between tall houses" in the second. Further enquiry reveals that some of these words also figure in the description of the jungle. A stretch of the river is described as "narrow, straight, with high sides", there are "high walls" of trees, the "high stillness of primeval forest". The word *deserted* only occurs three times in the text, and its other two occurrences are in descriptions of the African scene: "And the village was deserted, the huts gaped black, rotting(...)", "the waterway ran on, deserted, into the gloom (...)". Directing my computer in quest of other repetitions, I discovered that the word *ponderous* occurs only twice in the text. Though its second occurrence in "a ponderous door" may echo "doors standing ponderously ajar" and so serve to link Marlow's two city visits, it also echoes its first occurrence where it appears in a description of the progress of Marlow's boat upriver "between the high walls of our winding way, reverberating in hollow claps the ponderous beat of the sternwheel".

What is one to make of these inter-textual lexical connections? What do they hint at? What literary significance can we guess they might have? If, as Stubbs suggests, the use of *idol* and *voice* to describe both Marlow and Kurtz indicates some similarity between them, then the use of these other examples of repetition can presumably be said to have the same associative effect. If things that are described in the same terms take on a similarity, then just as Marlow assumes the likeness of Kurtz, so the city assumes the likeness of the river and takes on its darkness. This, we may suggest, is supported by other distributional facts that the computer reveals. As Stubbs points out, "the words *heart, dark* and *darkness* occur throughout the book, but increase in frequency at the very end". This is the textual hint. What possible literary significance might be assigned to it?

On, then, to the guesswork. And for this we need to set the computer aside for a moment, and look at the text for ourselves and consider its novel effects. The end of the book is where Marlow visits Kurtz's fiancée – the "Intended" – and he takes both the darkness and Kurtz's last whisper with him. At her door, as "the dusk was falling", he 'seemed to hear the whispered cry, "The Horror! The Horror!" She comes to meet him in the darkening room, "dressed in black", with "a pale visage", "dark eyes". On her appearance, "The room seemed to have grown darker". And as she speaks of the noble qualities of Kurtz, "with every word spoken the room was growing darker". Marlow listened. "The darkness deepened". As she talks, Marlow seems again to hear "the whisper of a voice speaking from beyond the threshold of an eternal darkness". The repeated words are like a sound track, a lexical leitmotif, that brings the room and the people in it into association with the African river that has been described in the same terms. And this is then confirmed by a quite explicit connection: a gesture of the Intended reminds Marlow of another woman – the "wild and gorgeous apparition of a woman" who appears so dramatically and ominously out of the jungle earlier in the narrative: "(...) I shall see her, too, a tragic and familiar Shade, resembling in this gesture another one, tragic also, and bedecked with powerless charms, stretching bare brown arms over the glitter of the infernal stream, the stream of darkness".

The two women become one and the realities of primitive savagery and apparent civilization are fused by the presence of a common darkness.

This is a darkness of deception and delusion as well. As Stubbs points out, the word *know* is, like *dark* and *darkness*, also evenly distributed through the text, often in negative form, but there is a cluster of positive instances at the end, mainly spoken by Kurtz's Intended. She knows that Kurtz was good and noble, and her belief is described as "a great and saving illusion that shone with an unearthly glow in the darkness, in the triumphant darkness".

And here we come to what (to me at least) is the thematic climax of the novel. Kurtz's last whispered words that have so haunted Marlow come back again: "The dusk was repeating them in a persistent whisper all around us, in a whisper that seemed to swell menacingly like the first whisper of a rising wind. 'The horror! The horror'".

The threefold repetition of the word *whisper*, insistently evoking the dark reality of Kurtz's world, is then immediately followed by another threefold repetition, and one that is an emphatic assertion of the counter-reality of the Intended's belief: "Don't you understand I loved him – I loved him – I loved him". For a moment, this reality prevails, to such an extent that Marlow is drawn into it himself and tells his lie to sustain it: "The last word he pronounced was – your name". Her reaction is first to give a light sigh, and then in the tense and darkened room she makes Marlow's heart stand still with "an exulting and terrible cry, a cry of inconceivable triumph and unspeakable pain". This cry is a dramatic and climactic moment in the novel. But it is also a textual echo. Where has the reader heard a cry before?

This, of course, is where the computer comes in. It reveals that the word occurs six other times in the text. The first two occur in the phrase: "a cry, a very loud cry, as of infinite desolation", which bears some formal resemblance to the Intended's cry, and breaks the stillness in a similarly sudden and startling way – but this time in the heart of darkness itself. As indeed does the third occurrence: "a cry arose whose shrillness pierced the still air". The other occurrences of the word relate to Kurtz – his "cry that was no more than a breath", his "whispered cry". But the cry of the Intended is not a whispered but "exulting", not one "of infinite desolation" but "of inconceivable triumph". And here there is another echo, surely.

Back to the computer. And I find that the word *triumph* occurs only twice in the book. Its only other occurrence appears just before Marlow arrives at the Intended's door, when he describes the death of Kurtz in terms of "a conquering darkness", and as "a moment of triumph for the wilderness". It is not now the darkness that is triumphant, and in contrast to all the vague and menacing indeterminacy that pervades the book, we have a straightforward assertion of absolute certainty, which Marlow repeats. " 'I knew it – I was sure!' She knew. She was sure".

Just how Marlow is supposed to actually say these words we cannot know – in a tone of irony, incredulousness? But they serve to confirm this other reality which he cannot deny. He cannot tell her the truth – to do so would have been to condemn her to the other darker world – "It would have been too dark – too dark altogether".

"[T]oo dark altogether". Here I am teased by another verbal echo, faint but persistent. What does this phrase remind me of? I check the concordance for *altogether*, and there it is: "too dark altogether", "too beautiful altogether". And this latter phrase takes me to an earlier scene in the book: Marlow's visit to another woman – his "excellent aunt". This aunt is a minor figure, and as far as her role in the story is concerned, seemingly superfluous. Why then is she there at all? Marlow describes the visit: "I found her triumphant. I had a cup of tea – the last decent cup of tea for many days – and in a room that most soothingly looked just as you would expect a lady's drawing-room to look, we had a quiet chat by the fireside".

Another lady's drawing room, but triumph here is associated with domestic normality – the cup of tea, the chat by the fireside. But it turns out that the aunt has the same kind of idealistic vision as does the Intended, and thinks of Marlow in the same way as the Intended thinks of Kurtz – as a kind of "emissary" or "apostle" with a mission, "weaning those ignorant millions from their horrid ways". Marlow comments: "It's queer how out of touch with truth women are. They live in a world of their own, and there has never been anything like it, and never can be". And he adds: "It is too beautiful altogether".

He expresses the same sentiment later, and in similar words, when, in his narrative, he anticipates the lie he will tell to the Intended: "They – the women I mean – are out of it – should be out of it. We must help them to stay in that beautiful world of their own, lest ours gets worse. Oh, she had to be out of it".

The aunt and the Intended are thus brought into association, both inhabitants of an illusory world of conventional ideals that has to be sustained by deception. A reality "too beautiful altogether" in contrast with the other reality which is "too dark altogether" – the darkness of some pervasive moral corruption that Marlowe senses but cannot clearly discern, and which, as Stubbs notes is reflected in the vagueness of his language.

But there are times when his language is not vague at all, and here we come to another aspect of the book as novel which the analysis of the text does not itself reveal. The intra-textual patterns I have been tracing can be taken as being indicative of the underlying theme of *Heart of Darkness*, and to lend support to the view that: "This is a novel about the fallibility and distortions of human knowledge". What a novel is about is something, it would seem, that a quantitative analysis of text is particularly well suited to identify: its theme is reflected by the frequencies of linguistic features and their distribution, as MS demonstrates so convincingly. But there is, of course, more to a novel than what it is about. Its theme only becomes significant by the manner of its representation, by the way it is activated by events and characters. What seems to me most striking about the intra-textual patterns that I have noted is the way they give dramatic expression to the theme in the representation of the women characters and the events in which they figure.

The aunt and the Intended are associated in that they have in common the same idealistic view of the world, the same reality of conventional values. But the contexts of their appearance are in striking contrast: one a cheery drawing room, a quiet chat by the fireside, an atmosphere of relaxed normality, the other a somber and sepulchral room, the atmosphere charged with intense feeling, and dialogue as different from a casual chat as it is possible to imagine. Neither woman is described in any detail. In fact the aunt is not described at all. She is "excellent" and that's all. We have no indication about what she looks like. The Intended is hardly less sparely described – just one or two simple monosyllabic adjectives: "fair hair" "pale visage", "dark eyes". Why this absence of descriptive detail, one might wonder. In the case of the aunt, one might suggest that since she is a minor character no description is called for, but then other minor characters are described in some detail. One of the women in the office where Marlow goes to get his job, for example, is described in very particular terms – warts and all indeed: "Her flat cloth slippers were propped up on a foot-warmer, and a cat reposed on her lap. She wore a starched white affair on her head, had a wart on one cheek and silver-rimmed spectacles hung on the tip of her nose".

The aunt and the Intended are by comparison featureless. As such, they seem to function more as thematic symbols than as individual characters: the aunt as representing conventional normality, defined by the typicality of her drawing room, and the Intended as representing too the darkness of delusion and deception in which she is embroiled. But there are other figures that do not blend in with the thematic background, but are starkly foregrounded against it. The most striking instance of this is "the wild and gorgeous apparition of a woman" that, as pointed out earlier, Marlow explicitly associates with the Intended. This is how the woman is described:

> She walked with measured steps, draped in striped and fringed cloths, treading the earth proudly, with a slight jingle and flash of barbarous ornaments. She carried her head high; her hair was done in the shape of a helmet; she had brass leggings to the knee, brass wire gauntlets to the elbow, a crimson spot on her tawny cheek, innumerable necklaces of glass beads on her neck; bizarre things, charms, gifts of witch-men, that hung about her, glittered and trembled at every step.

There is nothing vague or indistinct about this description. The vivid impression the woman's appearance makes on Marlow is etched on his mind in exact verbal detail, and the description stands out as particular and precise because the words in it are infrequent. It is this that makes the woman stand out against "the gloomy border of the forest", "the immense wilderness". But at the same time she is also "like the wilderness itself, with an air of brooding over an inscrutable purpose". The clarity of the perception registered in this descriptive precision contrasts with the vaguely expressed sense of strangeness and foreboding and accentuates it. As Stubbs notes, much of the language of the text, the recurrence of words to do with darkness, uncertainty, negation and so on reflects the underlying theme of the novel. In a way they serve as a backdrop, a mise-en-scene. But it is the events and characters, figures against this ground, that activate the theme and give it dramatic force, create the literary significance that make the text into a novel. And these are often described in language that a quantitative analysis of the text would not register as remarkable.

The observations made in Stubbs (2005), particularly those that point out the recurrence of certain words and phrases, often themselves infrequent, in different parts of the text, have set me off looking for similar intra-textual links, and using them as hints to possible literary significance. Hints followed by guesses. And one bit of literary guesswork has set me in quest of other hints – infrequency lists, in concordances – looking for possible bits of textual evidence to support a particular literary interpretation. Hints and guesses. It is a fascinating exercise. But not one that Stanley Fish would be likely to approve of. For it is, of course, open to the charge of circularity. This does not, however, make it invalid as a process of exploring significance which I have been pursuing here. On the contrary, circularity of a kind, is an essential feature of this process, for, to quote T. S. Eliot again:

> (…) the end of all our exploring
> Will be to arrive where we started
> And know the place for the first time.
> (Little Gidding)

The Fish objection only applies to the positivist claim that stylistics establishes a correlation between linguistic features and literary effects so that one can be read off from the other. But this is not the claim that stylisticians generally make. What they are principally concerned with is not correlations but correspondences, with ways in which textual features can be adduced to give warrant to different literary interpretations, not to ratify one of them as definitive. Stylistic analysis does not seek to foreclose on a particular interpretation but to open up alternative possibilities. It does not claim to discover meanings which are inscribed in a text and which may have eluded literary critics, but to provide the means for exploring one's own reactions to the text. Herein lies its educational value – for it offers an alternative to the traditional teaching of literature. Rather than being the passive recipients of the second hand interpretations of literary critics, students can be enabled (empowered even) to take the initiative and engage actively and directly with literary texts themselves (Widdowson 1975, 1992).

Stylistics, then, is all about hints and guesses. As Verdonk puts it: "(...) it can serve not only to substantiate an impressionistic sense of meaning, but also to suggest the possibilities of reading other interpretations into a text" (Verdonk 2002: 78).

In his review of that book, Stubbs calls this a "weak" defence of stylistics and takes its author to task for not rising to the Fish challenge to "defend a stronger position" (Stubbs 2004: 129). In this article on *Heart of Darkness* Stubbs does rise to the Fish challenge, but interestingly does so by in effect arguing for the validity of the so-called "weak" position himself, justifying his stylistic analysis, very much along Verdonk lines, by concluding that: "(...) observational data can provide more systematic evidence for unavoidable subjective interpretation" (Stubbs 2005: 22).

As a text *Heart of Darkness* consists of objective 3rd person data that can be analysed by computer. As a novel, however, it can only be interpreted by 1st person subjectively. This means that what counts as evidence for interpretation can never be objectively determined, and any claim that it can (the "strong" position) is mistaken. Hints and guesses are all we can reasonably expect. But the point about the computer is that it can provide so many hints for us to guess the significance of. This is what makes Michael Stubbs' article so stimulating – his own textual findings set the reader off in quest of others. What, for me at least, is revealing about its "quantitative stylistic methods", is that the results of the analysis are so different from its effects: the very precision of the findings provoke very imprecise speculation about their significance. The more you pin down and quantify features of the text, the more aware you become that features of the novel cannot be pinned down and quantified. They remain elusive, subjective and variable, and cannot be reduced to textual terms. "But", as Stubbs says, "it is not the claim of stylistics that they can be, or should be". His kind of analysis does not tell us what *Heart of Darkness* means, but what it might mean to different readers. And herein lies its value, and particularly its educational value: it demonstrates ways in which textual features can be explored, and how such exploration can open up possibilities of novel interpretation.

10 The unrecoverable context

This chapter takes up again the issue of how texts are variously understood and vary in their effect depending on how they relate to context and pretext. The texts I am concerned with here were written by Shakespeare 400 years ago. What do they mean to us now, and what did they mean to his contemporaries?

To begin with, we need to note that Shakespeare produced texts of two kinds, written with entirely different pretextual intentions: the sonnets on the one hand, the play scripts on the other. The sonnets are texts designed to be permanent. A recurring theme is that their very composition serves to counteract mutability and mortality, to hold time itself in textual check. Shakespeare is here writing texts for posterity, and there is every reason to suppose that he took great pains to ensure that his texts survived in print, thus providing a recurrence of readings whereby he and his lover would, so to speak, be endlessly resurrected:

> *His beauty shall in these black lines be seen,*
> *And they shall live, and he in them still green.*
>
> *So long as men can breathe and eyes can see,*
> *So long lives this, and this gives life to thee.*

But for Shakespeare the playwright, things were apparently quite different. All the evidence here points to textual neglect and an indifference to posterity. The texts were composed as scripts to be publicly performed, only becoming a reality when activated by speech, not essentially written texts as such at all, and so not designed to be permanent. The writing was a means not an end in itself. Only that odd fellow Ben Jonson thought quaintly of plays as literature, and published them as his "works". Sonnets and plays were, then, texts of different kinds. One was a reading text, stable and designed for direct reception, with the assumption that its meaning, textually enclosed and complete, would survive intact over time. The other was a speaking text, unstable and indirect in the sense that it could only be apprehended by the discourse of performance, and not infrequently modified in the process. In this sense the plays depended on the immediate spatio-temporal context that the sonnets were written to transcend.

Note: Originally published in Bex, T., M. Burke & P. Stockwell (eds.). 2000. *Contextualized stylistics. A Festschrift for Peter Verdonk*, 229–241. Amsterdam/Atlanta GA: Rodopi.

https://doi.org/10.1515/9783110619669-014

Part of this context can of course be replicated. Indeed this has been done in the reconstruction of the Globe Theatre on the south bank of the Thames. This is a replica of the Elizabethan stage. But it cannot replicate the conditions of staging. To use a distinction proposed by Dell Hymes (Hymes 1974), it reproduces the *setting*, the physical circumstances of the context of performance. But it cannot reproduce the *scene*, the socio-psychological construction placed upon those circumstances so as to realize their significance as a cultural event, for this, obviously enough, depended on the customary ways in which the performance was originally apprehended. You can reproduce the Elizabethan stage, but not the Elizabethan audience.

One obvious feature of staging in the Elizabethan period was its dependence on language for framing the internal context of the play. The wooden O was open to the sky and there was little in the way of stage scenery, so whatever visual effects were called for had, for the most part, to be verbally created:

Think, when we talk of horses, that you see them,
Planting their proud hoofs i' th' receiving earth.
(Henry V, Act 1, Scene 1, 25–26)

The hurly-burly of battle is sometimes, of course, off-stage, as with the one the witches refer to in *Macbeth,* and represented second hand by commentary. Where it is on-stage, it is commonly presented by token figures and symbolic action, relying on the "imaginary forces" of the audience to project them inwardly and give them wider significance. But there are other features of staging which call for a more imaginative piecing out of the imperfections of the unworthy scaffold. Without the special electrical effects so common a feature of modern productions, darkness had to spoken into existence, conjured up somehow in the minds of an audience sitting in broad daylight. In general, then, the spatio-temporal dimensions of context had to be verbally projected in ways that present day productions on stage and screen have made redundant. All the blood and thunder of battle, darkness and day, sunshine and moonlight all can in modern productions be directly represented, particularly on screen, in an immediate direct appeal to the senses without verbal mediation. We do not *need* the language any more. So it is that what for the Elizabethan audience would serve the crucial function of locating where a particular scene takes place can these days become little more than verbal embellishment.

To take one simple example, from *Macbeth* again. At the beginning of Act 3, Scene 3, the men that are to murder Banquo make their appearance. On the Elizabethan stage, there would be no visual indication of what time of day it is, so this has to be provided verbally. One of the murderers obliges: "The west still glimmers with some streaks of day ... "

For the Elizabethan audience, sitting in the sun, this conjures up growing darkness. In a modern production the dimming of the lights on stage would make the murderer's speech redundant as contextual information: it simply adds a little poetic decoration. But we should notice that the murderer's words do not only serve to set the scene in time, making them functionally equivalent to "It's getting dark". The very 'poetic' elaboration serves to *create* the darkening evening, to invoke it, to call it into being. This becomes evident from the rest of the murderer's speech:

The west still glimmers with some streaks of day.
Now spurs the lated traveller apace
To gain the timely inn, and near approaches
The subject of our watch.
(*Macbeth*, Act 3, Scene 3, 4–8)

If the twilight is already visually provided, as it would be in a modern production, then of course the creative impact of these lines is, to some degree at least, bound to be diminished. And the greater the visual impact on the audience, then, obviously, the more likely it is to distract attention from the verbal representation. The speech here, then, does not only indicate the time of day to the original audience but actually *represents* it as a perceptual experience, gives it, one might say, not only a name but a local habitation.

But the very fulfillment of this contextualizing function creates something of a problem. For the language that fulfills it has to be spoken by somebody in the play. And this particular speech we have been considering does not seem to be the kind of thing that a murderer would actually say. It is true that this one is never identified by name or status (he may be a courtier, for all we know), nevertheless, these lines sound somewhat incongruous in the mouth of hired cut-throat. They do not seem to be in character. The issue here is the possible incompatibility between the contextualizing and the characterizing functions of Shakespeare's dramatic language. Contextualization is verbally rather than visually represented, but this can only be done by characters in the play. How then we do know when they are being used by the playwright simply as a mouthpiece for setting, and indeed, as we have seen, creating the scene, and when they are speaking in character, in their own voice? In the case we have been considering, for example, are we to think of the murderer as a character with a penchant for poetic expression?

This problem of possible incompatibility is not, of course, confined to Shakespeare. It confronts every playwright. At the beginning of any play, even one which can draw on modem technology for its staging or screening, the audience needs to be provided with contextual information of one kind or another: who the characters are in relation to each other, what past events are presupposed and so on. All of this is known to the characters *in* the play as part of their fictional world, but not to the audience outside the play, looking on. On screen, much of this can now, of course, be presented directly by flashback sequences, but on stage, it has to be done indirectly as a function of dialogue, and this has to carry conviction as "normal" interaction. The contextual information has to be naturalized. Tom Stoppard gives a comic illustration of what happens when it is not:

> MRS DRUDGE (into phone) Hello, the drawing-room of Lady Muldoon's country residence one morning in early spring? .. Hello!the draw ... Who? Who did you wish to speak to? I'm afraid there is no one of that name here, this is all very mysterious and I'm sure it's leading up to something, I hope nothing is amiss for we, that is Lady Muldoon and her houseguests, are here cut off from the world, including Magnus, the wheelchair-ridden halfbrother of her ladyship's husband Lord Albert Muldoon who ten years ago went out for a walk on the cliffs and was never seen again – and all alone, for they had no children.
> (Stoppard: The *Real Inspector Hound*)

We can account for the absurdity of this by invoking Grice' s co-operative principle (Grice 1975). Mrs Drudge, we may say, is violating the maxims of quantity and relevance in that she is off-loading more information than is required for, or is relevant to, the presumed purpose of the telephone call. But to say that is to assign her the role of character in a play, in which we would expect dialogue to have some resemblance to normal conversation. In this case, her flouting of the maxims results in implicatures which we interpret as indicative of her personality as a character-that she is garrulous, not very bright, insensitive to others, and so on. But if we take her to be the mouthpiece of the playwright, a contextualizing informant only, then what she says does conform to these maxims, to the extent that she is providing information which is relevant to the play. She is being co-operative with the audience. But the problem is that this results in her being un-cooperative within the enclosed world of the play itself.

One way round this difficulty of using characters as contextual informants and running the risk of triggering off unwanted implicatures is to take them out of the action of the play and have them directly address the audience as the chorus. This device, which shifts the mode of representation to narrative, is a device which Shakespeare, of course, quite often uses. He does so, as we have seen in *Henry V,* to overcome the narrow confines of the stage to represent events on a large scale. In *A Winter's Tale*, a chorus (figured as Time) conveniently fills the audience in on the 16 year gap between Act 3 and Act 4. In these and other cases the chorus bears independent witness, and provides a non-participant third person perspective on events. The chorus option seems not to be taken where the characters themselves are personally involved in the contextualization.

The Tempest provides a particularly interesting example of the problem that arises when contextualization *is* provided by the characters themselves. The events preceding the action of the play could conceivably have been narrated in a prologue. Instead it is Prospero who recounts them to Miranda (Act 1, Scene 2), and he does so at considerable length (100 lines and more), only interrupting his monologue to make sure that she is paying attention. Miranda's turns at talk are entirely determined by Prospero, and after a few minimal, and dutiful contributions to the exchange, she eventually (and not surprisingly) falls asleep. Prospero's contextualization here raises a number of interesting questions, and in considering them we come, I think, to a central issue about how the Elizabethan audience interpreted the use of language in dramatic representation.

To begin with, we might ask how convincing is this one-sided interaction within the play itself. Certainly it is not very co-operative conversation. Prospero is verbose and provides more information, it seems, than Miranda can readily take in. But it may be that she does not *need* to take it in because it is not *relevant* for her. This would depend, of course, on whether she has heard it before. It is quite irrelevant if she has. But if she has not heard it before, one cannot but wonder why she apparently takes so little interest in it, why she does not react in some positive way. Instead of being rivetted by such momentous events, her attention wanders and she nods off. One would also expect that Prospero himself would pause occasionally and elicit some kind of response to what would, after all, be an extraordinary revelation, rather than simply check that the channel is still open for transmission. This would suggest that Miranda *has* heard it all before, and it is redundant and so irrelevant. In that case an implicature of a Gricean kind results in respect to Prospero's character: namely that he has a way of going on about past injustices, talking about them obsessively to the only other human being on the island. Alternatively, of course, if we are to suppose that everything that Prospero says *is* indeed news to Miranda, her lack of response would reflect on *her* character too. Here is a very dull and unresponsive creature indeed, quite insensitive to her father's suffering. But this does not square with Miranda of the "piteous heart", who feels for the "poor souls" in the shipwreck and appeals to her father for their lives. Whether you assume that what Prospero says is relevant or not, the interaction between him and Miranda does not seem to carry conviction either way. The implicatures that arise about character (Prospero as paranoid or Miranda as moronic) do not seem satisfactory. So it would seem reasonable to abandon the idea (in this case at least) that contextualization and characterization can be complementary. If so, then the only alternative, it would seem, is to suspend the operation of the co-operative principle as it might apply to the dramatic dialogue, and edit out the unwanted implicatures. In other words, we simply take Prospero to be functioning here as a non-participant in the play proper, as in effect a chorus providing contextual information to set the scene, and relevant to the audience only.

But I would like to suggest that we can entertain conjecture of a different kind. We have been assuming so far that what the characters of a play have to say is to be interpreted in much the same way as we would interpret everyday speech off-stage. But a play is not the *replication* of everyday life, but a *representation* of an alternative reality. What is represented in dramatic speech, therefore, may not be what is normally associated with ordinary spoken interaction at all, in which case, it would then make no sense to expect conversational verisimilitude. I have already suggested, with particular reference to the murderer in *Macbeth,* that language was used in Shakespeare to represent the essential being of contextual features, and not just to indicate their outward appearances. I want now to suggest that the same point applies to the representation of character, that what we find in Shakespeare is language used by characters not only to engage in overt interaction, but to express their covert thoughts, feelings and perceptions, to represent the essential being of their inner selves. There is then, I suggest, a dual perspective at play, the inner and the outer, with characters constantly shifting from one to the other, and settling into neither. One might draw a pictorial parallel with portraits which show both full face and the profile of the subject simultaneously, thus integrating two perspectives in a perceptually impossible fusion. The Elizabethan audience, primed in these conventions of representation on stage, would not expect characters to be "realistic" by the criteria of "normal" speech behaviour. They would indeed be taken as *characters,* embodiments of character, persona, not persons. And as characters, they are representations not of people as such, but as constituted of natural forces both inside and outside them, different permutations of interacting humours and elements, human beings as microcosmic embodiments of the macrocosm. Here is another fusion: of inner character and external reality. It was not only that the characters spoke a context into being, but that context could also be the external projection of their inner selves. Context and character then cease to be distinct. So it is that the conditions of Elizabethan staging themselves provide for a mode of fused representation which the modem audience can no longer appreciate.

Consider the case of *King Lear*. In modern productions, on stage and on screen, the storm itself is perceptually presented, with special effects, visual and aural, designed to make a direct impact on the senses. And the more sensational the presentation, the more, one might say, is emphasis given to the physical privations that Lear suffers. At the same time, the significance of Lear's actual words diminishes, because they are no longer needed to set the scene. But what is *represented* in the scene is also changed, and changed radically, from what would have been apprehended by the Elizabethan audience. For in a modern production instead of having the one storm that Lear himself verbally creates, we have two: the aural/visual one of the staging, and the verbal one of the text. And they compete for attention, with the former, appealing immediately to the senses as it does, likely to prevail. There are indeed productions in which the staged storm is so dominant that the audience scarcely hears what Lear is actually saying and all they are left with is the gist and a general impression of passion. Note that, paradoxically enough, even if Lear's words *were* to be noticed, they would somehow have to be matched in ferocity with the staged storm to carry conviction in a modern production, with the consequence that the words would then fail in their creative effect.

Let us then speculate on how the scene might be understood by the Elizabethan audience as it is verbally represented on the bare stage. The first sign of the storm occurs in Act 2 Scene 4 as a stage direction (*Storm and tempest*), and signalled not verbally but by noises off, presumably by some rudimentary device (a wind machine, rolling cannon balls). The timing of its occurrence would not be lost on the Elizabethan audience. It comes after Lear has appealed to the gods to keep him from ignoble tears. It comes as a kind of response.

> Lear: *If it be you that stirs these daughters' hearts*
> *Against their father, fool me not so much*
> *To bear it tamely; touch me with noble anger,*
> *And let not women's weapons, water drops,*
> *Stain my man's cheeks ...*
> *You think I' 11 weep. No, I'll not weep.*
> (Storm and tempest)
> *I have full cause of weeping, but this heart*
> *Shall break into a hundred thousand flaws*
> *Or ere I' 11 weep. O fool, I shall go mad!*
> (Exeunt, Lear, Fool, Kent and Gloucester)
> Cornwall: *Let us withdraw; 'twill be a storm.*
> (*King Lear*, Act 2, Scene 4, 277–282)

For the Elizabethans, the external turbulence of the storm is not simply coincidental with the internal turbulence in Lear's mind but corresponds with it. And this correspondence would be taken not as a matter of symbolism but symbiosis: the disruption of natural order, or degree, in one place (as in the deposing, or disposing of a monarch) triggers off empathetic reactions of a cosmic kind. As Ulysses puts it in *Troilus and Cressida:*

> *Take but degree away, untune that string,*
> *And hark what discord follows.*
> (*Troilus and Cressida*, Act 1, Scene 3, 109–110)

So what discord follows the rejection of Lear, doubly deposed as both king and father at the hands of the "unnatural hags" his daughters? Lear mentions impending madness, Cornwall an impending storm. In the next scene (3. 1) we are given a vivid third person description of both:

> Kent*: Where's the king?*
> Gentleman*: Contending with the fretful elements;*
> *Bids the wind blow the earth into the sea,*
> *Or swell the curled waters ' bove the main,*
> *That things might change or cease; tears his white hair,*
> *Which the impetuous blasts, with eyeless rage,*
> *Catch in their fury and make nothing of;*
> *Strives in his little world of man to outscorn*
> *The to-and-fro conflicting wind and rain ...*
> (*King Lear*, Act, Scene 1, 3–11)

Here the disturbances, the two manifestations of discord, in the weather and in Lear's mind, combine. At the beginning of the next scene, Lear himself makes an appearance:

> Lear*: Blow winds, and crack your cheeks. Rage, blow.*
> *You cataracts and hurricanoes, spout*
> *Till you have drenched our steeples, drowned the cocks.*
> *You sulph' rous and thought-executing fires,*
> *Vaunt couriers of oak-cleaving thunderbolts,*
> *Singe my white head. And thou, all shaking thunder,*
> *Strike flat the thick rotundity o' th' world,*
> *Crack Nature's moulds, all germains spill at once,*
> *That makes ingrateful man.*
> (*King Lear*, Act 3, Scene 2, 1–8)

Now if, as in a modem production, a storm has been perceptually provided on stage or screen by special effects, then Lear' s speech, for all its vocative address and exclamatory power is essentially (like that of the Gentleman in the previous scene) *descriptive:* his words relate to a world that has a separate contextual existence. But if there are no such visual and aural provision of context (apart perhaps from rudimentary noises off) then the only storm we have is the one that comes out of Lear's mouth. He verbally creates it. His speech brings it into being. In this case, the vocatives actually *invoke:* He does not call *to* the winds and cataracts and hurricanoes, he calls them *up* as Prospero calls up the tempest. And the obvious effect of this, for the Elizabethan audience, is that the disturbances in the outer weather and inner state of mind converge. Lear, in effect, *storms:* his words project the discord which is raging *inside* him. Context and character are no longer distinct.

I would suggest that with modern staging, this dramatic representation of experience tends to reduce to the theatrical reproduction of weather, and the function, and effect, of Lear's speech is radically altered. And this is not an isolated instance. There are innumerable occasions in Shakespeare when the modern staged presentation of the context undermines the representation of the text. One thinks, for example, of the opening scene of *Macbeth*. Here again the provision of contextual effects outside those projected in the language of the witches shifts attention away from the reality which the language represents. As with Lear, the elements have no separate existence outside the witches: the blasted heath, the thunder lightning and rain are called up by their words. And if, distracted by theatrical staging, you do not attend to the words, then something of their dramatic effect is inevitably lost. And this effect again has to do with the fusion of context and character.

A modern audience, watching the play on stage or screen, will generally fail to notice the significance of what Macbeth himself says on his first appearance. Up to that point he has figured in the play (Act I Scene 2) only in third person description as news of his exploits are recounted to Duncan, and these are in support of the natural order. He is "valiant cousin", "worthy gentlemen", a paragon of good. But he has already been mentioned by the witches in the very first scene of the play. They arrange to meet him after the battle, and disappear with words that express the very discord that they represent: "Fair is foul, and foul is fair, Hover through the fog and filthy air" (*Macbeth*, Act 1, Scene 1, 11–12).

But the witches are agents of evil, unnatural discord, so the more emphatically Macbeth is presented as an agent of good, of the natural order, the more puzzling it becomes as to what the witches can possibly have to do with him. Act 1 Scene 3, and the witches appear again. The meeting is about to take place, and the puzzle resolved. Macbeth comes on stage with Banquo, and the Elizabethan audience would, I speculate, be particularly attentive to his first words as holding perhaps the clue to the mystery. Macbeth's first words are: "So fair and foul a day I have not seen" (*Macbeth*, Act 1, Scene 3, 38). The very words of the witches! Is it too fanciful to imagine a gasp of horror from the groundlings? Macbeth is condemned out of his own mouth. For all his apparent virtue, he is already tainted by evil.

These are cases, I would argue, of unrecoverable context. It is not only that much of the contextualizing function of Shakespeare's language in the location of the setting has necessarily disappeared with changed conventions of staging, but the representation of the inner selves of characters achieved through the very verbalization of context has disappeared as well. And disappeared for ever. We can, of course, learn about how the Elizabethans conceived of the interplay of microcosmic and macrocosmic forces in nature, their notions of degree and discord and so on, but we cannot directly experience them, we cannot feel them on the pulses. Nor can we recover their experience of language, their attentiveness to verbal nuance. The verbalizing of context was, in the absence of other staging facilities, a matter of necessity, but it also had the virtue of providing conditions for the integrated representation of context and character, and for creating dramatic effects of a particularly striking kind. But the appreciation of these effects depends not only on modes of thought but also on modes of listening which are to a great extent remote from modern experience. The original effects are lost on us, and lost *to* us for ever.

This is not all to say that the contemporary staging and screening of Shakespeare provides only an impoverished experience of the plays, but that it is inevitably a different one: one which is, I think, less essentially and intrinsically a verbally realized experience. There is no point in deploring this, or pretending that things can be otherwise: no point in talking about recovering the authentic or "real" Shakespeare, because the reality is in the eye, and ear, of the beholder. We can never see or hear the plays as the Elizabethans did. But what we can do is to try to understand how they would have seen and heard them, and this involves the close scrutiny of the language and its possible implications. This is the purpose of stylistics: to study the text and to speculate on its significance. We cannot thereby recover the unrecoverable context, but we can get an inkling of what it is that we have missed.

11 Macbeth and the third murderer. An exercise in forensic stylistics

The art of detection is the discovery of significance in what appears to be, and what usually is, insignificant, the picking up of what Autolycus, in *A Winter's Tale* calls "unconsidered trifles" and showing them to be worthy of consideration after all. So it is that things are brought to our attention which would normally pass unnoticed. As discussed in previous papers, in the linguistic detection work of critical discourse analysis, a single word can be identified as revealing an ideology otherwise concealed from us, and we see another world in a grain of lexical sand. In literary critical detection, a minor and apparently insignificant event or character in the plot can be recognized as having a key thematic relevance which has hitherto escaped our attention. T. S. Eliot's J. Alfred Prufock identifies himself with such a minor character:

> No! I am not Prince Hamlet, nor was meant to be;
> Am an attendant lord, one that will do
> To swell a progress, start a scene or two..-
>   (T. S. Eliot *The Love Song of J.Alfred Prufrock*)

But we might be so engrossed with Hamlet and the events centre stage that we have failed to notice what the attendant lords might be up to.

What I want to discuss in this paper is the role of one of the attendant lords not in *Hamlet* but in *Macbeth* by way of an investigation of the evidence in the criminal case in which this lord is implicated. Macbeth, it will be recalled, having murdered Duncan, next turns his attention to the despatching of Banquo and Fleance, and engages two murderers to do the deed. To their surprise, however, at the scene of the crime, they are joined by a third murderer. The identity of this third man has long been a subject of speculative debate by Shakespearian scholars. Commentators have pointed out that it is consistent with Macbeth's obsessive suspicion and sense of insecurity that he should send someone to keep an eye on the other murderers and make sure that the job is done properly. Someone. But who? It has even been suggested that it is Macbeth himself, but whoever it is, he would obviously have to be some person close to him, not just a servant, or any old retainer, but a trusty lieutenant, somebody he can confide in, who is party to his designs, a fellow conspirator perhaps. Who then is the third man? As I shall seek to demonstrate, the evidence of the text points, beyond all reasonable doubt, to one person: *Lenox*.

Note: Unpublished

Lenox, one might ask, who's Lenox? Never heard of him. Most people, if asked to list the *Dramatis Personae* of the play, would fail to mention him at all. He appears to be just one of the nondescript extras like Rosse, Angus, Cathness, Menteth – is just another attendant lord, a kind of Prufrock character. Lenox is not a prominent figure: he is indeed almost a non-entity. But this very lack of prominence is ideally suited to the highly significant low profile role that he has in the play- a role that the great host of Shakespearean scholars have hitherto failed to appreciate, a role which this present exercise in forensic stylistics will now reveal.

The part of Lenox is, it is true, a small one in respect to the lines he has to speak, but he spends a lot of time on stage. In many of the key scenes in the play, there he is in the background, a reticent and unnoticed presence. In Act 1 Scene 2: enter Duncan, Malcolm, Donalbain, and – Lenox. This is the scene in which Macbeth's heroic exploits are reported at considerable length. The only time Lenox opens his mouth is to make a single superfluous comment:

Duncan: *Who comes here?*
Malcolm: *The worthy Thane of Rosse.*
Lenox: *What a haste looks through his eyes! So he should look*
That seems to speak things strange.

There follows the scene when Macbeth and Banquo meet the witches, at the end of which Rosse and Angus appear, sent by the King to greet Macbeth with his new title of Thane of Cawdor. Then Act 1, Scene 4, enter Duncan, Malcolm, Donalbain, and, of course, Lenox, who, in this scene, has nothing to say at all. He is again in attendance when Duncan makes his fatal entrance under the battlements of Macbeth's castle: present, but again, silent. So whereas his fellow noblemen, Rosse and Angus have been busy furthering the plot – reporting on the battle and sent as emissaries to meet the victorious generals Macbeth and Banquo, Lenox apart from one brief utterance, has said nothing and done nothing. He is just there, always by Duncan's side, apparently just a token attendant lord and little more than a stage prop.

Then comes the high dramatic suspense of the killing of the King, and the sudden shock of the knocking at the gate. Enter the drunken porter.

Porter: *Here's knocking indeed! If a man were Porter of Hell Gate, he should have turning the key. Knock, knock, knock. Who's there, i'th' name of Belzebub (...)*

Knock, knock, who's there? Well, who *is* there. When the porter eventually gets round to opening the gate:

Enter Macduff and, believe it or not, Lenox!

Lenox? Why Lenox, one might wonder. So far in the play, he has been in constant attendance on Duncan –indeed that has been his sole function. So why did he leave the king on this night of all nights? Why was Lenox not at his usual post by Duncan's side last night? Why was he not present at the scene of the crime? We have here, surely, a significant absence, a highly suspicious circumstance.

So enter Macduff and Lenox. It is, of course, Macduff who engages in banter with the porter. Lenox, as usual, has nothing to say. His first utterance in this scene, and only his second utterance in the entire play so far, is prompted by the appearance of Macbeth.

Lenox: *Good morrow, noble Sir.*

It is then Macduff that takes up the conversational initiative:

Macduff: *Is the king stirring, worthy Thane?*
Macbeth: *Not yet.*
Macduff: *He did command me to call timely on him:*
I have almost slipped the hour.
Macbeth: *I'll bring you to him.*
Macduff: *I know, this is a joyful trouble to you;*
And yet 'tis one.
Macbeth: *The labour we delight in physics pain.*
This is the door.
Macduff: *I'll make so bold to call,*
For 'tis my limited service.

Macduff then exits through the door, leaving Lenox alone with Macbeth. One might expect that conversation would be awkward for both of them – for Lenox because of his apparently almost pathological reticence and for Macbeth because he is in an agony of suspense, knowing what Macduff is about to find. Macbeth is indeed appropriately curt. But the usually taciturn Lenox, whose previous contributions have amounted to just two brief and perfunctory utterances, suddenly and unexpectedly breaks out into eloquence. And he starts talking about the weather. This is how the exchange goes:

Lenox: *Goes the King hence today?*
Macbeth: *He does: – he did appoint so.*
Lenox: *The night has been unruly: where we lay,*

> *Our chimneys were blown down; and as they say,*
> *Lamentings heard i' th' air; strange screams of death,*
> *And prophesying with accents terrible*
> *Of dire combustion, and confused events,*
> *New hatch'd to th' woeful time, the obscure bird*
> *Clamour'd the livelong night: some say, the earth*
> *Was feverous and did shake.*
> Macbeth: *'Twas a rough night.*
> Lenox: *My young remembrance cannot parallel*
> *A fellow to it.*

How are we to account for this marked inconsistency of conversational behaviour on the part of Lenox? And why, when he does break into speech, does he talk about the weather? Comments on weather often serve a phatic function, of course, but only when they are brief and in passing. But Lenox is not brief. When in Oscar Wilde's *The Importance of Being Earnest* Jack Worthing talks about the weather, Gwendolen Fairfax comments: "Pray don't talk to me about the weather, Mr Worthing. Whenever people talk to me about the weather, I always feel quite certain that they mean something else".

So does Lenox mean something else? I think there can be no doubt that he does. Notice that his talking of the weather follows directly from his mention of the King, and, in accordance with pragmatic principles (as, for example, discussed in Grice 1975; Sperber and Wilson 1986) such juxtaposition of reference, of course, implies relevance. So what does the weather have to do with the king. As the Elizabethan audience would recognize immediately, it has *everything* to do with the king. For what Lenox describes is not just foul weather, but the cosmic disturbance of the natural world, the discord that follows from the disruption of degree, from the violation of the established hierarchical social order, held in place and presided over by the monarch. The violence of the night, the lamentings in the air, strange screams of death, confused events, the shaking of the earth: all this, as Lenox must know full well, can only betoken some corresponding cataclysmic destruction of degree in human affairs, such as would be brought about by the killing of the king. What does he mean by his speech then? What illocutionary force and perlocutionary effect are intended? There would seem to be two possibilities. One is that Lenox is signalling to Macbeth that he knows there has been foul play, and is probing him for reaction as a possible suspect? There is another, and perhaps more likely possibility. We have already noted Lenox's unaccustomed, and inexplicable, absence from the King's retinue that night. This might indicate, we might suspect, that he has himself conspired in the murder and is now indirectly seeking confirmation that everything has gone according to plan. Macbeth's response to Lenox is brief: "Macbeth: *'Twas a rough night.*' "

This might be taken as a cryptic confirmation: yes there has been a cosmic disturbance of degree, the deed is done and Duncan, as you are implying, is indeed dead.. Alternatively, this brushing aside of the portentous events that Lenox has mentioned as mere weather might be taken as a denial of their possible significance. Disturbance of degree? What disturbance?. Whatever the portents might suggest, the deed was not done after all and Duncan is still alive. At this point, Macduff bursts in on the scene.

Macduff: *O horror! horror! horror!*
Tongue nor heart cannot conceive, nor name thee!
Macbeth/Lenox: *What's the matter?*
Macduff: *Confusion now hath made his masterpiece!*
Most sacrilegious Murther hath broke ope
The Lord's anointed Temple, and stole thence
The Life o' th' building.
Macbeth: *What is't you say? the life?*
Lenox: *Mean you his Majesty?*
Macduff: *Approach the chamber, and destroy your sight*
With a new Gorgon. – Do not bid me speak:
See, and then speak yourselves.

Macbeth and Lenox then do indeed go off to see for themselves. Meanwhile, Macduff raves, the alarum bell rings, Lady Macbeth appears, then Banquo. Into this scene of confusion, horror and bewilderment, Macbeth and Lenox return. Macbeth indulges in extravagant lament. Lenox is, as usual, silent. Then the dead king's sons appear, to be told the dire news that their father has been murdered, and it is Malcolm who raises the key question:

By whom?

This is not addressed to anybody in particular, but who is it that chooses to reply? None other than Lenox. He, usually so reticent, takes this as his cue to speak, and he comes up with a ready answer.

Lenox: *Those of his chamber, as it seem'd, had don't:*
Their hands and faces were all badg'd with blood;
So were their daggers, which, unwip'd, we found
Upon their pillows: they stared, and were distracted;
No man's life was to be trusted to them.

Then Macbeth comes in with:

Macbeth: *O! yet I do repent me of my fury*
   That I did kill them.
Macduff is astounded at this, as well he might be:
Wherefore did you so?

And Macbeth replies with an elaborate explanation, so suspiciously unconvincing that Lady Macbeth creates a diversion by feigning to swoon.

Lenox meanwhile, has nothing more to say. When he identifies the servants as Duncan's murderers, he gives not the slightest hint that he knows they are now dead, that he himself has actually witnessed Macbeth killing them, without apparently doing anything to deter him. Why does he volunteer his testimony of the servants' guilt so readily, and why does he say nothing about their death?. And his reasons for accusing them are as unconvincing as Macbeth's justification for killing them. By having blood on their hands and faces and leaving their daggers unwiped the supposed assassins would seem to be have been intent on putting incriminating evidence on display rather than concealing it, and this surely should have aroused some suspicion that this was a put up job. Not surprisingly, they stared and were distracted – entirely normal behaviour, one would have thought, in the circumstances. In short, there is in Lenox's speech no substantial fact to support his conclusion that "No man's life was to be trusted to them".

Both the nature of the speech, and the readiness with which it is offered suggest that Lenox has been prompted to produce it, that he is puppet-like speaking the words that Macbeth has put in his mouth, playing the part that Macbeth has scripted for him.

So only twice in the play so far does the silent Lenox say anything of any substance. On the evidence of these two speeches, we can, I believe, reconstruct the crime of Duncan's murder as follows. Lenox, Duncan's apparently trusty attendant lord, is suborned by Macbeth and persuaded into a conspiracy to murder him. Lenox finds an excuse to absent himself on the night of the crime, leaving his royal master exposed. When the deed is done, Lenox, as instructed by Macbeth, identifies the servants as the perpetrators of the crime.

Having played his part in the conspiracy, he then fades again into the background, and resumes his role as attendant lord. But now, of course, he is in the service of Macbeth. His right hand man, fellow conspirator, bound to him by common guilt. The only person Macbeth can trust.

And so naturally he is the one who is sent to keep an eye on the two murderers, and give them their instructions. It is none other than Lenox who is the third man, lying in wait in the gathering darkness to do execution on Banquo and Fleance.

But the attempt is botched and Fleance escapes, and from then on, things start to fall apart for Macbeth, as Lenox, always in continual attendance, is in a unique position to witness. And as Macbeth's fortunes decline, Lenox, true to type, shifts his allegiance elsewhere. We see him playing his customary deferential role with minimal utterance as usual:

May it please your Highness, sit,

Goodnight and better health
Attend his Majesty

What's your Grace's will

And so on.

But behind the scenes, Lenox is treacherously consulting his own interests, distancing himself from Macbeth, and changing sides once more.

There is one curious circumstance in the play which, on a superficial level, could be taken as evidence against identifying Lenox as the third murderer, but, properly interpreted, only serves to indicate the onset of his treachery against Macbeth, and to emphasize the Machiavellian cunning of the man. At the beginning of the scene just after the murder of Banquo, he enters with Macbeth and the other attendant lords. Shortly afterwards, the first murderer makes his appearance to give his report of Banquo's death and Fleance's escape. So why has Lenox neglected to tell Macbeth already? One might suggest that he intended to do so, but did not find the right moment and is pre-empted by the first murderer, whose sudden appearance takes him by surprise. He would, after all, have had to hurry back from the scene of the crime to be ready for the banquet. But there is an alternative and a more satisfactory explanation: that Lenox never intends to tell Macbeth about what has happened, and simply uses the lack of time as a pretext for not doing so. Why then would he want to behave in this way?

Lenox, previously loyal to Duncan, has been suborned by Macbeth to be his accomplice, an accessory to the king's murder. What could possibly persuade Lenox into such momentous treachery, the sacrilegious nature of which he is he is only too aware of, as we know from his exchange with Macbeth, which we referred to earlier, before Duncan's murder is discovered. The only plausible explanation is that Macbeth, to gain his complete complicity, has told Lenox everything about the witches' prophecy, including of course, that part of it that concerns Fleance. So Lenox is fully aware of the necessity to kill Fleance and of the implications of his escape. Knowing therefore that Macbeth's conspiracy has failed in one crucial objective and suspecting that this is likely to have baleful consequences, he is already, true to character, reconsidering his own position. So at this moment, he stays silent and bides his time.

Further evidence that Macbeth has confided all to Lenox comes to light in the following scene. I refer here to what often appears as Act IV Scene 1 in the printed play, with Act III Scenes V and VI intervening. This order is obviously erroneous. The text of the play first appeared in the Folio (there is no Quarto) as almost certainly printed from a prompt- copy, which usually took the form of loose sets of manuscript pages. This being so, there was always the possibility of scenes being changed in their sequence, and there is internal textual evidence that indicates quite clearly that the scene sequence of Act III as printed in the Folio version must be mistaken. At the end of the banquet scene we have been referring to, when the Lords (including Lenox) have left, and just before retiring for the night, Macbeth expresses his intention of seeking out the witches:

Macbeth: *I will tomorrow*
     And betimes I will, to the Weird Sisters.

This is a clear indication that the next scene should be the meeting of Macbeth and the witches early the following day – that is to say what is now printed as Act IV Scene I.

And it is here that we find further evidence of Lenox's complicity. Macbeth meets the witches alone. After they have conjured up their apparitions, they chant, and dance and vanish. Then Macbeth says:

Macbeth: *Where are they? Gone? – Let this pernicious hour*
     Stand aye accursed in the calendar!-
     Come in, without there!

And, not surprisingly, who should come in but Lenox, and Lenox alone. The first remark that Macbeth addresses to him is revealing:

Macbeth. *Saw you the Weird Sisters?*

The Weird Sisters. The definite article is telling in that it signals shared knowledge: that Macbeth knows that Lenox knows all about the witches already. And this is borne out by Lenox's reply which confirms this: there is no trace of puzzlement, nothing along the lines of "Weird Sisters? What Weird Sisters? What are you on about my Lord" but a simple negative:

Lenox: *No, my Lord.*

There can be no question that Lenox knows everything about the witches, and is completely in Macbeth's confidence.

The confidence is, of course, misplaced. The next scene in which Lenox appears is the erroneously placed Act III, Scene VI. This occurs "somewhere in Scotland" and must take place at some considerable time after the scene just referred to. Here, Lenox has already not only distanced himself from Macbeth, but is inciting rebellion against him. This is the first and only time in the play when Lenox is a prominent figure – or is anything but an attendant lord. It is the third occasion when he produces anything more than a brief perfunctory utterance. This time he gives voice to a speech of, for him, quite unprecedented length, one which, furthermore, is apparently only the last of a series in a campaign to expose Macbeth. But he has to be cautious not to incriminate himself by too direct a denunciation, and so has to proceed indirectly by suggestion and insinuation. Hence the length of the speech.

Lenox: *My former speeches have but hit your thoughts,*
Which can interpret further: only I say,
Things have been strangely borne. The gracious Duncan
Was pitied of Macbeth: marry, he was dead:-
And the right-valiant Banquo walked too late;
Whom, you may say (if't please you) Fleance kill'd,
For Fleance fled. Men must not walk too late.
Who cannot want the thought, how monstrous
It was for Malcolm, and for Donalbain,
To kill their gracious father? Damned fact!
How it did grieve Macbeth! Did he not straight,
In pious rage, the two delinquents tear,
That were the slaves of drink, and thralls of sleep?
Was that not nobly done? Ay, and wisely too;
For 'twould have anger'd any heart alive
To hear the men deny't. So that, I say,
He has borne all things well: and I do think,
That, had he Duncan's sons under his key
(As, and't please Heaven, he shall not) they should find
What 'twere to kill a father; so should Fleance.
But, peace!- for from broad words, and 'cause he fail'd
His presence at the tyrant's feast, I hear
Macduff lives in disgrace. Sir, can you tell
Where he bestows himself?

This, we might say, is richly ironical, coming from somebody who, all the evidence suggests, conspired in the murder of Duncan, connived at the murder of the two servants, and actually participated in the murder of Banquo.

As Duncan says of the executed Thane of Cawdor:

> *There's no art*
> *To find the mind's construction in the face.*
> *He was a gentleman on whom I built*
> *An absolute trust.*

But there *is* an art to find the mind's construction in what people say, and in offering this example of forensic stylistics, I have, in a humble way, been practising it. And it leads to the indictment of Lenox. He too is a gentleman on whom absolute trust was built – first by Duncan, then by Macbeth. And he betrays them both. In discovering the truth of his treacherous nature, and detecting his crimes, we can see how the theme of deception so central to the play as a whole is also enacted through the small part of the unnoticed, unconsidered, minor character of one of the attendant lords.

Section 4: **English as a lingua franca**

Preamble

This book is an exploration, from a particular theoretical perspective, of the nature of language use and learning. The language that has the widest range of use in the contemporary world is English. Its use as an international lingua franca serves the needs of communication brought about by the increased movement of people, across borders, both free and enforced, and the vastly extended networks of digital interaction. The question arises as to how far this globalization of English, its expedient appropriation as a lingua franca, calls for different ways of thinking about the language. And if it does, then what are the implications for the way English might be designed as a pedagogic subject? And how far, more generally, can language use and learning be taken as separate and distinct processes – a question that takes us back to the issues discussed in Section 2 about the relationship between linguistics and applied linguistics.

A key issue concerning the linguistic description of ELF as a use of language relates to the immediately preceding discussions in Section 3. There what was stressed was the essential indeterminacy of language, how its use can be pragmatically adapted to accord with different contextual and pretextual factors. When English is used in communication within a community of its native speakers, its users can rely on shared lingua-cultural presumptions about what is socially customary and appropriate on different occasions of use. In this case, what can be described is how the members of a particular community conventionally use their communal language to communicate with each other. But how do people manage to communicate in English and relate to each other when these conditions of communal commonality do not obtain? How do the majority of users of the language as a lingua franca make adaptive use of English as a communicative resource?

What is of particular significance in ELF study is that in raising such questions, emphasis shifts away from ways in which language is used in communication to the nature of the communication itself, which a familiarity with how it is conventionally given linguistic expression tends to conceal. This leads to the rejection of the idea that effective communication is a function of conformity to preconceived norms, and a recognition that it is a continual adaptive process whereby users make expedient use of the linguistic resources at their disposal to express themselves and to relate to others. What now is of focal concern is not the incidental conformity of language use but its essential creativity. And so it is that creativity figures as a prominent theme in the chapters in this section, including that entitled "Creative Incompetence" which concludes it.

This last chapter, like the last of the previous section, is one of those referred to in the introduction that is tongue in cheek, satirical, mock-academic in manner. But, as with the other chapters in the same vein it has a serious point to make.

When users of English produce non-conformities, what is it that determines whether these are to be stigmatized as linguistically defective, evidence of incompetence or taken to be communicatively effective, evidence of creative capability? And how far does this depend on who is identified as the user? Such questions have to do with the legitimacy of ELF as language use and also with its implications for language learning which are taken up again in the next section.

12 ELF and the inconvenience of established concepts

What I want to do in this chapter is to explore the wider implications of ELF, as both a phenomenon and an area of study, for an understanding of the nature of language and the conventions of linguistic description. In doing so I shall be taking up issues already raised in ELF research, particularly in Seidlhofer 2011, and relating them to the broader epistemological theme of how the way we think about things in general is conditioned and constrained by what is customary and schematically conventionalized as normal. This, of course, has always been a familiar theme in philosophy and the site of continual contention between scholars of opposing positivist and relativist persuasions. But it is a theme that, as I shall argue, takes on a particular relevance in relation to ELF.

To begin then with a very simple formulation of the theme: how, in general, do we think about things, and what role does language play in the process? Let me take a literary quotation as a starting point:

human kind
Cannot bear very much reality.

This is taken from T. S. Eliot's poem *Four Quartets*, a central theme of which is the elusiveness of personal experience and how limited language is in capturing it. And yet, language is just about everything we have got to deal with it. Individual experience, the implicit reality of our personal selves, is something we are aware of but can only be conveyed by being reduced to explicit conventional means. As George Steiner puts it:

> Each communicatory gesture has a private residue. The "personal lexicon" in every one of us inevitably qualifies the definitions, connotations, semantic moves current in public discourse. The concept of a normal or standard idiom is a statistically-based fiction ... The language of a community, however uniform its social contour, is an inexhaustibly multiple aggregate of speech-atoms, of finally irreducible personal meanings.
>
> (Steiner 1975: 47)

And so what we do, and what we have to do, is quite literally, to come to terms with reality by reducing personal experience to common knowledge by means of language. We impose a stability on what is continually in flux, or otherwise, in the words of Othello "Chaos is come again". It needs no chaos or complexity theory to tell us that natural phenomena, including human behaviour, are

---

Note: Orginally published in 2012. *Journal of English as a* Lingua Franca 1 (1). 5–25.

https://doi.org/10.1515/9783110619669-017

unpredictable, elusive of conceptual control. And yet control them we must in some degree for our very survival, and so we convert actual experience to abstract knowledge and encode it in language so that we have things to think and talk about and can impose some order on the world. But this order is bound to be a kind of fictional representation of reality. And this connects with what Eliot writes elsewhere in *Four Quartets*:

> *(...)There is, it seems to us,*
> *At best, only a limited value*
> *In the knowledge derived from experience.*
> *The knowledge imposes a pattern, and falsifies,*
> *For the pattern is new in every moment*
> (East Coker 80–85)

What Eliot says here applies also to the experience and knowledge of language itself. Steiner refers to "the concept of a normal or standard idiom" as fiction because it fails to capture the facts of "irreducible personal meanings": it is a reduced version of the irreducible. But linguists *do* deal with such fictional concepts as a normal or standard idiom of the language of a community. They are in the business of imposing patterns on experience and these too are in this sense falsifications of limited value. The question is: what is it that sets the limits on value? Linguists, like everybody else, cannot avoid imposing patterns on experience and deriving abstract constructs to think with – they cannot make sense of language unless they do. This, as Thomas Kuhn points out (Kuhn 1970), is how any disciplinary enquiry makes sense of experiential data: it establishes paradigms of normality which set conceptual limits as a necessary condition for enquiry, but which, at the same time, necessarily constrains its scope. For such constructs and patterns, such paradigms of enquiry, can only have a relative validity: they are what Seidlhofer (2011) refers to as "convenient fictions", representations of reality which are suited to certain purposes, relevant to certain circumstances. This is what sets the limits on their value.

So, as far as English is concerned, the question is what value these constructs have for an understanding of how the language is now known and experienced. As Seidlhofer points out, the radically changed circumstances of the use of English as a lingua franca should prompt us to think again about how convenient conventional constructs are, what relevance established ways of thinking have for the purpose of understanding ELF as a mode of use and its implications for the teaching of English as a subject.

One construct in particular that ELF prompts us to think again about is the familiar one of competence and its connection with performance. Non-native users of ELF can be, and usually are, characterized as incompetent when their performance does not conform to standard native-speaker norms. The criterion applied to their achievement in learning is taken to apply equally to what they do with this learning in actual use: non-conformity is equated with incompetence. Yet, as research in ELF makes abundantly clear, such "incompetence" does not prevent ELF users from performing very competently as communicators. They do not know English in the same way that native speakers know it, so how *do* they know it? Do they have a different kind of competence, and if so, what is it? What, after all, is competence – a cue for Chomsky to make an appearance in this chapter.

For the concept of competence was, of course, identified by Chomsky as the proper object of linguistic description and he defined it as the perfect knowledge of a language of "an ideal speaker-listener in a completely homogeneous speech community" (Chomsky 1965). This has often been roundly condemned as an arid formalist abstraction that fails to capture the experienced reality of language as a means of communication in social contexts. There is no such thing as an ideal speaker-listener or a homogeneous speech community: it is a fiction. Very true. But this does not invalidate the construct as a convenient abstraction. The question is: how convenient is it, for whom and for what purpose.

Sociolinguists, like Labov, naturally take a very different view of what the proper object of linguistic description should be: "The object of linguistics must ultimately be the instrument of communication used by a speech community; and if we are not talking about that language, there is something trivial in our proceedings" (Labov 1970: 33).

Since Chomsky is obviously not talking about "*that* language", his proceedings would in this view be dismissed as trivial. But we need to note that Labov's own proceedings are themselves not fiction-free in that he retains the abstract construct of a speech community. For there *are* no distinct speech communities out there, just as there *are* no distinct languages or varieties of language that these communities speak until sociolinguists define them. Although sociolinguists may deplore the formalist constructs of ideal speaker-listeners and homogeneous speech communities, similarly ideal constructs are still tacitly presupposed in their descriptions of different languages and varieties and speech communities. They too deal in convenient fictions. As indeed one of the most distinguished among them openly acknowledges: in reference to how distinct varieties are separated out from the continuity of linguistic variation, Peter Trudgill makes the point: "How we divide these continua up is also most often linguistically arbitrary, although we do of course find it convenient normally to make such divisions and use names for dialects that we happen to want to talk about for a particular purpose as if they were discrete varieties" (Trudgill 1999: 122).

As I have argued earlier, there is nothing at all reprehensible about such pretence. It is a methodological necessity and without it we would be hard put to it to make any sense of the world at all, linguistic or otherwise. But it is also important to recognize that these distinctions can only be of relative validity.

In the light of this, it is interesting to consider how Trudgill himself makes use of these convenient distinctions and for what purpose. He is co-author of a book (now in its fifth edition) called *International English*, subtitled *A guide to the varieties of Standard English* (Trudgill and Hannah 2008). In reference to British English the authors say: "As far as grammar and vocabulary are concerned, this generally means Standard English as it is normally written and spoken by educated speakers in England and, with certain differences, in Wales, Scotland, Northern Ireland, The Republic of Ireland, Australia, New Zealand and South Africa" (Trudgill and Hannah 2008: 5).

These "certain differences" are taken to define the international varieties of this Standard. But which differences are certain cannot be identified with certainty. It may suit the purpose of a guide to present variation in English as if there were distinct varieties but, as Trudgill himself says, which variable data counts as evidence of a variety and which does not is ultimately a matter of arbitrary and convenient decision. It may also suit the purpose of a guide to presuppose that there is a pre-existing and stable standard norm against which differences can be measured, and to presuppose furthermore that these differences are normal in the usage of educated speakers who are native to these countries located in what Kachru refers to as the "Inner Circle" (Kachru 1985). Unless such a norm is presupposed, there can be no way of identifying which variations count as permissible variants of the standard and which do not. The difficulty here, of course, is that whereas these different countries can be objectively identified by reference to secure geo-political criteria, there are no such obvious criteria for defining who is an educated speaker, or even indeed who counts as a native, let alone what constitutes the standard language. So it is impossible to establish distinctive varieties on empirical grounds: they are essentially abstractions, convenient fictions.

The process of distinguishing those differences which are distinctive and variety-defining from those that are not would seem to be closely akin to Chomsky's proposal for establishing the grammaticality of sentences. Here is Chomsky again: "The fundamental aim in linguistic analysis of a language L is to separate the grammatical sequences which are the sentences of L from the ungrammatical sequences which are not sentences of L and to study the structure of the grammatical sequences" (Chomsky 1957: 13).

Similarly, it would seem that the fundamental aim in describing varieties of Standard English (henceforth SE) is to separate out the acceptable variants of

SE from the unacceptable variants, and to study the features of the acceptable variants. In both cases, there is the presumption that there is a stable norm by reference to which certain linguistic features can be identified as legitimate and clearly distinguished from those which are not. It is, of course, the same presumption that provides the basis for identifying the non-standard English of ELF users as deviant and evidence of incompetence.

But the norm is elusive. As has been frequently pointed out, distinguishing grammatical from ungrammatical sequences turns out, to say the least, to be a difficult thing to do. Thus linguists may claim grammaticality for the examples they cite, selected conveniently to lend support to their analysis, only to find that other linguists challenge the claim. Alongside the asterisk * denoting ungrammaticality might appear a question mark ? signifying "not entirely sure", or two question marks ?? signifying "not at all sure: perhaps grammatical – up to a point".

Up to a point. But up to what point? This is the question that is considered by Geoffrey Sampson in an intriguing article entitled *Grammar without grammaticality* (Sampson 2007). Quoting the statement from Chomsky we have already cited, Sampson proceeds to argue against the position that there is a clear-cut distinction between what is a grammatical sequence in a language and what is not. He takes a quotation from a novel by John Mortimer entitled *Dunster*, in which occurs the sequence:

> But then, as I have made it clear to you, I worry.

"This", Sampson says, "does not correspond with his own usage". He would have omitted the *it* and written:

> But then, as I have made clear to you, I worry.

Which, then, is the grammatical sequence?

Bearing in mind that this second sequence would probably be favoured as the correct option, do we then mark the first sequence with an asterisk * – definitely ungrammatical, or at the very least a question mark ? – grammatical up to a point. Sampson feels it would be inappropriate to make judgements of this kind in this case:

> Mortimer is highly educated (Harrow and Brasenose) and has lived by the spoken and written word, combining a career at the Bar with a prolific and successful output of intelligent fiction (...). And Penguin books normally seem to be carefully copy-edited. On the face of it, one would expect that if Mortimer and Penguin between them let a sentence into print, I ought to be happy with it from a grammatical point of view.
>
> (Sampson 2007: 3)

Here again, the educated native speaker is invoked as representing the authoritative norm. And Mortimer, one might add, is not only "highly educated" but has been honoured by his monarch and is a knight of the realm. Obviously a man with such impeccable credentials cannot possible be charged with improper linguistic conduct. There must be some way of granting grammatical status to his sentence. And Sampson does indeed find a way. By means of a somewhat intricate syntactic analysis, he is able to conclude that in spite of appearances the Mortimer sequence does actually conform to grammatical rule after all. So it is not that one of these sequences is grammatical and the other not, but that both are permissible variants. It just happens that Mortimer has chosen one, Sampson the other. And by reference to corpus data, Sampson illustrates that this is not an exceptional case: variants of this kind, each an equally valid alternative, are of quite frequent occurrence. Sampson elucidates the way he sees things by means of an extended metaphor:

> The grammatical possibilities of a language are like a network of paths in open grassland. There are a number of heavily used, wide and well-beaten tracks. Other, less popular routes are narrower, and the variation extends smoothly down to routes used only occasionally, which are barely distinguishable furrows or, if they are used rarely enough, perhaps not even visible as permanent marks in the grass, but there are no fences anywhere preventing any particular route being used, and there is no sharp discontinuity akin to the contrast between metalled roads and foot-made paths – the widest highway is only the result of people going that way much more often and in far greater numbers than in the case of narrow paths. (Sampson 2007: 10–11)

This, I find, an attractive image, almost allegorical in its appeal – it conjures up a John Bunyan- like vision of a field full of pilgrim-like language users all taking various paths across the grassland towards ... well towards what? Not Bunyan's Celestial City, but some destination or other, one would suppose. At the very least, one assumes that the different routes would have to get to the other side of the field. Those that go round in circles, or end up where they started would not, presumably, be considered a legitimate part of the network of pathways, but what of those that meander into detours? What latitude is allowed for divergence? And since "there are no fences anywhere preventing any particular route being used" does any path taken across the grassland count as a route, no matter how indirect? And what of paths that have not yet been taken but might be? No allowance seems to be made for grammatical possibilities other than those that have been attested as actual usage. But whose usage? Who is to be recognized as relevant for deciding on paths which count as legitimate variants and which do not? Who are the pathfinders?

What started Sampson on his enquiry into variation, it will be recalled, was the dilemma posed by an apparently ungrammatical expression used by a highly educated native speaker, John Mortimer in his novel *Dunster*. The statistical analysis that gives rise to this vision of a network of pathways is based on a corpus of native speaker written English. Throughout the discussion, reference is made to speakers of English, but it is clear that this is shorthand for educated native speakers/writers of the language. It is their usage that is taken to be the norm, and only the variants they produce, which Sampson calls *Dunsters*, are recognized as legitimate paths through the grammatical grassland. So it is that Mortimer's *as I have made it clear to you* is said to be an admissible variant of *as I have made clear to you* on the grounds that as he is highly educated he can be trusted to produce exemplary English – "a model", says Sampson, "for the kind of English I think of myself as aiming to speak and write" (Sampson 2007: 3).

But what if this expression were to be produced by somebody without such impeccable educational credentials? Or what if an expression is in a kind of English that Sampson would not wish to aim to speak and write – *as I have made you clear*, for example? Would this be considered a *Dunster* as well? Presumably not: You cannot do a *Dunster* unless you are both educated and a native speaker.

These are the same conditions of acceptability that have to be met for variants to be given the status of Standard English in Trudgill & Hannah's guide. They too invoke the notion of the educated native speaker, but without giving any indication as to how one might determine whether a speaker counts as educated or not. Everybody attending school is educated up to a point, but at what point do they become educated enough to be categorized as users of Standard English? Presumably they would not all need to have gone to Harrow and Brasenose College Oxford. Perhaps some other prestigious public school would do, or some other university? And what of non-native speakers, users of ELF for example, who get educated in English? May it be that some kinds of education can cancel out the handicap of non-nativeness? If so what kinds?

A moment's reflection makes it obvious that the concept of the educated native speaker is simply an idealized construct, a convenient abstraction which is, paradoxically enough, on a par with Chomsky's ideal speaker -listener. The difference is that Chomsky is quite explicit that his speaker listener is indeed a non-existent ideal abstraction, accessible only to intuition, whereas Trudgill & Hannah and Sampson seem to assume that educated native speakers actually exist as an observable group of language performing people in the real world, although they do not feel obliged to provide any criteria for identifying who they are.

They feel no obligation, I think, because the concept of a standard language or variety is already established by fiat and does not need to be inferred from an analysis of actually occurring language data. For what constitutes a standard is not the language produced by its native users, educated or not, but that which linguists have codified. What makes a language or a variety standard is, as indeed Trudgill and Hannah themselves acknowledge, that: "[I]t has been subjected to a process through which it has been selected, codified and stabilized, in a way that other varieties have not (...) whose grammar has been described and given public recognition in grammar books and dictionaries, with its norms being widely considered to be 'correct' and constituting 'good usage' " (Trudgill and Hannah 2008: 1–2).

In other words what is standard is decreed by authority, although which authority is left unspecified: the language "has been subjected to a process (...) has been selected, codified and stabilized" by some unmentioned agency. In effect the standard is a construct based on what linguistic tradition has deemed to be worth codifying, which is then carried over and assumed to be valid in subsequent linguistic descriptions. The public recognition of this validity is then assured by publication in what are conveniently called standard works of reference. And so a convenient construct becomes an established convention. For one needs to note that the grammar books and dictionaries that are referred to here are not newly compiled each time from scratch from empirical data, but are adapted versions of previous grammars and dictionaries. Thus the illusion is perpetuated that these descriptions are the empirically substantiated accounts of the actual language, whereas what they represent is essentially versions of conventionalized constructs that are sanctioned by linguistic tradition. Let me stress again that to say this is not to dismiss such constructs. As I have argued, we cannot do without them if we are to impose some order on reality. Again, however, the question is what purpose and what interests define how convenient particular constructs are.

The descriptions I have been considering so far are concerned with competence in the Chomskyan sense, with what ideal speaker-listeners know of the encoded properties of their language. Nowadays, of course, with the development of computerized language corpora, there are grammars and dictionaries which radically depart from linguistic tradition and set out to describe the actually occurring language of "real" speakers. These are descriptions not of what people are surmised to know of the language but what they actually *do* with their knowledge. They are performance descriptions that deal not with the first person data of the linguist's own introspection but with the third person data of observed usage, actual language behaviour.

There is no doubt that corpus linguistics, in reinstating the significance of performance, constitutes a fundamental change of approach to language description. The shift of focus from 1st person data derived from the speculative introspection about the abstract code, to the observed 3rd person data of actual usage, clearly reveals aspects of linguistic reality that were previously unnoticed or disregarded. But not all aspects. Corpus linguists have sometimes suggested that their approach to description supersedes all previous approaches in that it deals with factual data and so captures "real" language, the language that can be attested as what real people produce. But what is described is only partially real – real up to a point. It too is an abstract version of reality.

In the first place, what is "real" is selected from what is assumed to be "normal" English and the data are selected as representative of "the language" by tacit reference again to this undefined category of educated native speakers. And now it is their usage, their performance, rather than their competence, that is represented as the ideal. It is their linguistic behaviour that defines *the* language. And this description of usage is also an abstract construct in that it is only a partial account of the reality of language experience. For corpus descriptions tell us what linguistic forms have been produced by this representative group of users, but not why they produced them and to what pragmatic ends and purposes. If we refer again to what Labov says should be the object of linguistics – the use of language as an instrument of communication – it is certainly not *that* language that is the object of description of corpus linguistics. What is described is linguistic text dissociated from communicative context – what linguistic forms are *manifested*, not the communicative functions that they are used to *realize*: the textual product is abstracted from the discourse process. But these linguistic forms are only real for the language user as a by-product of this process and so corpus descriptions do not, and cannot, capture the reality of language as experienced by its users (for further discussion see Widdowson 2003, 2004).

So the account of language that corpus linguistics provides is also an abstraction, at a remove from experience. It deals with performance, but only with the form that performance takes, and abstracting that form from its natural communicative function in use makes it into an analytic construct, another kind of fiction. This does not mean that it is without value, but the value is bound to be limited. And again the question is: what are its limits? How convenient a fiction is it?

As I have already argued, you can only make sense of what you actually do, or of what other people actually do, by relating it to some construct of abstract knowledge. So you can only make sense of performance as the realization of some competence or other. And here we come to the crucial question of the relationship between the concepts of competence and performance. One can accept that an exclusive focus on linguistic competence fails to account for the various ways in which it is acted upon in contexts of communication. But equally, an exclusive focus on the form that performance takes fails to account for what linguistic knowledge is being drawn upon in the process.

Dissociating competence from performance and isolating it for analysis may be a misrepresentation in that it disregards how such knowledge is actually acted upon, but it is this competence that makes the performance a reality. The ability to communicate presupposes some knowledge of linguistic means. You cannot just perform: you have to perform *something*. Performance is the actualization of abstract knowledge so it has to presuppose competence of some kind or another. Corpus linguists, in claiming to have captured the essentials of the language that has eluded other linguists, would seem to suppose that we can dispense with the distinction between competence and performance altogether: that what people produce *is* the language, the real language.

But the point is that competence provides the dynamic that drives the meaning making process and no matter how extensively you describe its performative products, its generative potential remains undiminished and is, as Chomsky has said, the essential source of creativity. This is why its reality cannot be captured by corpus descriptions, no matter how extensive. For these descriptions are examples of how this potential *has been* exploited in the past for certain communicative purposes by certain groups of users, but not how it *can* be exploited for *other* purposes and by *other* users.

To return to Sampson and his linguistic grassland, what corpus descriptions show, and can only show, is the "network of paths" already taken, and those which have hitherto been the "heavily used, wide and well beaten tracks" as distinct from the "less popular routes". But as I pointed out earlier, these paths and tracks and routes are only those which are made by authorized pathfinders – the educated native speakers who provide the corpus data. What is not recorded is what tracks others, the non-educated or the non-native, might have made to find their way through the linguistic grassland. And what cannot be recorded, of course, is what other tracks it might be possible or expedient to make in the future, whether you are an educated native speaker or not.

As far as English is concerned, there are innumerable other people apart from educated native speakers that are finding a way across this metaphorical field, and there is no reason why they should follow the well trodden paths of native speaker custom and convention which may well not suit their purposes. But there is a prevailing assumption that this is what all users of English ought to do – stay on the beaten track, do not stray, keep off the grass.

So it is that the way users like non-native speakers of English as a lingua franca make their way through the language is said to be deviant. Their performance, as I said earlier, is generally taken as evidence that they are incompetent. And they are judged to be incompetent on two counts: not only is their knowledge of the language imperfect in that they do not conform to the abstract encoding rules that are said to constitute native speaker competence, but they do not know how to perform properly because they do not conform to conventions of actual native speaker usage either. They do not stay on track. This, however, is to accept the validity of equating competence with conformity to native speaker norms. But quite apart from the fact that the very concept of native speaker competence lacks any clear definition, there is plenty of evidence that it is irrelevant and that ELF users can get by very well without it anyway.

So how do they manage to do it? They cannot perform without competence of some kind. If they do not have native speaker competence, what kind of competence do they have? And how do they act upon it in their performance? To return to points I made at the beginning of this article: we can only ever make sense of anything by generalizing from particulars. We deal in preconceived constructs all the time: we convert *samples* of actual experience into *examples* of abstract categories, and this conversion process necessarily extends and elaborates these categories according to convenience. We cannot cope with the *data* of experience until we have converted them into conceptual *evidence*. In this sense, paradoxical though this may seem, we can only make things real by making them abstract, and we learn how to do this in the very process of learning language. And most of what we know of the world is not directly derived from perceived experience but taken over on trust from ready-made conceptualizations. Most of our knowledge is second- hand. So it is not just linguists that deal with abstract constructs as convenient ways of making sense of things. We all do it and we could not survive if we did not.

So it is by reference to what we know, to our competence, our abstract construct of linguistic reality, that we take bearings on our experience and interpret data as evidence of something familiar. The abstracting process goes on all the time. Consider how we make sense of conversation. As those who have recorded ELF interactions will know well enough, the actual data of conversation is highly complex and confusing and it is often very difficult to make out just what is going on. This is the difficulty that the ethnomethodologists set out to deal with in their conversation analysis: "What the parties said would be treated as a sketchy, partial, incomplete, masked, elliptical, concealed, ambiguous, or misleading version of what the parties talked about" (Garfinkel 1972: 217).

From the outsider perspective of the analyst, what is said, the actual text that the participants produce may be sketchy, partial, incomplete, ambiguous and so on, but this a problem for the analyst, not the participants themselves. This is because they are only processing textual data as evidence of the discourse process and have no difficulty abstracting what is talked about from what is actually said. This is the only way in which the interaction can be made real for them. And the task of the analyst is to produce a similarly abstract version by inferring discourse function from textual forms, and as any ELF researcher knows, the problem is to know how far the analyst's version can correspond with that of the participants. Or indeed *should* correspond. For of course, the analysis may be informed by pretextual purposes and the analyst may be intent on placing a particular construction on the text to reveal significance that the participants may not be aware of (for further discussion see Widdowson 2004).

Deriving discourse versions from textual data will always be a tricky and controversial proceeding. There is no way, as far as I can see, of determining the validity of the different constructs that are abstracted from the data. Each is a different representation, a different take on reality. Each, therefore, to refer back to the quotation from *Four Quartets* cited earlier "imposes a pattern, and falsifies". Each is, in this sense a kind of fiction.

In the case of conversation analysis, the constructs are derived from actual data. But there are also abstractions which are unconnected with specific instances of actually occurring language use. Here we can make a connection with representations of talk that are overtly fictional as in the dramatic dialogue of a play. The playwright Harold Pinter, for example, is often praised for the naturalistic way his characters carry on their conversations. Their talk somehow rings true. But these dramatic dialogues are not actually true to life. Performance on stage is entirely different from how language is performed in actual contexts of use – one has only to compare a scene from one of Pinter's plays with the transcripts of actually occurring talk to see how remote they are from what goes on in real conversation. Though they are not true to life, the dialogues somehow carry conviction – they represent a reality that the audience recognizes and responds to, based on their schematic knowledge of conversation they are familiar with. They recognize that Pinter has abstracted something essential about human interaction and has represented talk by editing out the distractions of what would be actually said. So it the effectiveness of the performance on stage depends on the competence of the audience. Unlike Garfinkel, Pinter is not dealing directly with the data of actual occurrence, and so his version of talk is not required to be substantiated by adducing evidence of its validity. Garfinkel is in this sense translating from an original and Pinter is not. But both Harolds – Garfinkel and Pinter – are in the business of devising fictional representations, versions of reality that edit out the particulars of actuality. But they are fictional in different ways as relevant to their different purposes. Their validity is relative: it depends on our recognition of this relevance. We would not take the script of a play as a valid example of conversation analysis, or vice versa. But each has its own validity and there are times when acknowledged fictional representations of reality in literature give enlightening insights into how people experience language beyond the scope of the supposedly factual account of linguistic analysis. One might add that this suggests an area of comparative enquiry, as far as I know still under-explored: the difference between literary and linguistic representations of language in use. This would bring to the fore the uncertain relationship between fact and fiction in human affairs that I am considering in this article.

So what I am saying is simple and obvious enough. We make sense of things by abstracting from the actual. What we do, our performance, is a partial, incomplete, elliptical, masked expression of what we know, our competence – in this respect Chomsky surely got it right. We can only perform language and understand other people's performance of it by reference to some abstract construct or competence or other, And ELF as a natural use of language is no exception. Some abstract construct or other. But which? That is the question.

The main impediment to an understanding of the concept of ELF is the assumption that the only relevant and legitimate construct is native speaker competence. But non-native ELF users cannot know English as native-speakers know it. Native-speaker knowledge is abstracted from the experience of primary socialization whereby language, culture and social identity are naturally and inseparably inter-connected. Non-native speaker ELF users experience the language very differently, as an extension of a language resource they already have, acquired through secondary socialization and separated from these primary and inherent connections with culture and identity.

We need abstract constructs, I have argued, because they represent our realities and without them we cannot make sense of the world. But these constructs represent different realities, different socio-cultural schemata, values, beliefs, ways of thinking, that are appropriate to certain purposes, relevant to certain circumstances. One can see, of course, why it is politically and commercially expedient to represent a language, particularly English, as a well- defined and self-enclosed entity with fully competent native speakers to provide its norms of correctness. But these norms are determined by cultural and identity factors that no longer apply outside native-speaking communities. One can see that once such a construct of English is established as convenient fiction it becomes taken for granted and there is no need to question its validity: attitudes harden and the fiction takes on the force of fact. But when purposes and circumstances change, when English gets globalized as a lingua franca and becomes common property, and thus as a means of expressing other cultural values, other identities, then there is the obvious need to adapt our representations of reality. The old conditions of relevance and appropriateness no longer apply. "The old order changeth, yielding place to new ", as Tennyson has it. Or if it does not, surely it should.

Non-native speaker ELF users have some kind of "competence" in English: they could not function in the language otherwise. Although, as I have said, their linguistic knowledge may be seen as deficient when measured against NS norms, the only measurement that is generally recognized as valid, this does not prevent them from communicating efficiently. So they have some kind of *communicative* "competence". This is the cue for Dell Hymes to make his appearance.

To remind you, Hymes proposes that there are four criteria for establishing how far somebody is communicatively competent in a language: the extent to which they can judge whether and to what degree a sample of a language is possible, feasible, appropriate and actually performed. He says: "There is an important sense in which a normal member of a community has knowledge with respect to all these aspects of the communicative systems available to him. He will interpret or assess the conduct of others and himself in ways that reflect a knowledge of each (...)" (Hymes 1972: 282).

We should note that although he does not say so explicitly, reference to "a normal member of a community" implies that it is, again, native speaker competence that Hymes has in mind. What else can a normal member of a community be but an ideal speaker-listener under a different name? And the norm that this normal member conforms to can only be that of the native speaker. You obviously cannot make judgements about whether and to what degree a language sample is possible, feasible, appropriate and actually performed without reference to established norms that define *a* particular language as the property of *a* particular community. Thus whether and to what degree a sample of language is contextually appropriate means, or has certainly been taken to mean, appropriate to native speaker contexts and whether and to what degree it is done means actually produced by native speakers. On these criteria, of course, the non-conformist ELF users remain communicatively incompetent. And their conduct is indeed interpreted and assessed as such. But as has already been noted, what is appropriate in native-speaking contexts and what native speakers actually perform are essentially irrelevant for ELF contexts.

So what if we dispense with the normal member of a native speaking community? What if we forget about making normative judgements and ask instead, how ELF users construct their own reality by making appropriate and feasible use of language that is not possible in these terms and not normally performed by native speakers? In the Hymes scheme, the four factors are presented as separate and unconnected components with no indication of any priority or relationship between them. The formally possible comes first in the list, but there is nothing to suggest that this implies some kind of primacy, and there is no discussion about how, for example, the appropriate factor affects the possible – how, in other words, contextual functions have a determining effect on the encoded forms of a language. But if we are to understand how communication is actually achieved, we need to consider how these factors relate to each other. Hymes provides what he calls "a linguistic illustration" of his four factors: "[A] sentence may be grammatical, awkward, tactful and rare" (Hymes 1972: 281). But communication is not a matter of identifying the property of sentences, but of knowing how these factors connect and combine to make effective communicative use of the language – how, for example, one can relate the feasible with the appropriate to say something that is tactfully awkward, or when it is appropriate to produce an expression which is rare or ungrammatical to achieve a particular pragmatic effect. Communication is a function of the dynamic interplay across these different factors and it cannot be described simply by identifying them as separate components.

Use of the language in ELF, as research has amply illustrated, provides abundant evidence of how its users relate these factors. The possible is generally subordinated to the feasible and the appropriate, and what is, or more strictly has been, actually performed becomes irrelevant. It does not matter, in other words, whether the language conforms to established code rules or usage conventions so long as it is intelligible and pragmatically effective. Indeed, users, freed from the constraints of conformity, will typically increase feasibility by reducing the irregularities and exploiting the redundancy of the standard code, and will produce lexical re-alignments of formal features as contextually appropriate to their purposes. Thus their alternative version of the possible is motivated by functional need, and in this respect what we see in ELF is an entirely natural, and indeed inevitable, process of linguistic evolution, consistent with the Halliday dictum that the form a language takes is a reflection of the functions it has evolved to serve (Halliday and Matthiessen 2004).

The essential point to make here is that this process of functionally motivated de-formation and re-formation continues, which is why communication, in ELF or any other natural language, depends not on conformity but on non-conformity with established norms of the formally possible and the actually performed. These established norms have been derived from ways in which the language has feasibly and appropriately functioned for particular groups of users in the past, but they are no longer of necessary relevance to other users in the present. Adherence to these norms does not, as is often claimed, ensure effective communication but on the contrary will tend to make it more difficult. ELF has often been equated with fossilized learning. But if anything is fossilized it is these norms – fossils, it would seem, set in stone.

And so non-native speaking ELF users may develop their own construct of the possible as a function of what is feasible and appropriate for their purposes, by exploiting the potential for meaning making inherent in the language, what I have called elsewhere the virtual language (Widdowson 1997, 2003). Descriptions of ELF already give some indication of the nature of this construct, and identifying its essential features is, I think, one of the major challenges of ELF research in the future. What findings already seem to show is that ELF involves a reconsideration of the concept of the possible itself. In Hymes this would seem to be equated with grammatical competence as defined by Chomsky. ELF users, as we know, can communicate without conformity to the standard grammar: they take what they need from it and leave the rest. But what is it that regulates which features they take and which they leave?

This raises the very general question of what the communicative function of grammar is anyway. There are, after all, times when we can get by very well without it, when the use of words alone is both feasible and appropriate. This suggests that grammar serves only a subordinate and auxiliary role – we call on it as an expediency when it is necessary to make a more explicit connection between lexis and context. If we make use of grammar when it is not necessary, it is likely to impair communication rather than improve it. What we see in ELF interactions is just this expedient use of grammar, and ELF users will naturally focus on those grammatical features which have a high degree of communicative valency, or potential, and will tend to disregard those features that do not. In other words, the construct of the possible in ELF represents the ongoing development of a genuinely functional grammar, where linguistic forms are pragmatically motivated by contextual function in contrast to Halliday's functional grammar, which is essentially the static semantic record of how functions in the past have become encoded in the standard language.

I have been talking about the wider implications of ELF from a sociolinguistic perspective. What then of the pedagogic perspective? What are the wider implications here? How does all this connect up with English language classrooms? Most ELF users are erstwhile EFL learners and their construct of English typically has its origins in the classroom. It is there that it has been abstracted from the actual language performance they have been presented with and practised in. So it is no surprise that ELF and learner English are in many respects formally alike: it would indeed be surprising if they were not. As we know, this is generally taken as evidence of failure in that this formal likeness is unlike Standard English or approved conventions of native speaker usage. But this is to focus on form without regard to the functional motivation that gives rise to it.

The question that needs to be asked about ELF users and EFL learners alike is this: why is it that they develop their own abstract construct of the language? Why are learners so perverse in their refusal to learn what teachers tell them to learn? It is not that they do not learn *something*, but that they get little credit for it if the something they learn does not measure up to what they have been taught, even if they can put it to effective use. So if it is not what is taught that determines what is learned, what does? It is an obvious fact that in English language classrooms there is always at least one other language present. Learners learn the new language by referring it to the language or languages they already know: although English is generally *taught* monolingually, it is actually *learned* bi- or multilingually (for further discussion see Widdowson 2003). I would suggest that, primed by the experience of their own language, learners quite naturally focus attention on what is functionally salient, give intuitive priority to what is feasible and appropriate, and filter out linguistic features that are surplus to communicative requirement. In short, they develop their own functional grammar. This is not, and cannot be, the same as what they have been taught. But this represents success, not failure.

For this really is communicative language *learning*, as distinct from communicative language teaching, as it is generally practised, which only sanctions communicative activity that conforms to native speaker norms. Consider the version of the communicative approach that is now much in vogue: task based language teaching (expounded in detail in Ellis 2003). This sets out to teach learners what have been identified as the three basic components of competence: accuracy, fluency and complexity (see, for example, Housen and Kuiken 2009). All three of these are defined in terms of the standard language, and tasks are designed to ensure that their outcomes involve some focus on form so that learners can improve the accuracy and increase the complexity of their language as they move through stages of interlanguage towards the goal of a presupposed but undefined native speaker competence. So linguistic competence is taken to be the objective and communication the means for achieving it. Presumably, if learners are communicatively fluent without being accurate and complex in the approved way, that does not count as a successful outcome and you need to design another task.

This, I would argue, gets things the wrong way round. If learners achieve a communicative outcome without being accurate and complex, what you need to think about if you are really interested in communication, is how they manage to do that, and then design tasks that get them to keep on doing it. There is a good deal of concern that learners might not notice linguistic features, and tasks get designed to ensure that they do. But if these features are not noticed, the question is why not – and why should they be. It may well be that they are not taken to be communicatively salient and so not worth noticing.

Learner achievement is generally measured in terms of *quantity*. But I would argue that *how much* learners know of English is of little importance. It is *how* they know it that really matters. And here we might note that a good deal, perhaps most, of what is difficult for learners about the language is just those features that have an identifying function for native-speakers but are communicatively redundant. What is most difficult, and most resistant to teacher correction, is probably what is most dispensable. But these are the very features that teachers tend to spend most time trying, in vain, to teach.

Learners construct their own version of the language they are being taught and this gets carried over and developed further when they escape from the classroom and become ELF users. This version is generally taken to be an interlanguage, an interim and inadequate stage of acquisition. The pedagogic task is, in this view, to move learners on towards the final goal of native speaker competence, following the directions determined by the teacher on the advice of the researcher in SLA. This is not unlike the quest for the Holy Grail: the goal is unattainable, not least because it is an illusion. And not only unattainable, but irrelevant anyway. It is surely time to think of a possible alternative.

Research on ELF gives an indication of what form such an alternative might take. This research makes clear that ELF users can make effective use of English despite their failure to conform to the kind of competence prescribed by their teachers – one might indeed say *because* of this failure. For in failing to conform they have developed their own construct, a kind of competence of their own. They have, in Halliday's terms (Halliday 1975) learned how to mean in English, and this provides them with a *capability* for further learning as they exploit and extend this competence as and when this is functionally necessary for different communicative purposes in different contexts of use (for a discussion of capability, see Widdowson 2003). It would seem to make sense to try to understand what learners know of English, how they know and use it: to identify what aspects of the virtual language learners abstract from the data, what they filter out and focus on, what they notice, what they focus on as salient and essential and what they edit out as not – what, in short, they *make* of the language. And then to adjust teaching accordingly. This would be the use of learner language: not to identify what is to be corrected, but what is to be encouraged – a genuine learner-centred approach.

What form such adjustment might take is, of course, an open question. And it is bound to be constrained by factors beyond the control of practising teachers – like the reference books and teaching materials that they have to work with, the persuasive authority of teacher-trainers, especially those who are native speakers of English, and, above all, the exigencies of assessment. All of these conditioning circumstances are themselves unlikely in the near future to adjust to the changing role of English in the world and its pedagogic implications. But there will be some room for manoeuvre. The first step is to raise the awareness of teachers that there is an alternative way of thinking about the subject they teach, based on an understanding of English as a lingua franca.

And here I return to my central theme. We make sense of the world by relating the actual particulars of experience to abstract constructs of knowledge, and these constructs are always in some degree fictions of relative validity and value. Cultures and paradigms of enquiry represent their own realities according to purpose and convenience. They make different conceptual distinctions, know things in different ways. The study of ELF is, I have argued, of particular significance in that it prompts a reappraisal of established, taken for granted ways of thinking about language, especially English. I have argued that, convenient though these ways may be for some purposes and for some manifestations of the language, they are an encumbrance when it comes to understanding how English is used as a lingua franca. Many years ago, John Sinclair made the insightful point that developments in corpus linguistics produced "new material" that also prompted a reappraisal of conventional thinking: "The categories and methods we use to describe English are not appropriate to the new material. We shall need to overhaul our descriptive systems" (Sinclair 1985: 252).

Although this is not at all what Sinclair had in mind, his comments are especially pertinent to ELF. Here too we have "new material", and great amounts of it, for which the categories and methods conventionally used to describe English are not appropriate. Here too we need to "overhaul our descriptive systems" and deconstruct our established concepts. And this, as I have argued, involves a quite radical rethinking about the relationship between what we know about the language and what we do with it, between competence and performance, between form and function, between learners and users of English, and between the teaching and learning of the language as a subject.

13 ELF and the pragmatics of language variation

The study of English as a lingua franca is a relatively new area of enquiry which has inspired a great deal of research and the tendency, quite naturally and properly, has been to focus on its relationship with current ideas. But as someone who has been around for a long time, my own tendency is to relate the present to the past and to look for continuities. Though such retrospection can have its disadvantages of course, it can also provide a different perspective which might show ELF in a new light. So my purpose is to provide a kind of synthesis of past and present thinking and to trace a continuity of enquiry so as to bring into sharper relief what I believe to be the crucial significance that ELF research has for the study of language and language learning in general.

Over recent years, a number of publications have made the point that an understanding of language depends on recognizing that it is unstable, dynamic, intrinsically variable and that the way it is used simply cannot be accounted for by supposing that it is a static system of rules that users conform to. This is often presented as an innovative insight into the nature of language, revealed by postmodernist thinking about performativity, complexity theory and the sociolinguistics of globalization and a radical departure from previous unenlightened approaches to linguistic description. This new conceptual order is said to provide the essential theoretical framework for ELF research (Baird et al. 2014).

Innovation can, of course, be inspiring and there will always be the tendency for people to be influenced by ideas in vogue. But what is innovative is a matter of perception, relative to contexts of time and place. As now formulated, the idea that language use is variable, adaptive, emergent may have all the appearance of novelty but, in the disciplines of the social if not the physical sciences, the idea is really far from new. Over forty years ago, for example, long before complexity theory made its appearance, a book was published with the title *New Ways of Analyzing Variation in English* (Bailey and Shuy 1973). This is a compilation of papers, all reporting research into inherent linguistic variability, research indeed that conceives of English very much in complexity theory terms as "a dynamic system that emerges and self-organizes from frequently occurring patterns of language use" (Larsen-Freeman and Cameron 2008: 111).

One of the contributors to this 1973 volume was William Labov – indeed the volume is dedicated to him as recognition of his ground-breaking work on the description of variation in English. I want to suggest in this talk that a

---

Note: Originally published in 2015 *Journal of English as a Lingua Franca* 4 (2). 359–372.

https://doi.org/10.1515/9783110619669-018

consideration of Labov's descriptive work on the complex and adaptive variability of English leads to a much clearer understanding of the essential nature of ELF than does the speculative invocation of complexity theory. Baird et al. tell us that "[c]omplexity theory provides principles that embody non-fixity, incompleteness, and non-linearity within approaches that are held to be consistent with empirical enquiry of various kinds" (Baird et al. 2014: 177).

Although Labov is not referred to in the article, it is just such principles that informed his extensive empirical enquiry into language variation that made such a mark in the 1970s. Labov does get a brief mention in the Larsen-Freeman and Cameron book. He even gets a nod of approval: complexity theory, we are told, "would find merit" in his approach to the study of variation" (Larsen-Freeman and Cameron 2008: 87).

Labov's way of analysing language was new at the time precisely because it challenged the established way of thinking about language as essentially an abstract static model of competence and focused attention on features of performance, on how language was actually and variably realized in contexts of use. This shift of focus represented a much more radical departure from established ideas about language than generative grammar, which, as Chomsky himself acknowledges, follows the same traditional line as de Saussure in restricting the scope of linguistic description to the formal properties of the language system. It was not that Chomsky or de Saussure were unaware of the complexities of language use. On the contrary, it was because language use was so complex and so variable that they believed it to be elusive of systematic description and so made the methodological decision to exclude it. Labov's achievement was to demonstrate empirically that there were aspects of complexity that could be systematically accounted for in a linguistics of performance or parole. In the words of what is probably his most cited paper, Labov's aim was "The study of language in its social context" (Labov 1970, 1972) and essentially with its variability in use. Since ELF research is also concerned with the variability of English in different social contexts, it seems reasonable to suppose that his work might be of some relevance.

The best known of Labov's work has to do with how the variable occurrence of linguistic features correlate with social class and reflect social values. His aim is to show that there are variable rules which operate within certain varieties of English. But he is also concerned to assert the legitimacy of these varieties as the means of communication for the communities that speak them. Thus in a celebrated paper, "The logic of nonstandard English" (Labov 1969a), he argues that what was then called non-standard Negro English (subsequently Black English Vernacular and African American English), was not, as was commonly supposed at the time, a defective version of the language which made its speakers verbally deprived, incapable of logical thought and effective communication, but a different version, with its own system of rules, and no less cognitively and communicatively effective than Standard English within the community of its speakers.

Labov's argument against the notion of verbal deprivation finds an obvious resonance in ELF study. Here, too, researchers have had to contend with the fixed idea that uses of English which do not conform to approved Standard English norms must necessarily be defective, and its users verbally deprived. They, too, have to contend with the educational establishment's insistence that such users have to be shown the error of their ways and subjected to remedial treatment to get them to acquire the proper language. ELF scholars, then, share Labov's view that people are perfectly capable of communicating effectively without conforming to the norms of the standard language – that indeed such conformity may well result in ineffective communication.

But there is a crucial difference in that they are not talking about the same kind of people. Labov is talking about intra-community communication, about people communicating within a particular community which conforms to the norms of its own distinctive variety. In so doing he is seeking to validate Black English Vernacular or African American English as an English in its own right, with its own rules and its own communal conventions of appropriate use. His case for the legitimacy of its departures from the standard rests on the argument that these departures are regular and systematic and constitute a separate variety: "All linguists who work with non standard Negro English recognize that it is a separate system, closely related to standard English but separate from the surrounding white dialects by a number of persistent and systematic differences" (Labov 1969a: 32).

Here Labov is making common cause, not with an ELF but with a WE (World Englishes) line of enquiry. Scholars working with manifestations of English in different Outer Circle countries also recognize them as constituting separate systems with their own persistent and systematic differences. In this respect, Labov's paper can be seen as supporting a World Englishes agenda – a precursor of that so-called paradigm.

So we can see this paper as genuinely seminal in that it has within it the seeds of two separate developments in the study of variability in English. One of these considers how variable linguistic features constitute a variety associated with a particular community. The concern here is the validation of a way of using language as the expression of communal identity. Thus just as there is a distinctive English that is used by the community of African Americans, which we might call Ebonic English, so there are distinctive Englishes used by the communities in various ex-colonial countries: Indian English, for example.

Although these two Englishes are located in different Kachru circles – Ebonic in the Inner and Indian in the Outer, their status as independently legitimate expression of communal identity is the same. And this status depends on recognizing that variations that are not in conformity with Standard English norms are so internally regular as to constitute systems in their own right. That is the WE line of development. Obviously, then, from a WE perspective, what is of primary concern is the identification of varieties as correlated with communities in the traditional definition of groups of people who share the same primary socio-cultural space.

The other line of development is the study of ELF. This follows from Labov's demonstration that a capability for effective communication is not dependent on conformity to Standard English rules and norms of usage. However, what Labov argues is that there is still conformity but to the rules and norms that define a different system, a different dialect or variety. This is where ELF study parts company with Labov. Because what is clearly evident in the use of ELF is that communicative capability not only does not depend on conformity to Standard English norms but that it does not depend on conformity to the norms of any other variety either. And here, too, is the essential distinction between ELF and WE. The study of ELF considers variability not in terms of variety at all but as the variable use of English as inter-community communication, as communication across communities. There is a marked tendency for scholars working in the so-called WE paradigm to deny the validity of such study. For them, it seems, variation is only of significance as evidence of variety and there really is little point in studying it otherwise. Many sociolinguists appear to share this view. Even when it is deemed worthy of study, as, for example, in the work of Edgar Schneider, the unsystematic variation of ELF use is really only of interest to the extent that it is an interim phase on the way towards variety status (Schneider 2012).

Variety status is achieved when variations become conventionalized and so settle into what is taken to be a systematic state, in other words, when variation is taken to be regularized to the extent that it constitutes language change. But since language is, as both Labov and the complexity theorists have made abundantly clear, intrinsically variable, dynamic, emergent, continuously in flux, the identification of a variety depends on supposing that variation is in a state of suspended animation. In other words, it is an ideal construct, a convenient fiction. What ELF study does is to focus on the process of variation itself, on what motivates the variable use of linguistic resources in the achievement of communicative purposes in different contexts of use. I would suggest, then, that whereas WE clearly follows the sociolinguistic tradition of variety description with a primary concern for the relationship between language and community, the study of ELF is essentially an enquiry into the relationship between language and communication, how linguistic resources are variably used to achieve meaning. The study of ELF is, in short, an enquiry into the general pragmatics of variation. So what does such a pragmatic enquiry involve?

Generally speaking, as with sociolinguistics, the study of pragmatics has focused attention on language used within particular communities. It has been principally concerned with how meaning is achieved between parties who share the same linguacultural background, who can rely on mutual schematic knowledge to complement the language they use. Pragmatically speaking, language in use only serves an indexical function, pointing to some contextual reality external to language, and meaning is achieved only when this external context is engaged. Obviously, the more familiar the context, the less language is needed to make the indexical connection. So it is, for example, in speech act terms, that if parties share a frame of reference, little language may be needed to make an appropriate reference. Similarly, if they share a knowledge of the ways a particular illocutionary act is conventionally expressed, its force can be readily recognized with minimal linguistic effort. This is not to say, of course, that indexical connections are always made as intended and that intra-community communication always proceeds smoothly. Indexical meanings have often to be negotiated. But the point is that most of the conditions for effective communication among language users who share communal linguacultural knowledge are already in place and only need language as an auxiliary means to activate them.

What one needs to bear in mind is that effective communication does not depend on the language itself being precise but on its being appropriate to context and purpose. Users of a language in a particular community are communicatively competent in that they are aware of the local conventions that regulate their social behaviour. They know what Hymes refers to as rules of use – rules, as Labov puts it, which "(...) will show how things are done with words and how one interprets these utterances as actions: in other words, relating what is done to what is said and what is said to what is done" (Labov 1969b: 54).

But these are, of course, local rules which only apply within the limits of the community. They do not apply to ELF communication, where there may well be no set of preconceived agreed communal conventions that can be taken for granted, no such self-evident linguacultural commonality that users can depend upon. This means that there will often be a greater reliance on language to co-construct the necessary pragmatic conditions on line and extempore in the very process of communicating.

With ELF we see the use of linguistic forms functioning to pragmatic effect before our very eyes, so to speak. ELF users have to co-operate to establish common ground. But they cannot do this by simply following the maxims of Grice's

Co-operative Principle, for this again presupposes the existence of shared communal values. Grice describes his principle in the following way: "Make your conversational contribution such as is required, at the stage at which it occurs, by the accepted purpose or direction of the talk exchange in which you are involved" (Grice 1975: 45).

The maxims Grice proposes are not, as is sometimes mistakenly supposed, unconditional in their application. They are always related to an "accepted purpose or direction" of talk. In other words, they are subject to the mutually accepted conventions that define different genres or kinds of communication. So if you are giving a funeral oration, for example, in accordance with the convention that one does not speak ill of the dead, in not telling the truth about the deceased, you are not flouting the quality maxim but adhering to it, regulating its application as appropriate to the accepted conventional purpose of your talk. In this case, you would indeed be flouting the maxim if you told the truth: "Arthur as we all know was a drunk whose embarrassing company we tried to avoid". The flouting of a maxim results in what Grice refers to as an implicature and creates an effect – in the case of the funeral oration, the effect would perhaps be outrage or amusement. But for all I know there may be communities where it is entirely appropriate to be explicitly frank about the dead and their vices, perhaps as a kind of vicarious confession on their behalf to purify their souls in preparation for an after-life.

The point is that the recognition of a flouting crucially depends on your knowing how the maxims operate as conventionally appropriate to different kinds of communication in your community; if you do not know what these agreed communal conventions are, you cannot recognize the flouting and there is therefore no implicature. Conversely, if you are ignorant of these conventions, you obviously run the risk of producing unintended implicatures and creating an effect you might wish to avoid. Thus what you say might be heard as flouting the quantity maxim and so to be over-elaborate, verbose, pretentious. Or, not familiar with the conventions of idiomatic use current in a native speaker community, you may unwittingly fail to follow the manner maxim, create an unintended comic effect and find yourself a subject of ridicule. The point then is that Grice's Co-operative Principle presupposes that there are communicative conventions which are familiar to members of a particular community. So the question naturally arises: how do people co-operate, as ELF users do, if they are not members of the same community and so are not familiar with its conventions? How does co-operation work when users cannot rely on shared communal knowledge?

Generally speaking, scholars have apparently found it unnecessary, or inconvenient, to think of pragmatic processes in dissociation from the way they operate in particular lingua-cultural communities. There seems always to be the tendency to equate them with their particular realizations and to presuppose conventional normality, as with the Co-operative Principle. This is also the case with the so-called Idiom Principle, which closely relates to it. This principle, originally proposed by John Sinclair, derives from the incontrovertible evidence of language corpora that the texts that native speaker (NS) users produce when they communicate consists of recurring patterns, readymade idiomatic phrases, some of which allow for some internal variation, some of which do not. Sinclair concludes that the NS users who provide the data for his corpus do not compose their texts piecemeal on an open choice principle, but by the arrangement of preconceived prefabricated sequences. This is how he puts it:

> The principle of idiom is that a language user has available to him or her a large number of semi-preconstructed phrases that constitute single choices, even though they might appear to be analysable into segments. To some extent, this may reflect the recurrence of similar situations in human affairs; it may illustrate a natural tendency to economy of effort; or it may be motivated in part by the exigencies of real-time conversation.
> (Sinclair 1991: 110)

But the language users that Sinclair is referring to are NS users of English, and with such users, the idiom principle finds expression in particular collocational combinations or idiomatic wordings which recur in similar situations in the contexts of native speaker affairs. Here, one can see that such wordings make for communicative efficiency in that whole phraseological units will often be signaled by the occurrence of one or other of its verbal segments. But only, of course, if the users concerned are already familiar with these wordings. But what of users who are not familiar with them, ELF users for example, who are not using English in the recurrent contexts of NS affairs? If they do not conform to the particular idiomatic wordings that conventionally express the idiom principle, does this mean that their communication therefore necessarily lacks idiomaticity?

I would argue that all communication is in accordance with the co-operative and idiom principles, whether it conforms to NS usage or not. In ELF research we need to identify the processes whereby these principles are realized, in dissociation from the particular linguacultural ways in which they are conventionally realized. ELF users, as has been frequently pointed out, have the capability of communicating without conformity to NS norms. This means that they find their own ways of being co-operative and idiomatic on line in the very process of their interaction. In ELF interaction, the interlocutors cannot depend on shared linguacultural conventions and so they have to find common ground by developing their own local conventions in flight as it were, as appropriate to their own contexts and purposes.

The transcriptions of ELF interactions, in for example the VOICE corpus, provide evidence of this pragmatic process at work in the immediacy of the interaction. We see how interactants develop a common frame of reference, picking up and repeating words, phrases, fragments of talk to bind their discourse together, in effect creating their own idiom as they go along. Seidlhofer (2011: 139–142) has shown, to take just one example, how the word "endangered" is taken up and repeated in new collocational combinations by a group of ELF speakers and used as a referential link in the course of their interaction. One line of future research would be to identify the patterns of linguistic regularity that represent the locally emergent idiomaticity in ELF interactions. These words and phrases that have this idiomatic function will not necessarily conform to the idiomatic form of wording in NS usage – indeed, as Seidlhofer (2011: 134–137) has pointed out in her discussion of unilateral idiomaticity, the use of such conventional idiomatic forms may well be idiomatically dysfunctional precisely because they are not mutually recognized. Nor do these local idiomatic expressions have to be in English at all – they may be drawn from other languages, or they may be hybrid forms of significance only for those engaged in a particular interaction.

In the case of both the co-operative and idiom principles, when they operate within a particular community, they relate to, and depend on, mutually known social rules of use, conventions of what constitutes appropriate behaviour. And so they function to facilitate communication. But they also have an identifying function as markers of community membership. And this is why when the conventions are not conformed to, when users unintentionally violate a co-operative maxim, or get idiomatic wordings "wrong", they are exposed as outsiders and may well be open to ridicule. In language use within an established community, the communicative and identifying functions are in close correspondence. In ELF use they are not. On the contrary, they are intrinsically in conflict.

What we see in ELF communication is the establishing of common understanding, people finding ways of communing with each other and the emergence in effect of micro discourse communities. Such a common understanding, the formation of such a discourse community, is a microcosm of social communication. It is a variable use of language whose temporary conventions may not survive beyond a particular interaction. But sometimes, of course, they may, and then a particular mode of idiomatizing, a particular variation of use gets stabilized as conventional in a wider community, either in a primary social sense or as what has been referred to as discourse community

(Swales 1990)or community of practice (Wenger 1998). Then variation gets confirmed as change in that it becomes identified as a variety – a dialect, a register, a World English. But the point is that variation as an essential pragmatic process is continual and needs to be studied whether it eventually stabilizes as a variety or not.

And this is really, I think, where the crucial significance of ELF study lies. What we see in ELF is the pragmatic process of communication live, in action, laid bare, so to speak – open to observation if only we can rid ourselves of our preconceptions based on too much familiarity with the form that this process takes in particular languages or varieties of language in particular established linguacultural communities. It is, of course, just such familiarity that breeds contempt of ELF. What we see is actual use of what Pennycook (2010) calls "language as a local practice": language taking shape before our very eyes, its various forms motivated by pragmatic function, as its users appropriate, adapt, exploit the linguistic resources they have at their disposal. We see how form and function relate not as an established correlation but as an ongoing process.

And here we can make reference to another principle, one which Halliday has proposed: that the form a language takes is crucially determined by the communicative functions it is socially required to serve. As he puts it: "The particular form taken by the grammatical systems of language is closely related to the social and personal needs that language is required to serve" (Halliday 1970: 142).

This "function to form" principle is what informs the design of his systemic/functional grammar. But Halliday is concerned with how these communicative functions, the serving of the social and personal needs of a particular community, have already been conventionally encoded. What he shows is how form and function correlate in English as an established system. But of course, as with the co-operative and idiom principles, this principle of formal adaptability to function continues to apply to all language use. We can see its historical product in the particular encoded systems of Standard English, but these are just one example of the process, just as the particular idiomatic wordings we find in conventional NS usage are just examples of the process of idiomatizing . The principle continues to apply in the process of all language use. So when, as with ELF use, the language is required to relate to social and personal needs other than those served by NS English, it will naturally get adapted in various ways that are functionally appropriate to different contexts and purposes. Indeed, as with the co-operative and idiom principles, following this "function determines form" principle will often, perhaps usually, crucially depend on not conforming to the conventional ways it has been realized in particular linguacultural communities. Halliday talks about his grammar as representing what he calls the "meaning potential" of English. But this he defines as "a systemic resource for meaning".

So what he is referring to is how meaning is made by conforming to forms that have already been conventionalized and systemically encoded. The realization of meaning potential in his sense is, therefore, not essentially different from Chomsky's (1965) concept of creativity: the infinite exploitation of conventionally established encodings.

But again, the encoding possibilities inherent in English, as in any other language, are not exhausted by the way they have already been realized. In all uses of the language we find innovative grammatical and lexical expressions, variable encodings that are not sanctioned by established convention that exploit the hitherto unexplored possibilities in what I have referred to as the virtual language. This is what I mean by the pragmatics of variation. These variations, these departures from the norm, may be accepted as pragmatically appropriate in NS contexts of use – perhaps as motivated violations of the Gricean maxim of manner to achieve an effect by creating an implicature. But the same acceptance is not so readily extended to the exploitation of virtual language potential in the use of ELF contexts. This, instead of being seen as an entirely natural process of pragmatic adaptation, crucial for effective communication has, on the contrary, generally been dismissed as defective communication.

And this perverseness is rooted in the persistent failure to dissociate the pragmatics of communication in general from their conventional realization, on the assumption that you cannot language without doing it in an established language, that you cannot commune unless you do it in an established community. To accept such an assumption is to be in denial of the essential reality about human language that both Labov and the complexity theorists recognize: that it is intrinsically variable and could not function as a means of communication otherwise. Particular variations may settle into the relatively stable form of a variety, and describing such varieties, as World Englishes scholars do, is an entirely legitimate sociolinguistic thing to do. But this kind of sociolinguistic enquiry is, as I have argued, quite different from the study of ELF, the focus of which is on the pragmatics of variation as such.

And it is this focus that makes the study of ELF of particular potential relevance to language pedagogy. Times have changed, but ideas about language teaching have not changed to keep up with them. Outmoded thinking, sustained by the publishing and testing industries and institutionally endorsed by the specifications of the Common European Framework of Reference, still perpetuate the old orthodoxy that the objective of language learning can only be the acquisition of competence defined as conformity to native speaker norms. Even when the emphasis takes a pragmatic turn and shifts to communication, the focus is not on the communicative use of language, but on how native speakers use it. The objective is still conformity. Now it is not only that learners have to achieve accuracy by keeping to the rules of the standard language, what they learn also has to be authentic in that it corresponds with actual native speaker usage. Now that corpus linguistics can provide a detailed description of such usage, the argument goes, learners can, and should, be taught this "real" language, the very patterns of native speaker idiomatic wordings that I referred to earlier as essentially irrelevant as far as ELF users are concerned to the extent they are not appropriate to their contexts of use. The "reality" of native speaker usage cannot simply be transferred to classroom contexts either and is as irrelevant to the learning as to the use of communicative capability. In both cases, the "authenticity" of native speaker use is irrelevant if it cannot be authenticated (for further discussion see Widdowson 2003). So, in communicative language teaching the objective is still conformity. But, as research into ELF shows so clearly, conformity and communication do not correspond outside the conventional limits of native speaker contexts. Indeed, here effective communication would seem to depend on non-conformity, on exploiting linguistic resources in creative ways as appropriate to other contexts.

I have argued that the unique advantage of ELF study is that it can give us insights into how communication actually works by the local exploitation of linguistic resources. It seems reasonable to suppose that such insights might suggest a rethinking of what is relevant and realistic as a learning objective. This is all the more reasonable since the orthodox insistence on conformity has, generally speaking, resulted only in failure. For all the teachers' efforts, and for all the shifts and changes in methodological approach and technique, most learners perversely fail to conform. They persist in the error of their ways, and cannot, it seems, rid themselves of what is taken to be the pernicious interference from their own language. But then the question arises as to why this should be so. One reason could well be that what learners are doing is acting on the experience of their own language, and so using their English together with their own language as a pragmatic resource, seeking to communicate in a natural way. In spite of the efforts of the teacher to get them to communicate as "proper" monolingual native speakers do, they would seem to naturally seek to communicate as multilingual ELF users do. In other words, one might suggest, the reason for the learners' linguistic abnormality is that they are trying to use the language in a normal communicative way, with linguistic form determined by pragmatic function.

This would provide some explanation of what has been depicted as perverse learner behaviour. Returning for a moment to the idiomatic patterns of NS usage that I discussed earlier, Alison Wray, well known for her corpus-based description of such patterns, expresses puzzlement as to why, if such patterns are, as is claimed, so communicatively effective, learners do not learn them more readily, as she puts it: "(...) why learners do not feel more empowered to harvest L2 input in larger chunks in pursuit of painless routes to effective communication" (Wray 2012: 236).

But this is only a puzzle if one supposes that the harvesting of such idiomatic chunks does indeed make for effective communication and, as I have argued, on the evidence of ELF it clearly does not. And if learners instinctively follow an ELF line in their learning, as I suggest they do, they will not see the harvesting of such chunks as increasing communicative empowerment. Learner resistance to the imposition of native speaker norms and the instinctive learning along ELF lines would also explain why so many so-called learner errors are in areas of grammar which have little if any communicative value but only serve an identifying function. It would also explain the resemblance, often noted, between the linguistic features of much ELF usage to that of learner language. English learners and the ELF users they will become, both naturally and instinctively put the linguistic resources at their disposal to pragmatic use and so act on their communicative capability.

The difference of course is that learners are discouraged from doing this and forced into unnatural conformity. What this means is that the teacher's prescription of competence in effect prevents the learners' development of capability. One can only conclude that it is not the learners' own L1 that interferes with the learning of English – on the contrary, it is reference to L1 experience that facilitates it. What really interferes with the effective learning of English as a means of communication is the way it is currently taught and tested. And it is teaching and testing that define what counts as learning. Success is not positively assessed in respect to what is learned but negatively in respect to how far what is learned measures up to what is taught. Learners are not so much learners as teachees. The pedagogic relevance of ELF is that it points the way to a genuinely learner-centred approach to English language teaching.

Time to conclude. In this chapter I have argued that relating the current study of ELF to certain descriptive and theoretical enquiries in the past helps us to identify and explain the distinctive nature of ELF as having to do not with the sociolinguistics of language variety but with the pragmatics of variation. I have indicated how this perspective relates to current ELF research and its possible development in the future, and have suggested its implications for English language teaching. Many of the issues I have mentioned have already been addressed in the ELF literature and my purpose has been to reformulate them within a wider historical context. In doing so, I wanted to point to the need for continuity in enquiry by showing how present thinking can be informed by past ideas, but also reciprocally how past ideas get revised by present thinking.

14 ELF, adaptive variability and virtual language

In Barbara Seidlhofer's critical discussion of the nature of ELF (Seidlhofer 2011), there is a chapter entitled *Standard English and Real English*. The conjunction implies that there is both a distinction and a relationship between two. But as Seidlhofer points out, the two are commonly conflated: the established way of thinking is to assume that Standard English is the real language, and so is accorded official status in linguistic description and in language pedagogy.

But what kind of reality does Standard English represent? The concept is regularly invoked, but its definition is uncertain. It is generally equated with the equally uncertain notion of native speaker competence, as in the following definition of British English: "As far as grammar and vocabulary are concerned, this generally means Standard English as it is normally written and spoken by educated speakers in England and, with certain differences, in Wales, Scotland, Northern Ireland, The Republic of Ireland, Australia, New Zealand and South Africa" (Trudgill and Hannah 2008: 5).

To describe what is normal obviously depends on the definition of an abstract norm, but then how has this norm been determined? This is left unexplained and all we can do is to take what the authors say on trust. Similarly we have to assume that the authors have reason to suppose that there is a distinct category of educated speakers. But again, there is no indication of how this abstract category might be defined. All speakers have had some education, so what level of education do they have to reach to be categorized as educated? The notion of Standard English has, of course, been much discussed in the sociolinguistics literature (e.g. in Milroy and Milroy 1991; Bex and Watts 1999; Crowley 2003) but a clear definition of just what has proved elusive, as indeed some sociolinguists concede:

> (...) "standard English" still seems to me to be a "confused and confusing" territory for sociolinguistics, and probably much more so than we should be comfortable with. "Standardness" and "non-standardness" are too deeply ingrained into sociolinguistic theory and methods for us to dispense with received perspectives and begin again, conceptually. (Coupland 2000: 632)

One can acknowledge that the concepts of Standard English and native speaker competence are convenient constructs. It is difficult to see how any linguistic description can dispense with such abstractions. Chomsky has been

Note: Originally published in Pitzl, M-L & R. Osimk (eds.). 2016. *English as a* lingua franca: *perspectives and prospects. Contributions in honour of Barbara Seidlhofer.* Mouton de Gruyter.

much berated for concept of the "ideal speaker–listener in a completely homogeneous speech community" (Chomsky 1965: 3). But the ideal speaker–listener is presupposed in the very idea that there is a native speaker competence, and research in SLA – Second Language Acquisition – is based on this presupposition. Similarly, the description of languages or language varieties as stable and separate entities associated with distinct communities of speakers obviously depends on an assumption of homogeneity (for further discussion, see Widdowson 2012b).

The expedient descriptive value of such concepts can of course outweigh their theoretical limitations. In linguistics, as in everything else in life, one has to assume some stability. To see things steadily one has to see them whole: one can only make sense of anything by ignoring particulars, and a theory of language, like any theory, can only provide insights by restricting the view. So concepts like variety, standard language and native speaker competence have their value and are well suited to "received perspectives". But what if these perspectives are not themselves well suited to changing circumstances which call them into question and create a need to think again conceptually?

Whatever its doubtful theoretical status might be, Standard English is descriptively enshrined in grammars and dictionaries as authoritative sources of reference. Over recent years, these have been based on corpora of native speaker usage and it is this now that is commonly claimed to represent "real English". But this in effect is a revised version of the standard which is still equated with native speaker norms. One can simply defer to the authority of these descriptions and ratify their reference status by accepting them as the officially sanctioned representation of the English language. Although this authorized version of native speaker English is taken to have a special and privileged status, it is, as is widely recognized, only one version, one variety of the language. There are many others.

But this raises the question of what it is that varieties vary *from*. Variation presupposes some kind of stabilized norm. One can argue that the non-conformist features of non-standard varieties can be identified by reference to Standard English, and this indeed is how they are usually identified. But this does not mean that for their speakers, there is a reference norm of Standard English from which these features vary. These varieties develop independently as naturally dynamic and adaptive uses of language. And if Standard English is also a variety, what is the norm that this variety varies from?

There are two conceptual problems about the notion of variety. One is that it is represented as a distinct and stabilized system in a state of arrested animation and so misrepresents the continuing natural dynamism of language use. In short, the identification of a variety depends on a disregard of the adaptive variability that is of the essence of natural language. The second problem is that even if one accepts that for some purposes the idealized description of varieties as stable and separate linguistic states is a legitimate thing to do, there is the difficulty of knowing what they are supposed to be varieties of. When one talks about varieties of English, how is this English to be defined? For reasons already touched upon, it cannot be Standard English, whether this is based on native speaker usage or not. This is only one version of the language, a variety that has been accorded a privileged status but of its nature not essentially different from any other. Like the others it is the exemplification of certain encoding principles, one set of realizations that have become conventionally established within a particular community. But a code is of its nature a generative device with the potential to be realized in all manner of various ways. It cannot be equated with the way it is realized in the standard language, or in any other variety. So we need to conceive of the code of English as a set of general encoding principles that are independent of their partial and selective use and that represents an inexhaustible potential for meaning making – a virtual language that allows for infinite adaptive variability in the way it is actually realized.

Contrary to what has at times been supposed (e.g. Vetchinnikova 2015), the concept of a virtual language is radically different from Saussure's langue. It is not a system of actual encodings: it is a generative encoding potential whose properties can only be inferred from its variable use. It is perhaps not too fanciful to liken it to astronomical phenomenon like a Black Hole: something that is not directly observable but whose presence can be inferred from effects that **are** observable. Similarly, I would argue, linguistic variability presupposes a virtual language. The essential point is that the lexis and grammar of an actual language, like that which is described as Standard English, or the "real" English of native speaker usage, is only a partial exploitation of coding possibilities.

And not only it is partial but it is also inconsistent. To take one or two brief examples. In Standard English certain lexical items like *break, open, close* are encoded as both transitive and intransitive verbs. But this encoding principle is virtually applicable to all verbs. It allows for verbs that are conventionally only intransitive to function transitively as well, as in *she smiled/her agreement, she agreed/his idea*. In this second example, as in many other cases, this transitivity shift can only be conventionally encoded by means of the adverbial particle of phrasal verbs: *she agreed to/with his idea*. These are for the most part idiosyncratic encodings, historical traces of past realizations that are inconsistent with the productive regularities of the code.

The virtual language also allows for a similar functional flexibility in the use of nouns. For example, it allows an extension of the use of the plural suffix to all mass nouns and not only those that have already been actualized as such in the standard language. Although expressions like *informations, evidences* and *advices* happen not to actually occur in standard English and are stigmatized as "errors" (see Seidlhofer 2011: 15), they are just as consistent with the encoding principles of the virtual language as are the Standard English forms *transformations, pretences* and *practices*. Again, the use of the encoding principle of verbal recategorization is restricted in Standard English to certain nouns and not others. But, in principle, it applies to all nouns. The use of the nouns *window* and *door* as verbs, for example, is not less consistent with the encoding principles of the virtual language than is the verbal use of the nouns *table* and *chair*. The difference is only that the latter happen to have become conventionalized and the former have not.

The same point can be made about virtual morphological principles of word-formation. Affixes like the prefix un- and the suffixes -less, for example, are in actual English conventionally attached to certain lexical forms but not to others. But there is the virtual possibility of extending this affixation principle to other forms as well. Word formations like *unsad* and *unsick* or *acheless* and *prideless* are just as consistent with this virtual encoding principle as are those that happen to have become conventionally established like *unhappy* and *unhealthy* or *painless* and *shameless*. When, as often happens, ELF users (or ELF learners) exploit the resources of the virtual language in this way, they may be told that they are overgeneralizing – wrongly following encoding rules that do not apply in these cases. But the rules **do** apply: it is just that users of English have hitherto not had occasion to apply them, or are inconsistent in their application.

It is, of course, not surprising that actual language is irregular and inconsistent in applying virtual language rules. On the contrary, the normal social functioning of a language requires it to be. The ways in which the resources of the code are put to use in actual language will naturally vary. As is pointed out in Sinclair (1991), actual usage is not a matter of composing messages in accordance with code rules, but follows an idiom principle whereby the language is produced and processed as already encoded phraseological units. As Sinclair puts it:

> The principle of idiom is that **a language user** has available to him or her a large number of semi-preconstructed phrases that constitute single choices, even though they might appear to be analysable into segments. To some extent, this may reflect the recurrence of **similar situations in human affairs**; it may illustrate a natural tendency to economy of effort; or it may be motivated in part by the exigencies of real-time conversation.
>
> (Sinclair 1991a: 110, my emphasis)

Such "semi-preconstructed phrases" are composites that, in varying degrees, are adaptable to communicative requirement. But their adaptation is necessarily in conformity to virtual encoding principles: they are not just randomly assembled.

Such phrases make for communicative efficiency, but only on condition that they are indeed available to the language users within that community who know them to be recurrent. But what of language users who are not, and do not know? Particular phraseological patterns can be said to "reflect the recurrence of similar situations in human affairs", as Sinclair puts it, but which situations and which human affairs? These are socio-culturally different across communities. What Sinclair seems to have in mind is native speaker users in the situations that recur in their communities. These patterns of particular encodings become conventional over time because they are serviceable for the contexts and purposes of communicative use in particular communities. And once conventionalized, they become markers of communal identity. But there is no reason to suppose that such patterns should be equally serviceable outside those communities. On the contrary, given the adaptive variability of language, there is every reason to suppose that they will not. Every use of language will naturally follow the idiom principle, but how this is actually linguistically realized is bound to vary. Acting on the principle necessarily involves variable adaptation according to context. So the idiomatizing principle cannot be equated with the semi-constructed phrases that are actually already available to a language user, assumed to be a native speaker.

The learning of a language necessarily involves the inferring of abstract encoding principles from their actual realizations and learners will quite naturally focus on those principles that have most communicative value for them. As far as the learning of English *as an L1* is concerned, this will involve a process of gradual conformity as learners acquire those principles and their particular usage realizations that have become conventional in the communities they are being socialized into. But as far as learning English *as an L2* is concerned, there is no such requirement of conformity: not all, perhaps not most L2 learners are learning the language in order to be socialized as members of native-speaking communities, or to identify with them. The contexts and purposes for which they will need the code as a communicative resource are other than those that obtain in such L1 communities. The encoding principles they focus on as having communicative value, and the way these principles are variably realized in patterns of usage, will naturally be other than those that have been established as conventional in L1 communities.

Adaptive variability is a necessary feature of all natural language use, but is particularly evident in the use of ELF because, apart from the fact that this has to relate to a wide range of different contexts and purposes, its users also have to find ways of accommodating to each other across their different linguacultural backgrounds. What ELF use reveals so clearly is the on-line enactment of the actual process of adaptive variability and therefore the essential pragmatics of communication. Where there is lack of conformity, it is entirely consistent with natural language development. To return to where I started, with the supposed reality of

Standard English. I have argued that there is nothing uniquely real about it, even when it is extended to include norms of actual native speaker usage. It represents particular realizations of a virtual code which by no means exhaust its conceptual and communicative potential. And it is this potential that is realized when the language is put to actual use, with users drawing on code resources in variable ways as appropriate to context and purpose: they do not communicate simply by conforming to established encodings, but also by realizing other encoding possibilities inherent in the virtual language. This is true of all users of English (and of any other natural language) whether they are so-called native speakers or not: if the language did not allow for such variation, it would be pragmatically dysfunctional. Adaptive variability, an intrinsic feature of language use, presupposes the availability to users of an unrealized meaning-making resource of a virtual language.

Seen in this way, as Barbara Seidlhofer and other researchers in ELF have consistently argued, ELF is communicatively normal. But especially in the field of English language teaching the idea still persists that it is an abnormal use of language in that its variations deviate from the encodings established as normal, and it is taken as self-evident that this abnormality necessarily makes ELF a reduced version of "proper" English, deficient as a means of communication, and so no different from learner language. In giving primacy to conformity over adaptive variability, this still widespread and influential pedagogic view actually misrepresents the very nature of human communication.

What seems to me to be of central significance of ELF study, in which Barbara Seidlhofer has played such a prominent role, is that it calls into question taken for granted assumptions not only about what "English" is, but what all languages are. In so doing, her work and that of other ELF researchers have challenged the institutionalized presumption that Standard English and native speaker norms of usage are real English and are the only variant version of the language that it is proper for people to use and to learn, in denial of the fact that it is clearly inappropriate as a means of international communication in a globalized world.

15 The cultural and creative use of English as a lingua franca

In Shakespeare's *Midsummer Night's Dream*, the fairy Puck proudly tells his master Oberon:

> I'll put a girdle round about the earth
> In forty minutes.

In Shakespeare's time, this was magic: something only fairies could do, impossible for mere mortals. In our time it is an everyday reality: on the internet we can put a digital girdle around the earth in seconds. We girdle as we google. The globalized world we now live in is very different from that of the Elizabethan age – indeed very different from any other age – and it calls for a radical reconceptualization of traditional notions of time and place, and also of community and communication. One major reason why we can now put a girdle around the earth so easily is that along with this international digital *medium* of communication there is also an international linguistics *means* of communication available to exploit it. This is English, English as a lingua franca, ELF. But obviously this is not at all the English of Shakespeare. Nor, perhaps less obviously, is it the language of the English, or any other community of its native speakers. It is indeed not really a kind of English at all but the variable use of the language as an expedient communicative resource. As researchers of ELF have pointed out, its very use raises the question as to what it means to talk about English, or any other language, as if it were a bounded entity and the property of a well-defined community of users. Neither communication nor community can any longer be defined in traditional terms when referring to the use of ELF in a globalized world.

Closely related to ideas about communication and community, and therefore of direct relevance to an understanding of ELF, are two other concepts which I would like to explore speculatively on this occasion. One of them is culture and the other creativity. Both are invoked in the work of researchers in ELF, who argue that it is of its very nature both creative in its non-conventional exploitation of linguistic resources (e.g., Pitzl 2018), and intercultural in that it mediates between people from different linguacultural backgrounds (e.g., Baker 2015). But what exactly does this mean? Behind the customary terms used in the study of language, as I suppose in other disciplines, often lurks an unresolved conceptual complexity. I suggest that this is the case with these terms creativity and culture.

Note: Published in 2016 *Lingue e Linguaggi* (19). 73–78. Originally presented as a Lectio Magistralis at the University of Salento.

Creativity first. The term, oddly enough, has been used to refer to what is distinctive in two directly opposing approaches to the description of language. The arch formalist Chomsky on the one hand claims that his generative grammar "accommodates the creative aspect of language use" (Chomsky 1965: 6). By this he means that abstract rules of syntax can be applied to produce, or generate, an infinite number of sentences. In this sense creativity is a matter of recurrent acts of conformity to rule. On the other hand, a functional approach sees creativity as the non-conformist exploitation of rules in actual usage, the attested instances of linguistic production as recorded in language corpora. So on the one hand, creativity is an abstract property of linguistic competence, on the other hand it is an actual property of communicative performance. However, in both cases, the property is taken to be an intrinsic and defining feature of language. Thus with regard to actual usage, as Ronald Carter puts it, "linguistic creativity is not simply a property of exceptional people, but an exceptional property of all people" (Carter 2004: 13).

Since this is a property of all people, it is hard to see how it can be exceptional – on the contrary it would be entirely usual and commonplace. In this view, everybody is creative. It is a feature of the ordinary pragmatic use of language and there is nothing unusual or extra-ordinary about it.

But this is again directly contrary to a third concept of creativity that which is associated with literature, with verbal art. Here creativity is indeed defined as an unusual and abnormal use of language which only exceptional people can produce. So the term creative writing, for example, has specific reference to prose fiction, plays, poetry. Being creative in this artistic sense is not at all the same as being creative in the general pragmatic sense – indeed, particularly in poetry, it depends on using language in an abnormal way, on *not* being creative in a general pragmatic sense. If every use of language were poetical, there would be no poetry. I will henceforth use the term pragmatic creativity to refer to its everyday occurrence, and the term poetic creativity to refer to its realization in the verbal art of poetry.

The two concepts of creativity, pragmatic and poetic, correspond closely to different ways of thinking about culture. The concept of culture has, of course, always been notoriously elusive of definition but we can, I think, accept the broad distinction that is generally made. On the one hand there is what has been called culture with a small c. This has to do with the ideas, values, conventions of behaviour which are customary in a particular community. This is what sociologists and sociolinguists are concerned with and which I will henceforth label societal culture. Since this has to do with what is usual practice in everyday life, societal culture encompasses pragmatic creativity – people exercise this kind of creativity in the ordinary activity of communicating with others in their community.

The second way of conceptualizing culture is that it has to do not with what is ordinary but on the contrary with what is extraordinary, not with the expression of everyday life but with the innovative representation of an alternative reality. Culture in this sense, culture with a big C, is music, dance, visual and verbal art, dissociated from the contexts of conventional social custom, discontinuous, often quite remote, from the familiar round of daily routine. This, of course, is how culture is conceived in the popular mind. For tourists arriving in Italy, for example, the culture they have in mind is certainly not societal, not the customary contemporary way of life of the Italian people, but artistic: the paintings of Botticelli, or Leonardo da Vinci. And as far as the written word is concerned, this culture is to be found in the sonnets of Petrarch or Dante's *Divine Comedy* rather than in the pages of *La Repubblica*. The point to be made about artistic culture is that it exists precisely because it is essentially different from societal culture, the representation of what Seamus Heaney has called a counter-reality (Heaney 1990).

Heaney uses the term in reference to poetry. This, as verbal art in its quintessential form, is what I shall be particularly concerned with here. Just as societal culture is served by pragmatically creative uses of language, so the artistic culture of poetry is served by poetic creativity. As I have said, if pragmatic creativity is a common feature of all language use, then it must sustain the usual purposes of communication in the contexts of everyday life, which is why the evidence of such creativity in English is so abundantly available in language corpora like the *British National Corpus* or the *Bank of English*. Since such corpora are designed to capture the features of normal usage, they do not as a rule include poetry and so reveal little of poetically creative uses of the language.

So what I am suggesting is that the terms *creativity* and *culture* are both used as labels for two quite different and indeed conflicting concepts and that we need to make a distinction between societal culture, which is served by pragmatic creativity and artistic culture, which is served by poetic creativity.

Creativity, whether pragmatic or poetic, is not a property of the text but of its discoursal interpretation. The recognition of creativity in uses of language depends on their being noticed as acts of intended non-conformity, deliberate departures from an expected norm. In the pragmatic case these departures are intended to have a particular perlocutionary effect – to make an utterance emphatic, ironic, amusing and so on. To be non-conformist in this way is to act against Grice's Co-operative Principle (Grice 1975). This he expresses as a set of default assumptions represented as maxims that people normally subscribe to when they communicate. When a maxim is violated, the effect is what Grice refers to as an implicature . The maxim that is of particular relevance to creativity is the so-called maxim of manner, which calls for perspicuity of expression. Thus when people communicate they would normally be expected to conform to this clarity condition, avoid obscurity and ambiguity and make their meanings as transparent as possible. Creative uses of language go against this maxim since they are of their nature non-conformist and unexpected and so they quite naturally give rise to implicatures.

But it must be stressed that these maxims relate to presuppositions of familiarity. So for example if in conversation with a fellow native speaker of English I were to say that somebody *had been barking up the wrong tree*, or *had shot himself in the foot*, since these are familiar idiomatic phrases they would not be noticed as maxim violations and there would be no implicature. If, however, I wanted to give a more incisive edge to my meaning, I could play on words, as the phrase goes, and creatively adjust the wording of these idiomatic expressions. I might say *he is barking up the wrong flagpost* or *he has just shot his whole political party in the foot*. Such rewordings *do* give rise to implicatures in that they depart from the customary patterns of use in order to achieve a special effect.

Such manipulation of established patterns of usage, however, is not only a feature of pragmatic creativity. It of course also occurs in what I call poetic creativity. Consider, for example, how the common phrase *happy as the day is long* is variably exploited by Dylan Thomas in these lines in his poem *Fern Hill*:

> *Now as I was young and easy under the apple boughs*
> *About the lilting house and happy as the grass was green,*
>
> *And as I was green and carefree, famous among the barns*
> *About the happy yard and singing as the farm was home ...*
>
> *Under the new made clouds and happy as the heart was long,*
> *In the sun born over and over,*
> *I ran my heedless ways ...*

Happy as the grass was green, happy as the heart was long: here again the effect of the verbal manipulation crucially depends on a familiarity with the conventional idiom: *happy as the day is long*. For anyone who does not have that familiarity – a non-native speaker of English, for example – there is no such effect and the creativity fails.

But then, if creativity works in the same way in poetic and pragmatic uses of language, how are these uses different? I would argue that pragmatically creative expressions are integrated into the normal communicative process, designed to be immediately understood in the context in which they are used and to function indexically in a conventional way – a way that, as I have argued, therefore sustains societal culture. If they caused a breakdown of discourse continuity they would fail in their intended pragmatic purpose. Poetic creativity, on the other hand, operates unilaterally and in contextual dissociation from the continuity of the normal communicative process. It does not function *indexically* to point to what is conventional and familiar but *iconically* to represent what is imagined as alternative counter realities, self- enclosed within the context of the poem itself.

How then is all this relevant to an understanding of the use of English as a lingua franca? Whether pragmatic or poetic in purpose and effect, both kinds of linguistic creativity necessarily involve the exploitation of the possibilities for meaning making which are virtual in the language code to produce patterns of language which do not conform to normal conventions of use. Much of ELF use can be described as creative in this general sense, as is extensively exemplified and discussed in Pitzl (2018). Here are just two examples from VOICE, the corpus of spoken ELF interactions compiled by Barbara Seidlhofer and her colleagues (VOICE 2013):

> the point of the whole things about quotas it's a very good idea but in the same time it's ... how to say it in english like knife with double blade..
> (VOICE 2013, POwsd372: 791–793)

> i feel that many times i am pulling the brakes and i'm really and i'm consciously doing it because i know that time is needed (VOICE 2013, POmtg314: 180).

Here too we find creativity in that it too exploits the potential of English in non-conformist ways. There is, however, a crucial difference. Consider again the pragmatic and poetic non-conformities I have discussed so far – *he has just shot his whole family in the foot, singing as the farm was home*. These are deliberate departures from a norm which is assumed to be known to the recipient – *he has shot himself in the foot, happy as the day is long* – and they are intended to be recognized as such, otherwise, as I have said, there is no implicature and the creativity fails. But this bilateral condition of mutual norm recognition typically does not apply in contexts of interaction between ELF users. If one or more than one of them is a non-native speaker, as is frequently the case, they exploit whatever linguistic resources they have at their disposal to get their meaning across and whatever non-conformities they produce are not usually intended to be noticed as such, and even if they are, the recipient may well not be able to ratify the intention. If the condition of mutual norm familiarity is not met, there is no implicature. In what sense, then, can ELF usage be considered creative?

According to the co-operative principle, an implicature comes about when a departure from the default norm is intended and recognized as such. The usual assumption is that this norm is preconceived, a schematic construct already known by the participants as a basis for their co-operation. But when ELF users co-operate in their communication, since they come from different linguacultural backgrounds, they cannot rely on such shared preconceptions. How then do ELF users from Lecce and Leicester, for example, or from Bangkok and Barcelona manage to communicate with each other? The answer, I suggest, is that they negotiate pro-tem norms online in the adaptive, emergent process of their very interaction. The co-operative principle still applies, as it must apply to all communication, but it is acted upon in ways that do not require conformity to conventional native speaker ways in which the principle is put into practice.

Most discussion of verbal communication deals with how meanings are achieved by speakers of the same linguacultural community – native speakers who have what is referred to as the same communicative competence. What we see in ELF use is how communication is achieved when this condition of shared competence does not apply – when users of English have to create the conditions for effective communication reactively and adaptively as they go along. By means of this pragmatic creativity, ELF users engage in the same kind of social interaction as native speakers do within their own communities. However, they do not do so in accordance with the conventions of the societal culture of a native speaking community. Coming as they do from different linguacultural backgrounds, when ELF users interact they constitute a microcosmic pro-tem community of their own and this calls for the negotiation of common ground by reconciling different cultural conventions. What emerges in this process is a kind of extempore hybrid culture, a mode of social behaviour which is specific to a particular and often transient community of ELF users.

Communities and cultures are not, of course, usually conceptualized in this micro and transitory way, but as stable and large-scale phenomena. But I would argue that an understanding of the nature of creativity in ELF leads to a reconsideration of these concepts too. As I indicated earlier, globalization has already brought about a realization that communities are not bounded entities but continually adaptive and emergent networks of social interaction. The same can be said of cultures. Although they too can be thought of as stable constructs defined by certain commonalities, they are, in fact, only temporary states of affairs, the present result of an historical process whereby individual experiences are abstracted into social conventions. And of course this process of variable acculturation never settles into a state, but continues as it adapts to new experience. So cultures can be seen as transient formations of shared perceptions and conceptions that emerge and vary in the process of communicative interaction. It may be convenient, and for some descriptive purposes entirely appropriate, to think of them as distinct and stable entities, but culture too, I would argue, is correspondingly a property of the communicative process: it is something that is performed and adaptively transformed on line as discourse participants converge on common ground.

The culture that evolves in ELF interaction through this natural process of pragmatic creativity is societal in the sense that it has to do with everyday communal reality. But it is not the everyday reality of the native speaker – it does not reflect or sustain customary shared ways of thinking or behaviour that constitute the societal cultures of particular communities. In this sense it represents alternative realities. But these are not the imagined counter-realities at a remove from the contexts of everyday life that are poetically created by verbal artists to represent their individual vision, but the actual immediate realities of here and now in a globalized world in which everybody is involved and implicated – the realities of international business and diplomacy, of values and ideologies in conflict and refugees in distress – realities that are of their nature constituted of different and often conflicting societal cultures and that can only be engaged with by reconciling these differences in some way.

And ELF, I suggest, provides a way. English has always been put to creative use: pragmatically in the communal process of social discourse and poetically in individual works of verbal art. But demands are now made on its creativity as never before as it is called upon to service the communicative needs of a culturally complex and variable community of users. This is the new globalized reality that English as a lingua franca has to express – not a counter reality that is the figment of the imagination of individual verbal artists but one that is an actual everyday social experience. As I said at the beginning, what for Shakespeare was something magical that could only exist in the imagination – *putting a girdle round about the earth* – has now become a commonplace reality – we girdle as we google. As the poet Tennyson puts it "the old order changeth yielding place to new" and the conventional old order ways of conceptualizing community and culture and creativity also need to yield to new ways of thinking more appropriate to the world we now live in. A brave new world? I am not sure how brave it is, but it is one we have somehow to come to terms with. And understanding the nature of English as a lingua franca, I suggest, offers us a way of doing so.

16 Creative incompetence

It is generally assumed that competence in a language is a matter of unconscious conformity to convention. If you are hesitant in your delivery, obviously groping for the correct grammatical rule or the suitable word, or, if, having groped unsuccessfully, you come out with garbled syntax or odd lexis, you obviously do not know the language properly. You are almost certainly a foreigner whose learning development has become arrested at some stage of interlanguage, having lamentably fallen short of the desired goal of native speaker competence. Or you could be a poet.

For poets – non-foreign, bona fide native-speaking poets – also quite consciously grope for the language they need, and come out with garbled syntax and odd lexis as a result. Here is an example in English:

> *Now as I was young and easy under the apple boughs*
> *About the lilting house and happy as the grass was green,*
> *The night above the dingle starry,*
> *Time let me hail and climb*
> *Golden in the heydays of his eyes, (...)*

These are the first lines of a celebrated poem by Dylan Thomas, and they bristle with deviant usage. True, Thomas was not English but Welsh, and we might seek to attribute the linguistic oddity here to that misfortune, but in fact English was his first language, so we cannot put this non-conformity down to incompetence. On the contrary, it seems as if Thomas is perversely using his competence to be deliberately non-conformist. So, for example, instead of keeping to normal idiomatic custom, as one would expect a native speaker to do, by using the familiar phrase *happy as the day is long*, he contrives the novel expression *happy as the grass was green* – a most peculiar distortion. If this were to appear in a student essay, we would be quick to underline it on the grounds that this is just not English and makes no sense. And *lilting house*? What is that supposed to mean? Do you mean *tilting house*? *Golden in the* "what" *of his eyes*?

So it would seem that the conscious effort of groping for a form of words is something that is done both by learners and users of an L2 and by poets using their L1. And in both cases, the result is a linguistic curiosity, an odd, anomalous kind of usage. But of course there is a difference. L1 poets have the competence to

---

Note: (Co-written with Barbara Seidlhofer) Published in Intemann, F. & G. Königs (eds.). 2006. *Ach!texte – Didak-Tick der (modernen, unmodernen uknd aussererirdischen) Sprachen. Eine etwas andere Festschrift für Claus Gnutzmann.* Bochum: AKS Verlag.

https://doi.org/10.1515/9783110619669-021

conform if they chose to do so, whereas L2 users do not. What motivates the groping of L2 users is the desire to conform, and what motivates L1 poets is exactly the opposite: they are intent on denying convention by deliberate acts of linguistic subversion. And these are designed to be noticed, and to be intrinsically part of the message to be conveyed. L2 users, on the other hand, would generally rather hope that their linguistic non-conformities will pass unnoticed and that they will have got their meaning across in spite of them.

How we react to linguistic non-conformity will depend on whether we think it was intended and meant to be noticed or just the unwitting reflex of incompetence. Here Grice's co-operative principle becomes relevant, and particularly the maxim of manner which calls for the avoidance of odd, obscure or ambiguous wording (Grice 1975). Deviations are likely to fall foul of this maxim, but only when they are taken as deliberate does any implicature arise. So since the phrase "golden in the heydays of his eyes" appears in a poem by Dylan Thomas, the reader is likely to suppose that the obscurity that arises from the flouting of the maxim is meant to be explored and some hidden significance discovered. If a foreigner were to come out with it, the likelihood is that it would be dismissed as gibberish.

So deviations or abnormalities are construed negatively as unintentional and deficient when produced by L2 English users (or learners) but positively as intentional and creative when produced by L1 English poets. But how do you know whether a deviation is intended or not? What about L2 users who feel the urge to be creative – poets, perhaps, who want to write poems in some language other than their L1? Consider another poetic line:

Do not go gentle into that good night.

Now let us suppose that this is presented to us as the first line in a poem written by an L2 English poet, an Egyptian let us say, a certain Hamadi Farouk (a name, as we shall see later, not randomly chosen), who has hitherto written in Arabic but who is now trying his hand at composing poetry in English. A nice line, we might tell him, shows promise, but there is just one thing: the fourth word here is grammatically an adverb, so it should be corrected to take the form *gently*. But as a matter of fact this line was not written by Hamadi Farouk. It was written by Dylan Thomas again. This makes all the difference. We now suppose that the use of this form is motivated, that it is a creative deviation that carries some significance, even though it might be hard to say what the significance might be. But then why should we take it as self-evident that a non-native-speaking poet is incapable of creativity, that if he uses the word in this way, it's just that he has got it wrong.

Consider another line of poetry:

You love not me.

Here there is a failure to follow the rule for encoding negation in English. The unfortunate poet (Hamadi Farouk perhaps?) apparently not only suffers from unrequited love but is afflicted with grammatical deficiency as well. A sad case. But at least he could try to complain in correct English and say *You don't love me* – who knows, it might help to improve his amatory prospects in the long run. It just so happens, however, that this sentence actually occurs in a poem written by Thomas Hardy, a bona fide native speaker of English.

> *You love not me,*
> *And love alone can lend you loyalty;*
> *I know and knew it. But, unto the store*
> *Of human deeds divine in all but name,*
> *Was it not worth a little hour or more*
> *To add yet this: Once I, a woman, came*
> *To soothe a time-torn man; even though it be*
> *You love not me?*

Now that the deviation is taken as intended, and repeated too at the beginning and end of the verse as part of the deliberate design of the poem, it creates an implicature, and we look to assign its significance. *You love not me.* Unlike the normal variant *You don't love me*, the negation is associated not with the verb but the object: it's not that you don't *love*, but that you don't love *me* (but perhaps somebody else). In this case, we see no deficiency. It does not occur to us to think that Hardy might have benefited from a course in remedial grammar.

So deviant wordings, it would seem, are only deemed creative to the extent that they are deliberate. Intention is the crucial factor. But there is a problem here: literary critics, or some of them at least, tell us that intention, far from being a crucial factor in the interpretation of poetry, is not really a factor at all, and to suppose otherwise is to fall prey to the so-called intentional fallacy (Wimsatt 1970). Even if we could ask poets what their intentions were in producing a particular wording, they may be quite incapable of telling you. For it is not the case that they are in complete command of the creative process and can direct it at will to do their bidding. It is more that they seem to get possessed by the process and words connect up with words in a chain reaction of associations out of conscious control. Poets are generally not good informants about how their poems came to be written. And they have no say at all in how they are to be read. There is no reason why the significance we assign to a certain wording should correspond with what the writer intended to mean by it (even if we knew what the intentions were) (for further discussion, see the introduction and notes in Widdowson 1992).

So it would seem to follow that whether a particular deviation in the wording of a poem is the result of deliberate intent or not is neither here nor there. If intentions are for the most part inaccessible, and irrelevant anyway, then it makes no difference whether the author of a particular poetic wording is a native speaker of the language or not. We can assign significance to it no matter who produced it: Dylan Thomas, Thomas Hardy, Hamadi Farouk – it makes no difference. Or does it? Surely, if you know that Farouk is the author, you will be primed to read his text in a different way. You will assume that having less access than a native speaker poet to the "total" resource of the language, being less aware of the potential to be exploited, his scope for meaningful manipulation is bound to be limited. That being so, you are likely to adjust your attention to the text and read it primarily as a language exercise rather than a poem and so notice its irregularities as evidence of incompetence rather than creativity.

Against this, however, it might be argued that Farouk's very lack of competence can be turned to poetic advantage. As was pointed out earlier, competence in a language implies conformity to convention, but in learning to conform, it is easy to lose sight of the vast potential for meaning making that remains virtual but unrealized in the language, unconventionalized and unused – concealed, so to speak, behind the patterns of normal usage. Since non-native users of the language have not been normalized into conformity, they can be said to have a more direct access to this unused potential, unhindered by customary convention. So it is that non-natives can activate meanings in morphological features that natives have neutralized in compounds, bring words that are semantically distinct into association on the basis of their sound, extend the scope of existing rules and regularities, exploit redundancy and so on. Of course natives can do all this too, and this, as we have seen, is what L1 poets do indeed do. But for them it is much more of an effort: they have to free themselves of the inhibiting influence of competence that non-native poets (like Farouk) have not yet acquired. It can be argued, then, that though lack of competence in the L2 can be considered a disadvantage in ordinary communicative encounters within a native-speaking community, as far as the writing of poetry is concerned, it is more than compensated for by an enhanced awareness of the virtual, un-encoded and un-conventionalized meaning potential that is immanent in the language itself. In short, for the L1 poet, deviations go against the grain, but for the L2 poet they are a natural outcome of incompetence.

Bearing all this in mind, the idea that creativity is the prerogative of the native speaker is clearly untenable. There may, of course, be occasions of use when creativity is inappropriate, or even improper, but that is another matter. In poetry, and that is our current concern, creativity is at a premium, and here the L2 English poet, for the reasons we have already put forward, should be recognized as having no less expertise in verbal artistry than the L1 English poet.

Coherent and cogent though we believe this argument for poetic parity to be, it does not follow that it will carry conviction. Regrettably, reason on its own will rarely prevail over prejudice. And this particular argument calls into question the privileged status of the English native speaker and promotes the cause of English lingua franca poetry. There is bound to be resistance and the argument will need all the support it can get.

Fortunately, help is at hand from a rather unusual quarter. It takes the form of the recent discovery in an antique bookshop in Pisa of a faded sheet of notepaper, found folded between the pages of a book. The book is itself remarkable, for it is a first edition of Shelley's long poem *The Revolt of Islam*, and in it are to be found manuscript emendations in what is believed to be the poet's own hand, written, one might speculate in 1821 or 1822 during Shelley's sojourn in Pisa immediately before he was tragically drowned in the Gulf of Spezia. This is a find of enormous interest, for, as was explained to us by Professor Umberto Fittibaldi of the University of Pisa (personal communication), it has always been known that Shelley was working on a revision of this poem for a second edition, but the changes he proposed never came to light. Until now. This is extraordinary enough. Even more extraordinary, however, as far as this chapter is concerned, is the sheet of notepaper that was found in the book.

It appears to be the last page of a letter, written in English in an uncertain hand. It ends with the salutation: "With esteme and hommage to you genius, I remain you humble poet brother", and, faint, though still legible, the signature: *Hamadi Farouk*. The text at the top of the page clearly follows on from a previous page, now lost. It reads:

> (...) frend who send to me your book of verses in October this year. I think what grete and boundless art and this honored sir inspire me to write also in your English language not just Arabic only and what theme I think more suted than historic personage and perilous shortage of human life and glory. So I set pen to page and here my poem. It called Ramesses II, who was great Pharaoh king from my country, ancient land of Egypt. It is sonnet.

Here, then, is an L2 poet using English with creative intent: a genuine and quite unique English lingua franca poem. It runs as follows:

> *Ramesses II*
> *There stands by Nile in Egypt ancient land*
> *Two vast grete trunkless leggs of crumbling stone,*
> *Quiver through sultry mist. Nearby on sand*
> *Half sunk is shatered head and face with frown*
> *And sneer of lips of king who gives command*

> Who make this face of stone has surely shown
> Stampd on these liveless things, but now alone
> Survive both king and sculptor skillfull hand.
> And words are there under these broken things:
> "My name is Ramesses Second, king of kings,
> Look at my empire, Great Ones, and despare!"
> Nothing remane besides, but ruin stay,
> And all around this ruin, boundless, bare,
> Lonely level sand strech far away.

Here, surely, by any standards, and for all the occasional oddities of spelling, we have a literary text of considerable aesthetic achievement, the creative use of English of a high order. We cannot but note, for example, the subtle patterning in the second line where the two-syllable words *trunkless* and *crumbling* are associated with assonance, and are given contrastive prominence in a line consisting otherwise only of monosyllables. We cannot but admire the way certain phrases not only powerfully evoke visual images of the desert landscape but also reflect the poem's underlying theme of the elusive mystery of time – phrases like *quiver through sultry mist*, and the last line *Lonely level sand stretch far away*, where sound and sense are perfectly harmonized to create the effect of the poem fading away into the timeless distance. Perhaps the most strikingly creative feature of Farouk's poem, however, is the total absence of any definite articles. Thus *sand, stone, ruin*, stripped of their conventional determiners, become indeterminate and timeless. This contrasts with the use of demonstratives in the phrases *this face, these lifeless things, this ruin* where it is the immediate spatial and temporal location that is emphasized. By this creative use of linguistic means, the poet aptly represents the dual perspective on time that is so central to the theme of the poem as a whole.

It would be hard to deny that here we have an accomplished example of verbal art which any native speaker poet would be proud to claim as his own. In fact, research has brought to light evidence that suggests that a native speaker poet did in fact claim them as his own – no less a poet indeed than the celebrated author of *The Revolt of Islam*, Percy Bysshe Shelley himself. The plot now thickens. We turn from Farouk's poem to the letter in which it was written.

We have no absolute proof, of course, that the letter was in fact addressed to Shelley, for its first part is lost, presumably for ever. However, the fact that the fragment was found in the leaves of the poet's own annotated copy of *The Revolt of Islam*, though only circumstantial evidence, is surely compelling enough for us to conclude that Shelley was indeed the addressee. At the beginning of this surviving page of the letter Farouk says that he received a copy of a "book of verses" in "October this year". But which book? Perhaps it was this very book *The Revolt of*

Islam, which was published in January 1818. But it might also have been *Alastor and Other Poems*, published in February 1816. Does it matter which book and which year? As we shall see, it matters a good deal.

Between the publication of these two volumes, Shelley, of course, wrote several other poems. One of them was composed in late December 1817 in a sonnet writing competition with his friend Horace Smith and published in *The Examiner* the following month – the well-known, much anthologized sonnet entitled *Ozymandias*. The title is highly significant, for it is apparently a Greek transliteration of one of the names of none other than the pharaoh *Ramesses II*. And even a cursory glance at Shelley's composition is enough to reveal how closely it resembles Hamadi Farouk's poem of that name.

> Ozymandias
> I met a traveller from an antique land
> Who said:two vast and trunkless legs of stone
> Stand in the desert. Near them on the sand,
> Half sunk, a shatter'd visage lies, whose frown
> And wrinkled lip and sneer of cold command
> Tell that its sculptor well those passions read
> Which yet survive, stamp'd on these lifeless things,
> The hand that mock'd them and the heart that fed.
> And on the pedestal these words appear:
> "My name is Ozymandias, king of kings:
> Look on my works, ye mighty, and despair!"
> Nothing beside remains: round the decay
> Of that colossal wreck, boundless and bare,
> The lone and level sands stretch far away.

There are so many similarities in the two texts that it is obvious that one must have been directly derived from the other, and the assumption that immediately springs to mind, of course, is that Farouk is the guilty party. Guilty, though, is perhaps not the right word. He was obviously not intent on deception: there is no attempt to disguise his debt to the original. On the contrary, it is made quite blatantly obvious, so the likelihood is that, since plagiarism is said to be the best compliment, Farouk's modified version was intended as a gesture of artistic obeisance, an act of "esteme and homage" as he puts it, to Shelley's genius. If so, it is to be hoped that Shelley had the good grace to write his admirer a courteous reply. But all this is on the supposition that *Ramesses II* was indeed directly derived from *Ozymandias*. But was it?

If *Ramesses II* is the derived version, then obviously it would have to have been written *after* the publication of *Ozymandias* in January 1818, and in this case the book of verses that Farouk refers to must be *The Revolt of Islam*, which appeared at the same time. But what if the book in question was *Alastor*, published two years earlier, and what if the year referred to in the letter is that same year, 1816, or even the year later – that is to say *before*, not after, Shelley wrote his sonnet? In that case, of course, it is *Ozymandias* that is the derived version, and Shelley the plagiarist.

To entertain such a conjecture seems ridiculous. It runs counter to our well-entrenched conviction that what native speakers write must be of more worth and of higher quality, be more *authentic*, than the efforts of non-native speakers. Non-native speakers imitate native speakers, and not the other way round. Everybody knows that. To suggest that Shelley's famous poem is a reworking – and not much of a reworking at that – of an original produced by an Arab who could not even spell properly is patently absurd. It is obvious that Farouk's poem is the derivation, and so the book of verses he refers to must be *The Revolt of Islam* (or perhaps even some later volume) and date of the letter must be 1818 (or perhaps even some later date).

Ridiculous though it may seem to be, there is, however, an additional piece of evidence that confirms that our conjecture is correct and that *Ramesses II* is indeed the original version. Poems that appear in print have often, perhaps usually, been through a process of revision with earlier drafts being corrected, rewritten, rejected. We are not generally made privy to the poet's labours, with what T. S. Eliot refers to as "the intolerable wrestle of words and meanings". Most early drafts of poems do not survive. Some, however, do. And it happens that there exists an earlier draft of the first lines of *Ozymandias* (printed in Rogers 1975: 320). And it is very revealing. We notice at once that the first four words are a verbatim copy of the Farouk poem:

> *There stands by Nile a single pedestal,*
> *On which two trunkless legs of crumbling stone*
> *Quiver through sultry mist; beneath the sand*
> *Half sunk a shattered visage lies, whose frown*
> *And wrinkled lips impatient of command*
> *Betray some sculptor's art, who* ...

Here we find words and phrases that do not appear in Shelley's final version. But they do appear in the Farouk poem. The opening four words are a case in point. So is the word *crumbling* and the phrase we have already identified as of particular aesthetic merit, *Quiver through sultry mist*. Since this first draft fragment was never made public in print, Farouk of course could not possibly have copied from it. Consequently, these expressions must be of his original composing. Shelley chose not to use them in his final version, but preferred to draw on other parts of *Ramesses II* instead. But draw on them he certainly did. There can be no doubt as to which is the original and which the derived poem.

As mentioned earlier, the writing of *Ozymandias* was occasioned by a sonnet writing competition between Shelley and Horace Smith, and Smith's sonnet on the same topic was published later in *The Examiner*. It is not entirely clear who it was who proposed the topic, and literary scholars have expressed some puzzlement as why, if it was Shelley, he should have selected it (Everest and Matthews 2000: 307). With this new evidence, however, we need be puzzled no longer: for if, as in all likelihood it was indeed Shelley himself who proposed the topic, he would have good reason to do so since he already had relevant poetic material at his disposal in the form of Hamadi's verses.

But what is significant about all this for our theme in this chapter is that it serves to make the point that L2 users of English can appropriate the language for their own self-expression just as effectively as can its native speakers. The use of English as a lingua franca is sometimes characterized in simple transactional terms: people use it as a tool, a handy but fairly rudimentary device for carrying out communicative chores, for getting things done. A far cry from poetry. But ELF is more than that. It is a resource for meaning making and the expression of individual identity and the awareness of other realities which cannot be confined by the imposed conventions of native speaker norms. Farouk does not have to imitate Shelley: he can also be creative in English. He does not have to copy other people: he can express his individual identity by using the resources of the language to write poetry of his own.

Section 5: **Linguistics in language learning and teaching**

Preamble

In accordance with the rationale for repetition as a design feature of this book, as explained in the Introduction, issues on the subject of language and its use discussed in the previous sections are taken up again in this section, which is centrally concerned with English as a pedagogically designed subject. English as a subject in this second sense has also been touched on several times in the preceding sections, but in this last section of the book, it is brought centre stage. Here such questions as how linguistic resources are put to variable communicative use are revisited and re-contextualized in discussions about their implications for how language, and English in particular, might be taught.

There is a particularly close association between these discussions and the issues concerning the use of English as a lingua franca in the immediately preceding section. The reason for this, as pointed out in the preamble to that section, is that ELF brings into prominence the essential features of communicative language use that it is the purpose of this book to explore. And just as ELF as a subject for linguistic study calls into question a number of well-established assumptions about the inter-dependency of competence, community and competence, so it also calls into question the well-established ways of teaching English which is based on the same assumptions. An enquiry into what bearings the study of ELF as use might have on the teaching of EFL – English as a foreign language – leads logically to a radical re-appraisal of institutionally sanctioned monolingual approaches to language teaching and testing.

All of the chapters in this section dissent from current orthodox thinking about language pedagogy. The last of them, however, differs from the others in that, like the last chapters in Sections 3 and 4, the dissention is expressed in a different generic key, being a satirical exercise in *reductio ad absurdum*. But as I argue in the Introduction, such exercises have their place. This one, like those others of this ilk, by virtue of its very absurdity, brings into sharp relief issues that have been discussed elsewhere in more serious academic vein.

17 The role of translation in language learning and teaching

As its title indicates this chapter sets out to consider the relationship between three activities: translation, language learning and language teaching. Nobody doubts that there is a relationship between the second and third of these, although as the history of language pedagogy makes clear, nobody seems to know just what this relationship should be. In the case of translation, the question is whether there is any relationship at all. In one entrenched tradition of pedagogic thinking, as Cook has pointed out (Cook 2010), translation has been outlawed not only as an irrelevance but an impediment to language teaching and his book presents a convincing argument for its methodological reinstatement as a classroom activity. Cook's focus of attention (and the title of his book) is translation in language teaching (TILT) and this of course involves a consideration of language learning. He comments:

> I could as easily have called this book "Translation in Language Learning" and used the acronym "TILL". "Teaching" and "learning" may not be reciprocal verbs, like "give" and "take" – it is possible to teach someone who learns nothing from being taught – but the two do generally go together. There is no significance in my choice of TILT rather than TILL. The book is about both. (Cook 2010: xxi)

My own view, as will become apparent, is that it is precisely the assumption of reciprocity – that the two "generally go together" – that needs to be questioned. For it generally also implies the presupposition that there is a dependent unilateral relationship between them: teaching is the cause and learning the effect, that in talking about TILT one is talking implicitly or explicitly about TILL at the same time. A similar cause-effect relationship is assumed in the extensive literature on task-based activities which are sometimes said to constitute task-based language teaching (TBLT) and sometimes task-based language learning (TBLL): the second is taken to be the necessary consequence of the first (see, for example Ellis 2003).

But this relationship is not a necessary or natural one. One might argue, indeed, that it is teaching which depends on learning rather than the other way round. We cannot be said to teach anything unless it is learned, but of course we learn all kinds of things without being taught, including language. This is readily accepted in the case of our L1. There seems no reason to suppose that

Note: Originally published in Juliane House (ed.). 2014. *Translation: An multidisciplinary approach.* Palgrave Macmillan.

https://doi.org/10.1515/9783110619669-023

the same does not apply to the L2. To be sure the data we draw on to learn our L1 is in some degree selected and organized by our social environment and the conventions of upbringing. These provide conditions for learning, but they do not determine what we learn. In the case of L2 pedagogy, on the other hand, what is taken to be learnt *is* so determined in that it is required to conform to what is taught. It is recognized that the process of independent learning takes place, as is clear from the "errors" that learners "commit" but even when these are seen positively as evidence of learning, the assumption remains that the learning has eventually to be directed towards conformity to teaching input. The learning process is seen only as a means to that end. But what if we focus attention on this process as an end in itself? What if we think of tasks or translation activities not as teaching devices to get learners to toe the line and conform but as providing conditions to activate the learning process, no matter how non-conformist the outcomes might be? What if we think first of the relationship between translation and language learning and only then consider the relationship between translation and language teaching – make TILT dependent on TILL and not the other way round? What I want to do in this chapter is to follow this way of thinking, and explore its implications.

To do so we need first to consider the nature of translation itself. As has often been pointed out, one difficulty about getting a conceptual grasp of the essential nature of translation is that the term itself is ambiguous. As a mass noun it denotes the process of translating, and as a count noun it denotes the resulting product. In the conventional use of the term, and especially as applied to the occupational activity of translators and interpreters, the two are assumed to be inseparably implicated, the process only engaged in as a means to an end product. But this can be misleading, for we need to note that it is perfectly possible to engage in the covert psycholinguistic process of translation without producing a translation as an overt result. One can be a transla*ter*, so to be speak without being a transla*tor* – and indeed, as I shall argue later, one has to be a transla*ter* if one is to make any sense of language at all.

Most definitions of translation, however, are concerned with what transla*tors* do. Here, for example, are two definitions almost 50 years apart.

> Translation is an operation performed on languages: a process of substituting a text in one language for a text in another. (Catford 1965: 1)

> Translation is the replacement of an original text with another text. (House 2009: 1)

In both cases, translation is said to involve the replacement, or substitution, of one text by another. Whereas Catford specifies that the two texts are in different languages, however, House does not, thus allowing for the operation to be performed within one language. This more general conception of translation could be taken to cover any instance of intralingual textual reformulation, including summary and paraphrase. House, however, makes a point of explicitly excluding these:

> Although such activities resemble translation in that they replace a message that already exists, they differ in that they are designed not to reproduce the original as a whole but to reduce it to its essential parts, or adapt it for different groups of people with different needs and expectations.   (House 2009: 4)

This raises a number of critical issues about the nature of translation which bear directly on the question of its pedagogic relevance that this chapter is concerned with. To begin with, the replacement of one text by another involves the rendering of an interpretation and so the translated text can never be a reproduction of the original as a whole but only a derived and partial version of it. Partiality is intrinsic to translation in two respects. Firstly, interpretation of the original, as of any text, involves a differential focussing whereby the main significance of the message is identified and in this sense the activity will always in some degree reduce the original to what are taken to be its "essential parts". Secondly, at the rendering stage, the second text will have to be recipient designed and this will necessarily involve some adaptation. In the case of conference interpreting, where the original is designed for known recipients, there is a requirement to reproduce it as closely as possible with minimal adaptation. But in other cases, recipients of a translated text may well be groups of people who are different from those for whom the original was designed, and who are very likely to have "different needs and expectations".

Both of these definitions of translation talk about the replacement of one text by another. Each of these texts is a determinate linguistic object which is the product of an indeterminate discourse process. The translator's task is to interpret the data of the original text as evidence of what its producer might have meant by it and then produce another text. This then provides data from which, in turn, its recipient has then to derive evidence for interpretation of what *this* producer might have meant by it. And, to complicate matters further, what meaning is intended is itself compounded of three elements: propositional, illocutionary and perlocutionary, to use the terms of speech act theory. That is to say, the text producer intends the text to make reference to something and in so doing to express some kind of illocutionary force to achieve some kind of perlocutionary effect.

All this poses a considerable problem for translation, and for text interpretation generally, and relates to the point I made earlier about differential focusing. If the force intended by a particular text is taken to be its most essential feature, this might entail some reformulation of its supposed reference, and the interpretation and rendering of reference and force might fail to capture its intended effect. In simple terms, one might get the intended reference of a text right, but fail to get the intended force, or get its intended reference and force right but fail to get the intended effect. What relative weight to give to these different aspects of meaning has long been recognized as a problem in the interpretation and translation of literary texts, especially poetry, where effect is particularly elusive. But it is a general pragmatic problem that in varying degrees has to be resolved in the interpretation and translation of any text.

So what reference, force and effect a text producer might have meant to convey, the discourse that is intended to be textualized, can only be indirectly inferred from the textual data: it is necessarily a function of partial interpretation – hence the indeterminacy. In the case of translation, the indeterminacy is twofold since it involves the interpretation of the reference, force and effect of two different texts – the original as interpreted by the translator, and the translated text as interpreted by its recipient. To spell out the process in more detail: a first person (P1) has meaning to express, an intended discourse (Discourse A), and designs a text accordingly (Text 1) which the recipient (P2) then interprets, thereby deriving a discourse from it (Discourse B), which may or may not correspond closely with Discourse A.

So far, this is a normal, necessarily indeterminate, pragmatic process that everybody engages in to make sense of language use. But translators then have further work to do. They have in turn to assume a P1 role and produce a second text (Text 2) which will not only incorporate their interpretation with reference to the first text but also be designed for a different P2 recipient – so the discourse (Discourse C) which is rendered as the translated text may vary in its degree of correspondence to the discourse (Discourse B) that the translator derived from the original text. And this rendered text, of course, is then interpreted by the recipient P2 to derive a further discourse (Discourse D). The whole complex process might be represented as follows:

P1 Discourse A→Text1 → P2 Interpretation 1→Discourse B
$\qquad\qquad\qquad\qquad\downarrow$
$\qquad\qquad$P1 Discourse C → Text 2→ P2 Interpretation→ Discourse D

It is often said, something always gets lost in translation. This suggests that there is some complete meaning inscribed in text which in principle can be fully recovered and conveyed. But there is no such inscribed meaning and no possibility of such recovery. It is not that something gets lost in translation, it is rather that different interpreters find different things, focus on different aspects of meaning, derive different discourses from a text. The claim that the translated text is a replacement of the original requires the translator to defer as much as possible to the intended discourse which of course presupposes that this can be identified on textual evidence. But texts do not themselves provide evidence but only data from which evidence can be inferred by interpretation.

The interpreting phase of the translation process is, as has already been noted, not restricted to the activity of translators. It is a process of pragmatic inference, of making meaning out of a text, that everybody engages in, and the text is an inert linguistic object unless and until this process is activated. So in the interpreting phase the translat*or* is doing what we all do as translat*ers*. But the rendering phase is not restricted to the activity of translators either. It is true that translators are always required to produce another text and we translaters are not – for them rendering is a necessary part of the operation. But when we *are* required to do a rendering, in the form of a summary or paraphrase, for example, we encounter the same problem of recipient design that I mentioned earlier, whether the rendered text is in the "same" or a "different" language. The problems posed by intralingual translation are the same in kind if not in degree as those posed by interlingual translation.

The essential similarity between intralingual and interlingual translation was noted long ago by George Steiner:

> On the inter-lingual level, translation will pose concentrated, visibly intractable problems; but these same problems abound, at a more covert or conventionally neglected level, intralingually. The model "sender to receiver" which represents any semiological and semantic process is ontologically equivalent to the model "source-language to receptor language" used in the theory of translation. In both schemes there is "in the middle" an operation of interpretative decipherment, an encoding-decoding function or synapse.
>
> (Steiner 1975: 47)

The sameness that Steiner is referring to, however, relates to the interpretative phase – what he calls the operation "in the middle" of "interpretative decipherment". But there are also correspondences at the rendering phrase as was pointed out earlier in reference to intralingual summary and paraphrase. These resemble the re-textualizations of interlanguage translation when, as they usually are, they are designed for second person reception. But the activity of summarizing is a very common feature of ordinary conversation, where it functions as a focusing strategy whereby interactants formulate on line what has been previously said. As Garfinkel and Sacks put it in their own inimitable way:

> A member may treat some part of a conversation as an occasion to describe that conversation, to explain it, or characterize it, or explicate, or translate, or summarize, or furnish

> the gist of it ... We shall speak of conversationalists' practices of saying-in-so-many-words-what-we-are-doing as formulating. (Garfinkel and Sacks 1970: 350, 351)

Some formulations might focus on referential meaning, providing a gist of what has been talked about while others might focus on force and/or effect bringing illocutionary or perlocutionary intentions out in the open, making them explicit as upshot. Although Garfinkel and Sacks are referring here to conversation, formulations are not, of course, confined to spoken conversation, but are a common feature in written language use as well (see Widdowson 1984, Ch. 8).

The general point to be made is that although we tend to think of translation as a distinct occupational activity practised by translat*ors*, it is essentially a commonplace pragmatic process – something we all do as translat*ers* of what other people say and write so as to accommodate it to our own schematic worlds. What we might call occupational translation is, of course, a special case of such a process with its own conditions of accountability: the mediating role of the translator necessarily imposes constraints on interpretation and rendering which generally do not apply to everyday communicative activity – and would impede effective communication if they did. It is knowing how to exercise such constraints that makes the occupation of translator a special, and a specialist activity.

So we can think of translation, not exclusively as the activity of translat*ors*, whose occupation requires special expertise, but as a general process of making meaning into and out of text, as a matter of the everyday experience of all language users. Making sense of language, deriving discourses from texts, is itself a learning process. We learn by making pragmatic adjustments to our schematic knowledge, extending our repertoire of conceptualized experience. The purpose of language teaching is presumably to continue that process: to get learners to develop and extend that experience by exploiting the resources of a different linguistic code. What language learners have to do is to learn how to be language users – in short, how to be translat*ers* in another language. In this sense, translation is not an extra or extraneous activity: it is intrinsic to the very learning process itself. This is not, however, the way translation has generally been conceived.

The received wisdom of one influential school of thought has a simple answer to the question of what role translation has in language teaching: none at all. Reasons for its rejection are discussed in detail in Cook (2010) but they would all appear to derive from the general assumption that any reference to the learners' L1 is an interference in their learning of an L2. Thus conventional L2 pedagogy does not encourage the extension of experience that I have referred to, but on the contrary cuts learners off from it. But although teaching seeks to impose this discontinuity, learners, of course, resist it. For they *do* refer to their L1 linguistic experience as a natural expedient of making sense of what is new by relating it to what is familiar. So although translation may be assigned no role in language *teaching*, it clearly plays a crucial role in language *learning*. Since this role is not overtly recognized, but is on the contrary suppressed, there is, as I have pointed out elsewhere (Widdowson 2003,Ch. 11), a fundamental conflict between the continuous process of bi- or multi-lingual learning and the discontinuous practice of monolingual teaching.

What this means, in effect, is that teachers create adverse conditions for learning, so that many, if not most, of the difficulties that learners have to cope with are pedagogically induced. In the end, the conflict is resolved in favour of teaching since the only institutionally recognized measure of success is the extent to which what is learned conforms to what has been taught: whatever else has been learned that is not sanctioned by teaching does not count. Learners are in effect assigned the role of *teachees*. Although one has often heard the cry "let the learners learn", their initiative remains under teacher control and is directed towards eventual conformity, and although a good deal of lip service has been paid to the idea of learner autonomy, this, of course, is still circumscribed by teacher authority, no matter how tactfully disguised.

And what is pedagogically authorized as a legitimate objective is *a* language, a quite distinct and different set of formal rules and conventions of usage from those which learners have previously experienced: French as distinct from German, English as distinct from Chinese, and so on. Language learning is understood not as the learning of a different realization of *language*, the continuation of previous experience and the extension of an existing linguistic resource, but the learning of *a language, an L2*, another and foreign language, a separate entity dissociated from the L1. But, as has already been noted, it is not so dissociated in the learners' mind. Indeed unless there is some association, no learning can take place at all: clearly learners can only make sense of the data of a second or foreign language to the extent that they can interpret it as evidence of language in general, as alternative realizations of what they are already familiar with in their own L1. So teaching that focuses exclusively on the L2 as something separate and distinct, closed off from the learners' experience of language through their own L1, has the effect of inhibiting the learning process.

And yet, the idea that language learning must necessarily be the learning of a different and distinct language is deeply entrenched. The language subject, defined as it is in reference to the description of a particular language unknown to the learners, is essentially teacher oriented. As such, learning can only be conceived of in terms of conformity. This remains the case even when there is a pedagogic shift of emphasis from linguistic to communicative competence for what is usually set as the objective is not the ability to communicate as such, but the ability to communicate in accordance with the norms of usage associated with the native speakers of a particular language. Communicative language teaching (CLT), at least as generally practised, is only concerned with encouraging learners to communicate by using language so long as the language was not their own L1 but the L2 they were being taught (for further discussion see Widdowson 2003, 2009).

This essentially monolingual concept of communication is carried over from Hymes' often cited paper on communicative competence, frequently invoked as providing the authority for a communicative approach to pedagogy. Hymes himself carries over the Chomsky concept of competence as having to do with knowledge of a particular language. Somebody competent in a language is said to be able to make a judgement about how far a particular sample of that language is possible according to its encoded rules, feasible, that is to say processable, appropriate to the context in which it is used, and actually performed. Such judgements can only be made against preconceived norms that are operative in a particular linguacultural community. As Hymes puts it: "There is an important sense in which a normal member of a community has knowledge in respect to all these aspects of the communicative systems available to him" (Hymes 1972: 282).

What is presupposed here is the existence of a distinct community and a set of rules and conventions that define its language, with the normal members of the community being the native speakers of the language. We are not all that far away from Chomsky's ideal speaker listener in a homogeneous speech community. In adopting Hymes' concept of communicative competence, as far as the pedagogic objective is concerned, learning a second language really is like learning the first (cf Ervin-Tripp 1974). Accordingly, the assumption that informs communicative language teaching (CLT), at least at it is most generally conceived and practiced, is that acquiring communicative competence necessarily means learning how to communicate in accordance with native speaker norms. It sets out to teach a particular way of communicating, what is supposed to be the native speaker way, abstracted as an idealized construct. Thus, as far as formal properties are concerned, only those which are described in standard grammars and dictionaries are admitted as possible. And what is deemed appropriate is identified, intuitively and impressionistically, only in reference to stereotypical native-speaker contexts of use.

In one respect, however, pedagogy departs from the Hymes proposal. Hymes makes the point that there is no necessary correspondence among his four dimensions of communicative competence: thus, for example, an expression might be possible but not feasible or not appropriate. One of the central arguments of CLT is that the structural approach it replaced was fixated on the possible at the expense of the appropriate, thereby presenting the learner with communicatively vacuous language (*This is a book. The book is here* – that kind of thing). So what CLT did was to link the possible with the appropriate so as to give linguistic form a communicative function. But the link took the form of a fixed inter-dependency: what is possible has also to be appropriate, and conversely, what is appropriate has also to be possible, with the appropriate and the possible always defined in native speaker terms. If students manage to communicate without conforming to what is conventionally encoded as possible this may be tolerated as an interim stage of learning but has to be eventually corrected so that the required conformity is achieved.

These two Hymesian dimensions of communicative competence are associated with what have been identified as the two basic constituents of learner behaviour: accuracy, which involves a focus on form, that is to say what is encoded as possible, and fluency, which involves a focus on meaning, that is to say what is contextually appropriate. In task-based teaching (TBLT), a currently much promoted version of the communicative approach, activities are designed to combine the two. Contexts are devised in the form of tasks which engage learners in solving problems that bear a resemblance to the "real world". So these tasks are represented as "creating contexts for natural language use" but at the same time are so designed as to involve a "focus on form" (Ellis 2009: 225). One of the key criteria for task design is that "learners should largely have to rely on their own resources (linguistic and non-linguistic) in order to complete the activity". But the only linguistic resource they are allowed to rely on is the L2 and not one they would naturally rely on, namely their own L1. Another key criterion is "There is a clearly defined outcome other than the use of language (i.e. the language serves as the means for achieving the outcome, not as an end in its own right)" (Ellis 2009: 223). But, again, learners are prevented from resorting to the obvious, and natural, means at their disposal for achieving a communicative outcome. They are not free to use any linguistic resource other than that of the prescribed L2. And they are not free in the use of this either: it is not enough that they use it fluently and appropriately to achieve their outcomes, they are required by the "focus on form" condition to use is accurately as well – that is to say in conformity to approved native speaker norms of what is possible according to the established encoding rules of the standard L2 language.

All of this obviously casts doubt, to say the least, on the claim that these tasks "create contexts for natural language use". What they actually do is to impose unnatural conditions on two counts: firstly, it is obviously not natural for learners to avoid their own language in these contexts, and secondly, even if they are induced to restrict themselves to the L2, the accuracy requirement obviously imposes an unnatural constraint on them in achieving their communicative outcomes. As Labov demonstrated long ago, focus on form, or, equivalently, attention paid to speech, is not naturally a feature of the contextually appropriate use of language (Labov 1972).

What I am arguing is that a pedagogic approach that defines what, in Hymes' terms, is possible and appropriate solely in reference to monolingual native speaker norms imposes unnatural constraints on learning and so creates difficulties which are in effect a function of the approach itself. As I have argued earlier, the consequence of an exclusive focus on the L2 is to cut learners off from their own experience of language and so to prevent them from engaging in the natural process of translating whereby the L2 is made real, realized, as an extension of that experience. In effect, the isolation of the L2 as a separate language dissociates it from language in general.

And this dissociation, and the difficulties it creates, are made even greater when another of Hymes' parameters is taken into account: whether and to what degree the language is actually performed. Again, this is generally taken to mean performed by bona fide native speakers – but now the native speakers are not ideal constructs with an abstract competence but actual language users whose performance can be recorded in corpora as factual data. Corpus linguists can now make available detailed descriptions of the actually occurring idiomatic patterns of native speaker usage. These patterns constitute other norms that learners are required to conform to if they are to achieve a native speaker level of proficiency in the language. The pedagogic stakes are accordingly raised. It is now not enough that their language should be accurate in reference to what has been encoded as possible; if it is measure up to the prescribed "real" or "authentic" language produced by native speakers it has also to be attested as idiomatically normal. Thus a recently published paper on the subject begins: "There has been general agreement in recent years that collocation is an important aspect of knowledge for language learners .... An increased knowledge of collocation not only allows learners to improve levels of accuracy, but it also aids fluency" (Webb and Kagimoto 2011: 259).

Another article in the same journal, *Applied Linguistics* (Martinez and Schmitt 2012) joins in this chorus of "general agreement". Like Webb & Kagimoto, they are actually talking about the description and learning of English, which they take for granted is that performed by native speakers. The authors cite one study that shows that "L2 speakers were judged as more proficient when they used formulaic sequences" and another that "... examined 170 written compositions from an EFL proficiency test and concluded that those with higher scores also tended to use more formulaic expressions than the lower scoring group". The authors conclude that "Given the importance of formulaic language, it can be argued that it needs to be part of language syllabuses" (Martinez and Schmitt 2012: 301).

But of course, the importance of formulaic language is only given if one accepts the premise that proficiency can only be measured against native speaker norms. Martinez & Schmitt take this as self-evident; and since there is as yet no reliable descriptive list of formulaic sequences that textbook writers, teachers and testers can draw upon, they have taken it upon themselves to repair this supposedly serious pedagogic deficiency by devising one. The result is their Phrasal Expressions List. It is, predictably, based exclusively on native speaker usage- but, even more exclusively, only on that manifestation of it that is recorded in the British National Corpus. Given the widespread use of English beyond the borders of Britain, this seems to be a particularly narrow prescription.

This widespread use provides abundant evidence that such a prescription is unnecessary and irrelevant. As Seidlhofer points out in her discussion of English as a lingua franca (Seidlhofer 2011), all natural language use will provide evidence of what Sinclair has referred to as the "idiom principle" (Sinclair 1991) and will have its formulaic or idiomatic features in that users will develop recurrent phrasal patterns on line on a least effort principle as they co-construct their interaction. Idiomaticity is part of the general pragmatic process. But the crucial point is that this process does not depend on the reproduction of established formulaic or idiomatic expressions. On the contrary, unless these are known beforehand as such by the parties concerned, they are likely to be dysfunctional (see also Seidlhofer 2012 for further discussion). Understanding this is not only a matter of understanding English as a lingua franca, but the understanding of the way any natural language functions as use. So as users of their own language, the natural inclination of learners will be to idiomatize the language at their disposal in a familiar pragmatic way, drawing on their own experience of how language works. In other words, they will naturally tend to make the L2 more functionally effective by translating it into their own idiom. The insistence that learners should be instructed in the particular linguistic forms that realize idiomaticity in native speaker usage can only inhibit them from doing this. Formulaic phrasing, like accuracy and fluency, is a function of communicative expediency. There is no virtue in producing conventionalized L2 formulaic sequences, or in conforming to prescribed native speaker norms of accuracy and fluency unless there are good pragmatic reasons for doing so. The only reason for learners to do so in the classroom is because the teachers require them to. For all the claims that the TBLT version of communicative language teaching creates "contexts for natural language use" it clearly does not. For contexts include participants and learner participants bring with them to the classroom the contexts of their own experience of language, which they would quite naturally bring to bear on achieving their communicative outcomes if they were not prevented by the pedagogic conditions imposed upon them. The tasks of TBLT are essentially teacher rather than learner oriented in that they are designed not to activate natural language learning but to impose an unnatural process on learners on the assumption that the only learning that really counts as such is that which conforms to what is pedagogically prescribed. Language learning is taken to be simply the reflex of language teaching and learners are, in effect, teachees – TBLL is just the consequence of TBLT.

But what if we were to focus on TBLL and take a genuinely learner-centred approach by allowing learners to react to tasks in a natural way without casting them as teachees by imposing the constraining conditions of conformity to L2 norms? What if we allowed them to draw pragmatically on all of the linguistic resources at their disposal to achieve their communicative outcomes? What if, in other words, we allowed them to be translaters?

As I argued earlier, translating can be seen as a general interpreting process of deriving discourse from text whether or not there is subsequent rendering of that interpretation in another text. As such, it is a natural pragmatic process that is applied to all language use, whatever language this is deemed to be *in*. All language users are translat*ers*. In the classroom, learners are presented with textual data, spoken and written, of all kinds and they will naturally seek to interpret it, make some kind of discourse out of it, convert the data into evidence of some meaningful message or other, instinctively making reference to their own linguacultural reality to do so. Language learners are also language users and they will therefore quite naturally do what all language users do: in a word, they will translate.

The process of translation is the means and the product in the form of a second text is the end. In language learning, there is textual input of one kind or another and a required textual output by learners but the purpose of this is to activate the process of learning. The *sample* of language has to be transformed into an *example* for learning to take place (see Widdowson 2003, Ch. 8 for further discussion). How far does this transformation process involve a translation process? Traditionally, the transformation is taken to be an intralingual operation involving only the L2, but of course learners will continually refer interlingually to their L1- in transforming sample into example they naturally translate. In so doing they are, like any language users, translat*ers*, drawing on whatever linguistic resources they might have at their disposal to make meaning. Denying them the opportunity to do this, and indeed penalizing them for making the attempt, has the effect of denaturalizing the learning process and alienating learners from their own linguistic experience.

So if translating is what learners naturally do, why not have teachers encourage them to do it? The usual answer, as has already been noted, is that this would distract their attention from what learners should be doing – learning another language and conforming to its quite different norms and standards as authorized by linguistic descriptions of native speaker competence. Inducing such learning has, after all, always been the time-honoured objective in language pedagogy. Where, as is frequently the case, a particular approach fails to reach this desired objective, another approach is proposed, and then another, always on the assumption that the objective is valid if only some way could be found of achieving it, some way of solving this problem of learner intransigence – if only learners could be trained to toe the line, if only their intake could be made to correspond with the teaching input. If only.

I would argue that the real problem is that the objective itself is misconceived. I would propose an alternative: instead of trying to teach *a language* as a set of distinct encoding rules and usage conventions, one would teach the properties of *language* in general as a means of conceptualization and communication which are variously realized through different languages. The objective so defined would represent an L2 not as something dissociated from the learners' own linguistic experience, but closely related to it and an additional resource in their linguistic repertoire. The pedagogy would be learner-centred in that it would exploit the learners' own experience of language, encourage them to recognize how another language can be used to realize meanings in alternative ways and give credit to what they achieve in making meaning, no matter what non-conformist or linguistically hybrid form this takes. The objective then would be defined in terms not of some illusory and unattainable native speaker competence but as the development of what I have referred to elsewhere as capability (Widdowson 2003, Ch. 9), that is to say the ability to translate as I have defined it – to derive discourse from text and to engage in what has come to be called languaging (see Swain 2006; Seidlhofer 2011: 98) by making use of linguistic resources expediently and creatively to make meaning that is appropriate to context and purpose. This capability would be an investment for further use and learning of language beyond the classroom as learners subsequently encounter it in its various realizations as different languages.

The earlier discussion in this chapter about the nature of translation led to the suggestion that it can be defined as a general pragmatic process of meaning making that is an essential feature of all language use. We are not all transla*tors*, but we are all transla*ters* in that we are all capable, in varying degrees, of interpreting texts so as to derive our own discourses out of them. This capability comes to the fore when we come across texts that are linguistically unfamiliar in one way or another. L2 language learning, I have argued, is essentially also a matter of exercising this capability and extending its application to other texts in another language. In this way, the other language is related to the L1 and becomes part of an expanded plurilinguistic repertoire.

As I said at the beginning, this chapter is concerned with the relationship between the three activities mentioned in its title. If language learning is defined only in terms of conformity to a teaching objective, and if this objective is defined only in terms of L2 native speaker competence, then there seem to be no very persuasive grounds for questioning the conventional doctrine of monolingual teaching. Translation might be resorted to from time to time as an optional extra, but its role would be peripheral at best. But if we think of learning and translation in the very different terms I have suggested here, then these relationships change quite radically. For in language learning that is not teacher-determined, I have argued, learners will draw naturally on existing language experience to extend their linguistic resource for making meaning. They will, in other words, engage in translating as a general pragmatic process, using whatever language they have at their disposal to learn more. Learning and translating become essentially the same thing.

Such learning would not be teacher-determined, but in a classroom context it would obviously need to be teacher directed in one way or another. So what form would this direction take? In rejecting the objectives and procedures of traditional monolingual teaching, we would clearly have to radically rethink its taken for granted assumptions about how and what language is graded, what activities are appropriate for encouraging and guiding learners as translat*ers* and crucially of course, how language proficiency is to be assessed. To return once more to the title of this chapter, the relevant question then becomes not what role translation has in language teaching, but rather what role language teaching has in translation.

So what would the role of teaching be in directing learners to develop the languaging capability through translating that I have argued should be the essential objective of learning? Such a radical shift in perspective would obviously have far reaching implications which would need to be carefully explored before any specific pedagogic procedures are proposed. Bearing this cautionary comment in mind, one might give an indication or two of what this changed way of thinking might involve.

Consider, for example, the question of grading. A focus on translating would recognize that difficulty is not a matter of the intrinsic complexity of the L2 but a function of the difference between L2 and L1. And so grading would apply to both languages and would depend on identifying particular semantic and grammatical equivalences across them which could be readily realized by learners. Decisions about what linguistic features are to be focused on and in what order would therefore necessarily be a local matter.

With regard to classroom activities, these too would obviously need to be bilingually designed. Consider, for example, TBLT, which was referred to earlier and which is so widely advocated these days. The basic principle of this approach would be retained – namely that tasks would be designed to get learners to achieve a communicative outcome by the use of their own linguistic resources. But obviously the inhibiting condition that these resources have to be drawn only from the L2 would be abandoned and with it the assumption that the purpose of tasks is to develop L2 competence along the dimensions of complexity, accuracy and fluency. Instead, tasks would get learners to make use of all their linguistic resources, but would be designed so as to constrain the use of the L2 where this is required to achieve a communicative outcome. The communicative outcome then becomes primary and the essential question for research in task design is to find out how different kinds of outcome call for a differential deployment of linguistic resources.

This chapter has suggested a way of thinking about the three activities mentioned in its title that brings them into a relationship other than that which is sanctioned by current pedagogic orthodoxy. As I have said, the implications for this way of thinking remain to be explored. So this chapter is not an account of any new advances that have been made. It is rather an argument for an alternative conceptualization which points in the direction of possible change in principle in conventional pedagogic thinking. Whether there will be advances in actual practice which follow this direction is, of course, a different matter.

18 Bilingual competence and lingual capability

Bilingualism is, of course, a familiar and well-explored topic – the number of publications where the term figures in the title would fill a library. One might suppose that everything that can be said about it has already been said, and said by scholars far better informed than I am. The fact that we have this conference on bilingualism, however, suggests that perhaps there are still aspects of the phenomenon that warrant enquiry, that from a different perspective, it raises issues that still need to be explored. The perspective I take is a pedagogic one. The teaching of foreign languages, and my particular concern is with English, is generally assumed to involve getting learners to be bilingual. But what exactly does this mean?

So, let me presume upon your patience and begin by posing, once again, the basic question: what does it mean to be bilingual? How is bilingualism to be defined? At a very general level, as the Merriam Webster dictionary defines it is "the ability to speak two languages" or as the Free Dictionary has it "using or able to use two languages".

But of course, as participants in this conference will know only too well, this raises a number of problematic questions. To begin with there is the assumption that there are such entities as languages, linguistic codes that are identifiably distinct. Where do such linguistic systems exist? One place where they would seem to have obvious existence is in grammars and dictionaries. If you want to know what English is, or French or Italian, you have only to refer to the description of such codes or systems in grammars and dictionaries – standard works of reference.

But these descriptions are of course the linguistic constructs of grammarians and lexicographers and as such, following the tradition of de Saussure, abstractions of *langue* from the actually occurring phenomenon of *parole*. And the identification of this code depends on the idea that underlying all the various and varying manifestations of *parole* there is a stable set of linguistic forms that represent *the* language, the standard language. What we call standard works of reference describe the standard language. Thus in reference to the language called British English: "As far as grammar and vocabulary are concerned, this generally means Standard English as it is normally written and spoken by educated speakers in England and, with certain differences, in Wales, Scotland, Northern Ireland, The Republic of Ireland, Australia, New Zealand and South Africa" (Trudgill and Hannah 2008: 5).

Note: Unpublished. Revised from a paper given at an international conference on bilingualism. University of Malta. 2015.

Presumably, by the same token, standard French or standard German or any other language is assumed to be what educated native speakers of French and German or any other language write and speak. The proper language is then essentially the property of a particular group of its users. But this assumption is not based on any empirical evidence. Corpus linguistics, of course, provides us with evidence of the actually occurring usage of educated native speakers, often with the claim that this is the real language. But this presupposes that such speakers can be defined in advance.

But such a definition is generally conspicuous by its absence. Quite apart from the difficulty of defining who native speakers are (Davies 2003), how does one determine whether they are educated or not? After all, most people have been educated to some degree, so what level do they have to reach to be categorized as educated? It has been suggested that the problem of defining the native speaker might be resolved by abandoning the concept altogether in favour of that of "expert user" (Rampton 1990). But of course this simply replaces one problematic indeterminacy with another. For how is expertise to be defined? The problem is that expert and educated are not absolute but relative terms – you can be expert and educated with respect to certain uses of language but not in others. One can only conclude that there can be no category of educated native speakers or expert users which can provide an empirical basis for the definition of a standard language.

Even those whose work is based on the concept of standard language are somewhat uncertain about it. As I have noted, Peter Trudgill assumes its validity and yet acknowledges that "there seems to be considerable confusion in the English-speaking world, even amongst linguists, about what Standard English is" (Trudgill 1999: 117). He is not the only linguist to recognize this.

> "Standard English" still seems to me to be a "confused and confusing" territory for sociolinguistics, and probably much more so than we should be comfortable with. "Standardness" and "non-standardness" are too deeply ingrained into sociolinguistic theory and methods for us to dispense with received perspectives and begin again, conceptually.
>
> (Coupland 2000: 632)

The message here seems to be that although the concept of a standard language is confusing, it is so deeply ingrained in sociolinguistic thinking and in accord with received perspectives that it is indispensible. This one might think is a rather odd position to take. One would suppose that if a concept is confused it compromises the validity of any description based upon it, and that it is indeed the very purpose of intellectual enquiry to question ingrained ideas and received perspectives.

Of course, one needs to recognize that any conceptualization of language is inevitably in some respects an idealized version of actuality. In actuality, language is elusive, heterogeneous, intrinsically unstable. We need no complexity theory to tell us that actual language use is always in flux, endlessly emergent and variable so that the concept of a language as a stable and bounded code is a convenient fiction. As Trudgill again points out, when talking about language varieties: "How we divide these continua up is also most often linguistically arbitrary, although we do of course find it convenient normally to make such divisions and use names for dialects that we happen to want to talk about for a particular purpose as if they were discrete varieties" (Trudgill 1999: 122). This is not to say that such convenient fictions are to be avoided: indeed they cannot be avoided. All abstract constructs are fictional in relation to actual lived experience and one cannot make any theoretical or descriptive statement at all without them. So one can readily accept that for some purposes, for some sociolinguistic theories and methods, the idea that there are discrete languages and language varieties is an indispensable assumption. Chomsky's reference to the ideal speaker-listener in a homogeneous speech community has been widely criticized by sociolinguistics on the grounds that that there is no such thing as the ideal speaker and that speech communities are not homogenous. But for his purposes it was a convenient assumption. But this does not prevent sociolinguists themselves from making similar simplifying assumptions for their purposes: for there is no such thing as a unitary standard language, or a discrete variety either.

The key issue is not whether one should avoid such convenient fictions, but how convenient they are, and for what purposes. For it is conceivable that for some sociolinguistic or other purposes their convenience may be at the expense of conceptual clarity. Consider, for example, the concept of language variety. A variety is defined in terms of its formal features and identified as a settled linguistic code. This of course is to represent the process of variation as in a state of suspended animation. But variation in use is a continual pragmatic phenomenon as users draw on their resources in all kinds of unpredictable ways as appropriate to different communicative contexts and purposes. Variation is of interest to variationist sociolinguists mainly as the causal origin of varieties. It is the state that the process leads to, the variety product so to say, that is the main focus of attention. But what of the process of variation itself?

Variety is a descriptive linguistic concept: it is defined in terms of the regular occurrence of particular encodings. The primary focus is on linguistic forms, though, of course, once these have been identified they can be correlated with social factors and communicative functions. Variation is, on the other hand, a pragmatic concept which has to do with the process of communication itself. What is significant here is not what linguistic forms occur but what motivates their use. The forms are of interest not because they can be identified as belonging to any particular linguistic code but because they are symptomatic of an underlying communicative function.

One familiar and much discussed kind of variation is code-switching defined as "the alternation of codes within a single speech exchange" (Bailey 2007: 257). Since this presupposes the existence of separate linguistic systems it is therefore an instance of bilingualism. Let us consider an example – taken from an article in a British newspaper:

> I've had a gay couple visiting from Paris. They arrived in a flurry of cashmere berets and chic luggage and disappeared into their room every couple of hours to make *l'amour*. They brought me some Mont d'Or cheese, which was so strong that my kitchen smelt like the laundry basket of the Lowestoft rugby team.
> (*from* Julian's Week. New Statesman 12.3.2007)

Here, we might say, we have a switch from English into French in the use of the word *l'amour* and the switch is signalled by the change of font. But what of the words "beret" and "chic"? These we might suggest do not count as switches because these words have been incorporated into English and no longer belong to a different system. Would this still be the case if their Frenchness were to be retained by pronouncing them in a markedly French manner? They would then surely have to be taken as code alternations. There are innumerable words of this kind – *restaurant, café, garage, rendezvous* and others. And what of "Mont d'Or". Does the use of this French name constitute a shift? If one pronounces it in the French manner, yes, if not, no?

It is obviously difficult to know when we have an alternation into another code or not. And even when there are relatively straightforward cases, as with *l'amour*, although there is clearly a bilingual alternation here, what evidence does it provide of the author's bilingualism? If I have only a few isolated words of another language in my linguistic repertory (or repertoire), without knowing the system they relate to, would making use of them count as code-switching? And could I claim to be bilingual? If this is so, then, it would be hard to find anybody who is not bilingual and monolingual speakers would be a rarity indeed. However, as Ervin-Tripp has pointed out, scholars have sought to resolve this indeterminacy: "Those who study code-switching like to reserve the term for maximally bilingual speakers who are known to have parallel options in both codes" (Ervin-Tripp 2001: 47). But what then does it mean to be "maximally bilingual". According to the editor of *The Bilingualism Reader* a maximal bilingual is "someone with near native control of two or more languages" (Li Wei 2000: 6). This again presupposes a definable native speaker norm. And this control presumably means having "parallel options in both codes". This would seem to suggest that there are speakers who can switch codes in all domains of use, in all communicative contexts. This surely corresponds to the Chomskyan concept of the competence of "the ideal speaker-listener ... who knows its language perfectly" except that to be maximally bilingual you have to know two languages perfectly. On this definition, nobody in actuality is maximally lingual in one code let alone two. So the question remains: how lingual in two languages do I need to be bilingual? This is a particularly relevant question in the field of language pedagogy, and I will return to it a little later.

Meanwhile, there is another and related matter that arises from our example. Even if we are able to identify a switch into a different code we are simply making a statement about the text as a linguistic object. But how are we to interpret it as discourse? What communicative function does the alternation serve. We move now from a formal linguistic to a pragmatic perspective. And from this perspective what is significant is how these expressions are meant to be interpreted: what the user meant by using them. What matters here is not whether the expressions can be assigned to a different code but that they are marked as signalling a communicative intent. And such marking does not depend on alternating between two linguistic systems but can be achieved equally effectively by using alternatives from just one. In other words, as communicative processes, there is no difference between code-switching and style-shifting.

> It has long been recognized that the processes which make a monolingual shift styles are the same as those that which make a bilingual switch languages ... Any theory of style needs to encompass both monolingual and multilingual repertoires–that is, all the shifts a speaker may make within her linguistic repertoire. (Bell 2001: 145)

What we see when we focus on the actual communicative process, rather than on the linguistic forms that are used, whether you categorize them as elements of different codes or styles, is the expedient exploitation of a repertoire of linguistic resource as required by some communicative purpose. As the purpose varies, so, naturally, the language varies accordingly.

It may well be, of course, as has been extensively documented in the literature (see, for example: Hernandez-Campoy and Cutillas-Espinosa 2012) that it is the purpose of the first person speaker to draw attention to linguistic features, which mark an alternation in code or style to express an attitude intended to have an effect on the second person recipient. As an example, consider again the passage about the gay couple and their berets and chic luggage and Mont d'Or cheese. The occurrence of a French word in an English text, or when read aloud, the French pronunciation of words of French origin like "chic" are marked co-textual deviations meant to be noticed. As such, in reference to Grice's Co-operative Principle, they flout the manner maxim:

Avoid obscurity of expression
Avoid ambiguity
Be brief (avoid unnecessary prolixity)
Be orderly
                Grice (1975: 45–46)

The same can be said of the phrase "in a flurry of cashmere berets and chic luggage". Here we have a shift into an elaborate style. To the extent that these switches and shifts are marked departures from straightforward description they flout the manner maxim and so result in implicatures. That is to say they designed to have a particular effect – to be humorous. And this effect is of course dependent on the second person reader or listener not only sharing an assumption of textual normality, but also of ratifying the attitude that these floutings represent. This is a kind of conspiratorial use of language – this French couple, you know, flurry of berets, chic luggage, l'amour – know what I mean (with a knowing nudge nudge, wink wink).

In this case, the first person text producer will pre-suppose a familiarity with conventions of use and cultural attitudes or otherwise the implicatures are not activated, the effect fails and there is nothing humorous about the description at all. We have all experienced occasions when such conditions of mutual familiarity fail when somebody tells a joke and we don't see the point, or don't find it funny.

So where there is no lingua-cultural mutuality, such alternations, whether designated switches or shifts, will have no such significance. This, for example, is very often the case with non-native-speaking users of English as a lingua franca. Coming from different lingua-cultures, they will frequently not be familiar with native speaker cultural norms or conventions of usage. What they do is what all natural language users do: they cobble a text together by means of lingual *bricolage* (to use a French word I happen to have in my own repertoire!), that is to say, expediently making do with whatever linguistic resource they have at their disposal to get their message across. In so doing they will frequently exploit the possibilities inherent in the code but which are unrealized in the conventionally established encodings of standard English. Although these non-conformities will usually be considered as deviant, equivalent to learner errors, they do not go against the Cooperative Principle, but on the contrary conform to it. This is how the principle is formulated: "Make your conversational contribution such as is required, at the stage at which it occurs, by the accepted purpose or direction of the talk exchange in which you are involved" (Grice 1975: 75).

In other words: make your contribution appropriate to context and purpose. Users of English as a lingua franca are involved in talk exchanges that require them to make their contributions communicatively effective, when they need to negotiate their meanings in contexts where the purpose or direction of the talk is not a matter of accepted convention. There will be occasions, of course, when it will be appropriate to use language that conforms to the established encodings of the standard language: but there will also be occasions when it is appropriate to exploit their linguistic resources in variable non-conformist ways.

What I am saying then is that being *lingually capable* to communicate is not at all a matter of being *linguistically competent*. By the same token you can, for your communicative purposes, be maximally capable in the use of linguistic resources from various sources without being maximally bilingual. From the perspective of the pragmatics of actual communication, performance is not just the variable realization of competence, variation is not simply evidence of variety, *parole* is not necessarily the actualization of a particular *langue*.

The first reading in *The Bilingualism Reader* previously referred to is an extract of an article written over 50 years ago and it begins: "Bilingualism is not a phenomenon of language; it is a characteristic of its use. It is not a feature of the code but of the message. It does not belong to the domain of 'langue' but of 'parole'" (Mackey 1962/2000: 26).

If this is so, then it makes little sense to talk about code-switching at all. The point is that *parole* as a use of language is an essentially pragmatic phenomenon and the language used does not have to be identified as *a* particular language. The problem is that *parole* has been persistently taken to be the actual manifestation of an abstract *langue*, the performance of a competence. But lingualism is the ability to exploit a linguistic resource to appropriate communicative effect, whatever the sources of this resource may be.

And yet the association of communication with particular linguistic codes and particular conventions of usage is, like the notion of standard language, so well established as to seem self-evident. It is so deeply ingrained, to refer again to the quotation from Coupland previously cited, that sociolinguists are understandably reluctant to dispense with it. And given that it has the imprimatur of sociolinguistic authority, it is not surprising that such an association is deeply ingrained also in the pedagogy of foreign language teaching.

Here the orthodox view is that the objective is to make learners maximally bilingual – to get them to acquire as close an approximation in another language to the competence they have acquired in their own and success is measured against native speaker norms. It is recognized, of course, that bilingualism is not just a matter of knowing particular linguistic codes but of having control over them, that is to say knowing how to put them to appropriate contextual use. So it is *communicative* competence that is taken to be the objective that foreign language learners should be directed at achieving.

But again this is defined as the competence of native speakers. The model of communicative competence that usually serves as the pedagogic frame of reference is based on that proposed by Hymes. To remind you, Hymes suggests that there are four constitutive features of such competence: to be communicatively competent is to be able to make a judgement as to whether and to what degree an instance of language is possible in the sense of conforming to code rules, feasible in the sense of being processible, appropriate to context and attested as actually occurring. But of course making a judgement about an instance of language with respect to these features presupposes a norm. As Hymes himself says: "There is an important sense in which a normal member of a community has knowledge with respect to all these aspects of the communicative systems available to him. He will interpret or assess the conduct of others and himself in ways that reflect a knowledge of each" ... (Hymes 1972: 282).

So what Hymes is talking about is not about knowing how language in general is used to communicate but whether and to what degree an instance of language conforms to the communicative conventions of a particular language which a normal member of the community that speaks it has knowledge of. We are back with something that suspiciously resembles the native speaker: the ideal speaker/listener in a homogeneous speech community who knows its language perfectly. To use language appropriately is to use it in conformity to the established conventions of the native speaker use of a particular language. And if there is no such conformity, then communicative conduct will be interpreted and assessed as inappropriate and evidence of communicative incompetence.

And it is just such an assessment that is carried over into language pedagogy, but with an additional assumption, not warranted by the authority of Hymes, that what is appropriate in these terms also has to conform to native speaker norms not only of what is possible but also what is attested as actually performed. In Hymes there is no hierarchical ordering of his features of communicative competence with any one being given primacy: they are represented as separate and independent, allowing for the fact, for example, that what is identified as impossible with respect to the code can nevertheless be communicatively appropriate, or what is possible may not be attested as having been actually performed. In language teaching, however, these features are seen as necessarily linked. The communicative competence that language learners are to acquire has not only to conform to what it is possible according to the standard code but also to what is appropriate in native speaker contexts of use, and increasingly these days appropriateness is conflated with what, on corpus evidence, native speakers actually perform.

So the idea that the objective of foreign language teaching is to make learners maximally bilingual, having equal competence and control in two languages, is deeply ingrained in the thinking of those concerned with second or foreign language learning. Thus, in the study of second language acquisition, SLA, as Herdina and Jessner (2002) point out:

> Most research on bilingualism has been based on the view of the bilingual as the sum of two monolinguals in one person with two separate language competences ... Consequently bilingual proficiency has generally been measured against monolingual proficiency. (Herdina and Jessner 2002: 6)

Such a view is sanctioned and promoted by no less an authority than the Council of Europe with its Common European Framework of Reference (CEFR). In its most recent version (Council of Europe 2018), although its can-do descriptors have been revised to avoid reference to the monolingual norms of "native-speakers", the reason for doing so is "because this term has become controversial since the CEFR was published" (Council of Europe 2018: 50). But the normative construct of the native-speaker has nevertheless been retained. In spite of the claim that "absolute statements have been adjusted", at the highest C2 grade of proficiency we find the descriptor "can recognize a wide range of idiomatic expressions and colloquialisms", which of course are distinctive of the language usage of native-speaking communities.

The can-do descriptors in the frame of reference may be intended to give credit to different linguistic abilities and put a positive spin on what would traditionally be negatively assessed as failure but they are nevertheless normative and prescriptive grades of proficiency in a particular language, calibrated from A1 to C2, with what is conceived of as degrees of native speaker proficiency. In this respect, it would seem that CEFR, for all its apparent innovation, is essentially based on the traditional assumption that the objective of foreign language teaching is to get learners to be maximally bilingual. The ideal speaker/listener who knows its language perfectly is still with us.

Most learners of course, not surprisingly, fall well short of this objective and defining success in relation to it results in a high degree of educational failure. I would argue that instead of persisting in this attempt to get learners to acquire competence in another language we should focus on the use of language in the communicative process itself, on getting learners to be not bilingually competent but lingually capable in using language pragmatically as a resource.

And here we might indeed consider Hymes' feature of the actually performed but instead of defining this in reference to native speaker performance, look at the performance of non-natives and how they manage to communicate – in the case of English, for example, in the use of English as a lingua franca, or ELF, contexts of interaction provide abundant evidence of lingual capability. ELF users' language is appropriate but with respect to contexts and purposes other than those of monolingual native speakers. And in making their language appropriate they draw mainly, though not exclusively, on the code of English as a resource. They thereby relate the appropriate to the possible, but the possible is not now to be defined in terms of established encodings, as it is in the Hymes' scheme – encodings that represent the standard language – but as encoding possibilities inherent in the code itself, a potential for meaning making that has not hitherto been realized – what I refer to as the virtual language (see Section 1).

I would argue then that the pedagogic objective in foreign language teaching should, realistically and relevantly, not be the bilingual acquisition of another language per se but the development of a capability for lingual communication in general. For such an objective, as far as English is concerned, the relevant model is not the monolingual native speaker but the ELF user. But although I have English in mind, the example of ELF is, I would argue, relevant to all foreign language teaching. Whatever the foreign is or second language is, what matters is not how far the learning of them makes learners maximally bilingually competent but how learners can make use of them to develop lingual capability.

What implications would such an objective have for what goes on in the classroom? To begin with, we would need to abandon the idea, also deeply ingrained, that foreign language teaching must focus exclusively on the foreign language and that any appearance of the learners' own familiar language is necessarily intrusive and disruptive of the learning process and should be suppressed. So the language is taught monolingually as a quite distinct and different set of formal rules and conventions of usage from those which learners have previously experienced. This dissociation has the obvious effect of making the foreign language more foreign. But of course the previous experience of learners cannot be suppressed – if it were, no learning would take place at all. For although the teaching is monolingual the learning process is not: learners will quite naturally draw on their own experience and relate the foreign language to the language that is familiar to them. Learning another language is bound to be a bilingual experience. When the inevitable presence of the learners' own language makes an overt appearance, it is negatively assessed as error: evidence of a learning failure and although it might be tactically expedient to be tolerant of such errors at times, they are still conceived of as errors that need to be eventually corrected. But although such nonconformities are seen as evidence of failure if the acquisition of bilingual competence is the objective, if the development of lingual capability is the objective, they are, on the contrary, evidence of success. For they show that learners are doing just what we would want them to do and should be encouraged to do: they are recognizing aspects of the foreign language as different realizations of language in general, as the continuation of previous experience, exercising their communicative capability to extend their repertoire of linguistic resource. So teaching that focuses exclusively on the foreign language as something separate and distinct, closed off from the learners' own experience of language, has the effect of inhibiting the learning process, and creating problems of the teacher's own making.

The argument for this reconceptualization of language pedagogy is that because it is consistent with the pragmatics of actual lingual communication it is in accord with, and not in conflict with, the natural disposition of learners. Furthermore, it provides an investment for further learning. For a lingual capability enables learners to make use of any subsequent linguistic experience to extend the repertoire of their resources to meet the demands of new contexts and purposes. If these contexts and purposes call for a closer approximation to "maximal" competence, then the learners as users will approximate because it is communicatively appropriate to do so and not otherwise. Bilingual competence of whatever degree – partial, minimal or maximal – is only achieved through the exercise of lingual capability.

My argument in this chapter is that the way language is taught should be consistent with the way *language* is used and not in conformity to how *a particular language* is used . And this means focusing attention on the communicative process itself and dissociating it from how it is realized in particular languages. Thus instead of persisting in attempts to teach learners to be bilingually competent in one or more language we need to develop in them a capability for use, an investment in what is currently referred to as "transferable skills" which, consequently, enables them to extend their lingual repertoire, subsequently, as and when occasion requires them to do so in the future. To put it another way, instead of trying to teach people how to be bilingually competent in a particular language, better to get them to learn how to extend their more general lingual capability. In a way, this is simply a foreign language pedagogy version of the old Chinese adage:

> Give a man a fish and you feed him for a day. Teach a man to fish and you feed him for a lifetime.

19 Competence and capability: rethinking the subject English

What do teachers of English do? They teach English, of course. Other teachers teach history, or geography or physics and they teach English. That is their subject. How they teach it may differ in all kinds of ways, and there is plenty of diverse opinion about the best way, but what they teach seems to be straightforward enough, and not a matter of dispute. In this chapter, I want to suggest that, on the contrary, there is a problem about what English is taught, and that this problem is at the very heart of TEFL – in Asia and everywhere else.

The English teacher's subject is English, and, in another sense of the word, English is also the subject of this chapter. To begin with a simple question, what do we mean by English? The question is simple, but the answer is not because English can obviously mean different things for different people. For people in native speaking communities in Britain, in the United States, in Australia, English is what they use quite naturally for communication in the continuity of daily life. It is an *insider* language, a familiar and essential part of their everyday social reality. For learners of English in classrooms it is an *outsider* language. It is not familiar, it is foreign. It is not part of the contextual continuities of their everyday social life. Generally speaking, it does not occur naturally but has to be *made* to occur by teaching. It is divided into discontinuous events called lessons that are fitted into the school curriculum between other subject lessons according to administrative convenience – once on Monday afternoon, perhaps, between history and physics, once on Wednesday, twice on Thursday.

So on the face of it, it is obvious that what English means for its native speaker users is quite different from what it means for its non-native speaking learners. There are two realities here, and the central pedagogic problem that teachers have to contend with, and have always had to contend with, is how these two realities can be related to and reconciled with each other. So this is the problem I want to explore. I make no claim that I can resolve it. My purpose is to raise awareness of the issues that I think crucially need to be taken into account in dealing with it. It is often said that teachers need to be reflective practitioners. All I want to do is to raise questions about the subject they teach that they might reflect on, or, as some people might say, reflect about.

The first thing I think it is worth reflecting about is the orthodox taken-for-granted assumption that it is English as a first or native language (ENL) that

---

Note: Published in the 2014. *Journal of Asia TEFL* 11 (4). Originally a plenary presentation at the 12 TEFL Conference, Manila, October 2013.

should be the objective for learners to achieve. The E of ENL is essentially the same as the E of the subject: English as a foreign language (EFL) or English to speakers of other languages (ESOL). It is ENL that is recommended as the E to be taught and tested as a subject.

So what is this ENL? We can identify three ways of describing it

1. **ENL = Encoded forms.**
    ENL is the English that has been codified as the standard language. Standard English – the English that has been described in authorized works of reference: The *Oxford Advanced Learners Dictionary*, The *Longman Grammar of Spoken and Written English* and so on. These provide norms of correctness for learners to conform to. Note that therefore learners are required to do what most native speakers do not do. Standard English is what grammarians and dictionary makers describe not what most NSs actually use – it is an idealization, an abstraction. But according to orthodox pedagogic thinking, if learners are to be linguistically competent, their English has to be accurate, they have to conform to the Standard, their English has to be correct: competence = conformity = correctness.

2. **ENL = communicative functions.**
    With the so-called structural approach, the E of the subject is the encoded language, the forms of the standard language and their encoded semantic meaning. With the communicative approach comes a change of subject. Now the focus is on how these forms are put to communicative use: their pragmatic function. The objective now is *communicative competence*. But again this is assumed to be the native speaker's communicative competence. Learners are induced to learn how native speaker communities use their language as appropriate to *their* social contexts – *their* acts of communication – how *they*, the native speakers, express greetings, apologies, agreements, disagreements, promises and so on. Learners are taught how to communicate, but only how to communicate like native speakers and their communication is required not only to be appropriate in reference to pragmatic convention but also correct in reference to the linguistic rules of the standard language. They have to communicate *on* NS terms and *in* NS terms. It is not enough for them to use their English resources to get their meaning across in pragmatically effective ways: they have to use their English accurately as well. Communicative function has to correspond with correct linguistic form.

    In the currently favoured version of this approach, task-based language teaching – TBLT, the activities that learners are taught to engage in are said to focus primarily on meaning rather than form but the meanings that they express still have to conform to norms of correctness and conventional native speaker usage. It is not enough for learners to achieve a communicatively successful outcome on their own terms; the outcome has to match up to native speaker standards. So there is not really a primary focus on meaning as such but on form – the approved native speaker form that the meaning takes. And now a third way of thinking of ENL.

3. **ENL = authentic usage.**
   In recent years there has appeared a third way of thinking of ENL which represents it in terms not of native speaker competence but of native speaker performance. With the advent of the computer, corpus linguistics is now able to reveal in detail patterns of NS usage – idiomatic patterns of linguistic forms that NSs have actually produced. This, it is said, represents real or authentic English usage. So since the objective of learning is to acquire the actual linguistic behaviour of NSs, then learners should, it is argued, be required to conform to the norm of these patterns of usage as well. The teaching objective now is to get learners to acquire not only the correct linguistic forms of standard English, and not only the conventional communicative functions that these forms can be used to express but also the actual idiomatic wordings that native speakers produce as revealed by a corpus. And so we get the corpus-based *Collins COBUILD dictionary* which claims to help learners with "real" English, and corpus-based *Cambridge Grammar of English* which carries on its cover a "real English guarantee".

So what is usually recommended as the English that teachers should teach as a subject is the English that is represented by standard encoded forms, by its communicative functions and its authentic performance in native speaker contexts of use. It is the English that native speakers know and use – *their* competence, *their* performance, *their* conventions of usage. EFL = ENL. This is the English to be taught and the English that learners are required to conform to. If they do not conform they are wrong. And there are plenty of books around that will tell them so. To take one example, at the beginning of Michael Swan's authoritative reference book *Practical English Usage* (Swan 2005), there are a number of pages with the heading printed in red – red for danger – *Don't Say it! 130 common mistakes*. Mistakes like:

It's often raining here
It can rain this evening
I gave to her my address
Please explain me what you want
I object to tell them my age
No doubt the world is getting warmer

The number of the unemployed is going up
I have much money

Don't say it! But learners do say it – and keep on saying it in spite of being told not to. Although it is these norms of native speaker English that are taught, it is not the English that is learned. As every teacher knows, learners stubbornly refuse to do what they are told and persistently fail to conform to these norms of correctness and conventional usage. English that is *taught* as a foreign language, ETFL, is not the same as English that is *learned* as a foreign language ELFL.

ETFL≠ELFL

Teachers set up ENL as the target language and try to help learners to hit the target but most of them miss it. All kinds of new methods and approaches have been proposed over the years to improve the learners' aim – the structural approach, the natural approach, communicative language teaching, TBLT, content and language integrated learning, all trying, and trying in vain, to get learners to conform to ENL norms and achieve NS competence.

So if learners do not learn ENL, why do we keep on trying to teach it? One answer is that only if you conform to these norms can you use the language effectively as communication. But none of these things that learners are told they must not say actually poses any problem of communication. And millions of people using English as an international means of communication, as a global lingua franca, produce "mistakes" of this kind and yet achieve communication appropriate to their purposes. We find such non-conformities in English usage all over the world – face-to-face exchanges, interactions over the internet, in business transactions, diplomatic negotiations and international conferences. When, for example, you listen to presentations in international conferences, you will hear plenty of these non-conformities, these so-called mistakes. So teachers themselves will be making the same kind of "mistakes" that they keep on telling their students not to make. This is not a criticism – on the contrary, it is simply a recognition that this is what English users quite naturally do in the real world. The use of English as a lingua franca – ELF – often, indeed usually, does not at all correspond with the norms of ENL. The globalized use of English as a lingua franca represents a different reality – a reality very different from that of the native speaker.

Let me give you one example. Here is Ban Ki-Moon, the Secretary General of the United Nations replying to a question in an interview about globalization

> ... the world is going through global communication and globalizations. The China is number 2 economic power in the world ... Combined economic power I think they can

play greater role than they have been doing now. While economic situation in Europe and other places are going down there is again expectation that the countries in this region can play better and greater role in the global situation ...

Ban Ki-Moon obviously has not acquired NS competence – or at least if he has, he does not act upon it. What he says is full of the kind of mistakes that teachers are told they must correct. *Globalization* is a non-countable noun that cannot be made into a plural. Don't say *globalizations*. Don't leave articles out of noun phrases: don't say *The China is number 2*, say *China is the number 2*. Don't say *play greater role*, say *play a greater role* and so on.

And it is not only that what Ban Ki-Moon says is ungrammatical and so does not conform to the norm of correctness. It does not conform to the norm of NS idiomatic usage either. To a NS ear, for example, there are oddities of phrase here. The world is *going through global communication*? The world is *experiencing, or, going through a process* of global communication would be more idiomatically normal. The economic situation in Europe is *going down* – no, that does not sound right. It should be something like the economic situation is *deteriorating*. And so we could correct Ban Ki-Moon's ELF and make it like ENL. This, we might say, is what he should have said:

> ... the world is going through a process of globalization and global communication. China is the number 2 economic power in the world ... I think that combined economic power can play a greater role than it has been doing up to now. While the economic situation in Europe and other places is deteriorating there is again an expectation that the countries in this region can play a better and greater role in global affairs.

We might suggest that the Director General of the United Nations should take English lessons to make him more competent, or at least to improve his performance, and while we are at it we might do some remedial work on his pronunciation as well, which also falls well short of NS standards. In this way we might hope to make his English more like that of a native speaker from Britain, or the United States, or Australia.

But why should he be required to use English like an Englishman, or American or Australian. He is a Korean, so why should he not be a Korean in English. Why should he deny his identity and assume the identity of somebody else? Ban Ki-Moon's English can be said to be incompetent in that it does not conform to NS norms, but this does not make him incapable of communicating. On the contrary, the interviewer has no problem understanding what he has to say – she does not say, *excuse me Secretary General, I think what you want to say is Countries in this region can play **a** better and greater role ... the economic situation is not are, deteriorating, not going down*. It is obvious that though Ban Ki-Moon's performance does not measure up to NS *competence*, it nevertheless shows him to have acquired considerable communicative *capability*. He would not otherwise be able to do his job, and there is no other job I can think of that makes such challenging demands on the use of English as a communicative resource. You may call his English defective in form, but it is nevertheless effective in function.

So where does his communicative capability come from? Like most other users of ELF, Ban Ki-Moon has been taught English at school. According to Wikipedia, he was "a star student, particularly in the English language", and furthermore he has a Master's degree from Harvard. But the English that he puts to use so effectively is not ENL – the native speaker English he has presumably been *taught* as a foreign language, it is not E*T*FL. What he puts to use is English as a lingua franca, ELF, which corresponds more closely to the English he has *learned* as a foreign language, ELFL. So ELFL can be said to contain ELF within it: *ELFL*.

What Ban Ki-Moon has done is what countless numbers of other users of English as a lingua franca have done, namely to subvert what they have been taught as competence so as to convert it into capability (for further discussion on the concept of capability see Widdowson 2003). Of course, some learners succeed in subverting and converting better than others. After all, to do so means to resist all the institutional pressures on them to conform, and there are penalties for not conforming. Non-conformity is associated with failure. So the development of ELF capability is inhibited by the teaching of ENL competence.

So why is it, we need to ask, that in spite of all these pressures, in spite of all the course books and reference books of the kind that you will find on display in the publishers exhibits at conferences, in spite of all the different approaches and techniques that teachers are recommended to follow, learners still do not learn what they are taught? The answer I suggest is not that we have not yet found the way to get them to hit the target but that we getting them to aim at the wrong target and this is because these norms of correctness and NS usage represent a reality that learners cannot engage with because it is radically different from their own.

To go back to the norm of authentic usage as revealed by corpora, for example, that learners are recommended to conform to. As one of its advocates puts it: "The language of the corpus is, above all, real, and what is it that all language learners want, other than 'real' contact with the target language?" (McCarthy 2001: 128). But how "real" can the learners' contact with actually performed "target language" really be? How, for example, would they make contact with the following sample taken from a corpus that McCarthy himself has been involved in assembling: a transcript of an authentic NS conversation.

S1. Now I think you'd better start the rice
S2. Yeah ... what you got there?
(4 seconds pause)
S2. Will it all fit in the one?
S1. No you'll have to do two separate ones
S.3 Right ... what next?
(17 seconds pause)
S.3 Foreign body in there
S.2 It's the raisins   (Carter and McCarthy 1997)

So what kind of contact would learners of English make with this text? In the first place, there are some things that would make it difficult for any reader, let alone learners, to connect with the text at all. "Will it all fit in the one? Will all *what* fit in the one *what*?" What are these people actually referring to? "Foreign body in there". In *where*? And what's all this about a foreign body. These difficulties arise because what we have here is a text without the context that would make it real for the participants in this interaction. The insider participants in this conversation are in the know about the context and can connect up with it. Outsiders like us are not in the know and cannot make the connection.

So contact with "real" language does not make it real for you unless you can replicate the context which gave it reality in the first place. If, as a learner, you are not in the know about what is going on, if you cannot *realize* what these people are referring to with these fragments of language, and how they are using them to relate to each other and to achieve their communicative purposes, then the fragments simply become a collection of linguistic forms – an interrogative sentence here, a noun phrase there. All you can do is focus on the forms isolated from their communicative function. What is real for these NS users is not at all real for NNS learners (for further discussion see Widdowson 2003, 2012).

And it is how learners engage with English to make it real for themselves that is crucial. So how would they do this? They can only do it, I suggest, by relating the language to their own reality rather than trying to relate it to somebody else's. Now a key part of that reality is the learners' experience of their own language. This is generally suppressed in E*T*FL but is active in E*L*FL because learners will quite naturally draw on this experience in their processing of this other language. They know how their own language works and will be naturally inclined to suppose that English works in the same kind of way – that what matters about linguistic form is how it gets adapted to serve a communicative function, that some parts of language carry more communicative weight than others, that many features of correctness are communicatively redundant and only serve as conventional markers of social identity in a particular community and have no real significance elsewhere. So something tells them – their own experience of language tells them – that correctness is not always needed for effective communication: that they can get by without it. Most of the so-called mistakes that are so persistent and which teachers spend so much time trying to eradicate have little if any communicative value – this is why learners keep on making them. They see no point in correction.

And we need to note that some of these so-called mistakes show that learners are capable of making creative use of the unused potential of English, and so are evidence of learning beyond conformity For example, the *Cambridge Grammar of English* claims to be a comprehensive guide to contemporary English: as I mentioned earlier, it carries on its cover a "Real English guarantee". It tells us, for example, that the expression *discuss about* is wrong. "*About* is not used with the verb *discuss*" (Carter and McCarthy 2006: 23). But learners *do* say "discuss about" as do many users of English as a lingua franca. So why do they do it? If you can quite "correctly" have a *discussion about* something and you can *think about* something, and *talk about* something, so *discuss about* would seem entirely regular. And this is not an isolated example: if, for example, you can, correctly, *complain about* something, why should *explain about* something be wrong? The same applies to *reflect about*. The *Oxford Advanced Learner's Dictionary* will tell you that that you can reflect *on* something and reflect *upon* something but there is no mention of reflect *about*, so learners, deferring to this authority, will assume it is incorrect. Don't say it! But learners keep on saying it. And not just learners – I have said "reflect about" myself in this chapter. And the expression "discuss about" is of frequent occurrence in the use of English as a lingua franca (see Seidlhofer 2011).

The point is that it is entirely natural to exploit the regularity within English in this way. What both learners and users are doing when they produce these forms is making strategic use of an existing encoding rule. And there is no negative effect on communication.

ELF users like Ban Ki-Moon, even if they know what the NS norms are, do not act upon their knowledge if in their contexts of use and for their purposes they are quite capable of making effective use of their linguistic resources without conforming to these norms. And this exploitation of the potential of the language is a continuing process. If and when contexts and purposes arise which do require a closer conformity to NS norms, then this capability for use will enable ELF users quite naturally to adjust their language accordingly. A capability for language use is also a capability for further language learning.

Linguistic forms serve communicative functions. As Halliday puts it: "The particular form taken by the grammatical systems of language is closely related to the social and personal needs that language is required to serve" (Halliday 1970: 142).

It follows from this that as the social and personal needs of users of English worldwide change, so the form of the language will naturally change accordingly.

NS competence is necessarily tied in with the contexts of use and the communicative purposes of NS communities, so it must also follow that if English is used by other people in different contexts and for different purposes, this competence no longer corresponds with their social and personal needs.

I began this chapter by raising the question of *what* teachers of English teach, and this, I have argued, leads us to think about *who* they are teaching it to. They are inter-dependently related, and how the subject "English" is conceived crucially depends on how this relationship is defined. The established way of thinking about the subject has been to give primacy to the *what* as the dominant factor in the relationship, with the *who* in a subordinate dependent role. What I have suggested is that this dependency should be reversed. One way of putting this is by reference to the meaning of the verb "to teach". Grammatically it can take two objects, separately or combined. Separately we can either have:

*Teachers teach **something**: Physics, History, English.*
Or:
*Teachers teach **somebody**: students/pupils.*

And these sentences can be grammatically combined in two different ways. One way:

*Teachers teach **English** to **students**.*

Here English is the direct object and is, one might say, given primacy. This I suggest is how the teaching of English is generally conceived with the primary focus on what is to be taught, what, defined in NS terms, is to be unilaterally transmitted to students: take it or leave it. But another combination is possible:

*Teachers teach **students English**.*

Here the focus is on the students. The dependencies, one might say, are reversed: instead of thinking first of the language to be taught and making students adapt to it, you think of the students first and make the language adapt to them. Another way of putting this is by reference to the acronym *TESOL*. This, as the name of a well- known association, stands for Teachers of English *to* Speakers of Other Languages. This little preposition, *to*, implies the very order of priority that I am arguing should be reversed: it is English *for* Speakers of Other Languages that needs to be taught: not an established and approved native speaker language which is unilaterally imposed but language they can naturally engage with as a communicative resource and that they can associate with their "other" languages, and so relates to their reality and to their requirements. Even such a small and seemingly trivial change of preposition might, by exploring its possible implications, lead to the kind of rethinking about the subject I have been arguing for.

To summarize what I have been saying, the orthodox assumption, or received wisdom of TEFL – in Asia and everywhere else – is that the English to be taught is English as a native language: ENL. The objective is to get learners to conform to norms of correctness and usage and so achieve NS competence. But this English that is *taught* as a foreign language ETFL is not what is actually *learned* as a foreign language ELFL. In spite of all kinds of expert recommendations about how to get learners to conform and achieve this competence in the so-called target language, most learners do not do so. Where ELFL does not match up with ETFL it is considered a failure. Little if any credit is given to ELFL since most assessment is based on what is taught not on what is learned.

The reason why learners do not conform, I suggested, is because ENL represents a reality that they cannot engage with because it is radically different from theirs. They will naturally seek to relate English the foreign language to the familiar experience of their own language and that this leads them instinctively to focus on those aspects of English that have most value as a communicative resource. Consequently, what is learned can be put to effective use when learners become users of English as a lingua franca. Their incompetence does not make them incapable as communicators. They have clearly learned a strategic capability for using the linguistic resources of English adapting them as appropriate to the various contexts and for the various purposes of global communication.

Earlier, I referred to two realities. The reality of ENL as an insider language and the reality of EFL as an outsider language and that the essential problem of TEFL as a subject was how these two realities could be related. My general point is that if we continue to base the subject TEFL on ENL then the realities will always be unrelated and cannot be reconciled. ELFL will always be at odds with ETFL and the result will always be, in varying degrees, a pedagogy of failure. But we can rethink the subject as it has been traditionally defined. And we can do this by taking account of a third reality that I talked about. This is the reality of English as a lingua franca, English as used across Asian and all other contexts in our globalized world, and which reveals quite clearly how users of the language are capable of effective communication without conforming to the norms of ENL. This capability, I have argued, has its origins in the learning of English as a foreign language – that *ELF* and *ELFL* are closely related. English now becomes more like an insider language – its features made less foreign and more familiar, related more closely to the learners' own reality. There has been much talk about learner autonomy, about teachers allowing learners to take the initiative. This way of thinking of the subject, which gives primacy to *who* rather that *what* is to be taught, would be a way of putting such ideas into practice.

So one way of rethinking our subject is to take our bearings not from ENL but from ELF, and to abandon the objective of NS competence in favour of encouraging and supporting the natural development in learners of communicative capability. TEFL would then not be a matter of teaching learners how to correctly accumulate quantities of language but essentially how to engage in the process of what has been called languaging (e.g., Swain 2006). – the strategic use of the resources of English to express themselves and communicate with others (for further discussion see Seidlhofer 2011). Such rethinking of course poses considerable challenges. But it also offers opportunities to make TEFL in Asia, and elsewhere, more effective and realistic as a subject, more real for learners, and more attuned to the changed role of English in a world which "is going through global communication and globalizations", to quote the words of a user of English as a lingua franca, and surely a role-model for any learner of English, the Secretary General of the United Nations, Ban Ki-Moon. I cannot claim to speak with anything like the same authority. But I hope I have said something in this chapter that teachers of English will feel challenges them not only to *think about* but also to *reflect about*, not only to *talk about*, but also to *discuss about* among themselves as professional practitioners critically concerned with the subject they teach.

20 Reversions

A modest proposal for the adoption of a radically innovative corpus-based approach to the teaching of poetry in English for students who have the misfortune not to be native speakers of that language.[1]

As many teachers will attest, poetry poses a pedagogic problem. Getting students to understand the meaning of poems in their own language is difficult enough, but it becomes well-nigh impossible when the poems are in a foreign language. One way of coping with the problem is to follow established and venerable tradition by providing students with ready-made critical opinion about poems so as to protect them from the traumatic experience of grappling with the original texts for themselves. Although there has been some criticism of this approach on the dubious grounds that students should be allowed some opportunity for independent response, little in the way of an acceptable alternative has been proposed. There have, it is true, been some misguided attempts, notably by the proponents of so-called stylistics, to engage students with the actual language of literary texts. These attempts, however, have generally proved disastrous in that they encourage an indulgence in interpretations which do not correspond with those legitimately sanctioned by expert critical judgement.

The central problem about poetry is that it tends to be couched in abstruse language which is beyond the limited competence of students to grasp, so that its meaning is only accessible to literary scholars expert in the exegesis of obscure text. For students who are unfortunate enough not to be native speakers, there is in addition the particular difficulty that the language in which poems are couched not infrequently fails to conform to the conventions of current usage, either because the poems are outdated or the poets perverse, or both. Whatever the reason for this non-conformity, it has the unfortunate consequence that such students are presented with texts that they are led to believe are of superlative linguistic achievement, but which are extremely misleading as models for their own language use. We are therefore confronted with the double dilemma that students are not only incapable of understanding the language of poetry, but have to be protected from it anyway as entirely unsuitable input for their own learning.

One way of resolving this dilemma is to abandon the teaching of poetry altogether, especially when it is in a foreign language. This course of action has

---

[1] (co-written with Barbara Seidlhofer) Published in Fill, A., G. Marko, D. Newby & Hermine Penz (eds.). 2006. *Linguists (don't) only talk about it. Essays in honour of Bernhard Kettemann.* Tübingen: Stauffenburg.

https://doi.org/10.1515/9783110619669-026

much to commend it. Poetry, after all, is of little practical use to anybody and has no commercial value. It makes no contribution whatever to economic development, which, in this enlightened age, is acknowledged to be the prime purpose of education to promote. The abolition of poetry would have the advantage of providing more time for the teaching of more profitable and cost-effective uses of language for specific purposes like animal husbandry, business management computer programming and the like.

However, it has to be conceded, if reluctantly, that a policy which advocated such a measure, though based on sound reasoning and in accordance with current educational principles, would meet a good deal of resistance from scholars of conservative cast of mind, many of whom are still in entrenched positions of considerable influence in the academic world. That being so, to seek to impose such a policy, at least directly, would be, to say the least, imprudent. There is, however, an alternative way of resolving the dilemma we have described, and this is the purpose of our chapter to propose, taking as a representative case, the teaching of English poetry to speakers of other languages.[2]

Our proposal is that the poetic texts in English that have been identified as educationally desirable on cultural or aesthetic grounds should be recast into alternative versions in which the language would not only be simpler to process, but would be in closer accord with current usage. These versions would therefore resolve the double dilemma referred to earlier by serving the dual function of making the comprehension of poems much easier while at the same time providing students with a reliable model for their own idiomatic use of the language. It is with this second function particularly in mind that we base these rewritten versions, or *reversions* as we shall henceforth call them, on the findings of corpus linguistics, adhering as we do to the well-established pedagogic principle that all learners of English should be required to conform as closely as possible to the norms of authentic native speaker usage that corpus descriptions now reveal with such unerring precision. The inestimable value of such descriptions is that they provide the authority for correcting deviation and for bringing the language of poetry in line with proper English.

Let us consider a typical example of the kind of problem that students encounter. Take Wordsworth's celebrated poem, *Daffodils*, a widely anthologized work which many a foreign student has had the misfortune of being subjected to. Its first verse runs as follows:

---

[2] Our particular concern is with poetry in English and with the pedagogy of English as a foreign or other language, but the principles and procedures we propose would be equally applicable, we would claim, whatever language is involved.

> *I wandered lonely as a cloud*
> *   That floats on high o'er vales and hills,*
> *When all at once I saw a crowd,*
> *   A host, of golden daffodils;*
> *Beside the lake, beneath the trees,*
> *Fluttering and dancing in the breeze.*

The phrase *lonely as a cloud* presents us with our first difficulty. Students, we must assume, will have been taught, in accordance with enlightened current thinking, how essential it is for them to learn formulaic phrases if they have any hope in achieving competence in English – phrases like *quiet as a mouse, fresh as a daisy, deaf as a post, sick as a parrot* and so on. They might reasonably suppose that here is another instance, incorporate the phrase into their active vocabulary, and in their laudable desire to sound like native speakers, use it with uninhibited abandon as if it were common and unmarked usage. One can readily imagine the following exchange:

A (student aspiring to NS usage): *So there I was in the middle of the dance floor on my own, feeling lonely as a cloud . . .*
B (real NS): (laughs) *Lonely as a what?*

Nothing is more likely to undermine the already precarious confidence and motivation of students than this kind of ridicule. But the difficulty that this phrase is likely to create is easily resolved by revising this first line to read:

> *I wandered like a lonely cloud*

In the second line, the word *o'er*, of course, needs to be corrected to *over* so as to be in conformity with current usage. The lexical item *vale* is another candidate for replacement. On corpus evidence, it is of very low frequency in contemporary usage, so low indeed that it is not included at all in Leech et al.'s invaluable register of word frequencies in English (Leech, Rayson, and Wilson 2001, which we will hitherto refer to as *the Leech register*) We obviously cannot run the risk of our students incorporating such a useless word into their linguistic competence. Fortunately, the word *valley* is available as a semantic equivalent. This is attested as occurring with a relatively high degree of frequency, being assigned three of the five black diamonds that mark frequency in the *COBUILD* dictionary.[3] The lexical

---

[3] Our reference is to the first edition of this admirable work, published in 1995. In a subsequent edition published in 2003, frequency bands have been unaccountably reduced from five to three. We might note in passing that such a reduction would seem to be pedagogically

item *float* in this line of the poem is marked in this dictionary as being in the same frequency band as *valley*, but this is misleading since we have it on the authority of the Leech register that in fact *float* occurs only half as often as *valley* in the British National Corpus. It is clearly a word of very little use. Luckily we can find an alternative and much more useful word to replace it, namely *pass*. This is awarded no less than five black diamonds in the *COBUILD* dictionary, and according to the Leech register actually occurs 10 times more often than *float* (204 vs. a mere 20 instances per million words). We are fortunate indeed to have such an extremely useful word available as a replacement. One might, to be sure, raise the somewhat pedantic objection that it lacks the semantic specificity of the word it replaces, leaving unspecified the nature of the movement concerned, but this can be readily inferred from its co-textual co-occurrence with the word *cloud*. One might reasonably suppose that language learners have some familiarity with clouds and so will know full well that clouds usually pass slowly as if floating and not at speed.

Corpus evidence is similarly invaluable in identifying the difficulty posed by the lexical item *crowd* in the third line. Here the problem is not that it is infrequent. On the contrary, the word even outscores *valley* in the frequency stakes (56 to 52 occurrences per million words according to the Leech register) and is assigned no less than four black diamonds in the *COBUILD* dictionary. So it is a highly desirable, if not indispensable, word for students to acquire. The problem here has to do with the abnormality of the collocational relations the word contracts in the poetic text. Consultation of a concordance will reveal that the lexical item *crowd* regularly collocates with words referring to human beings: *crowd of people, football crowd, crowd of well-wishers* and so on. Collocation with daffodils, or with flowers or indeed plants of any kind, is simply not attested. And a similar point can be made about *host* in the next line. On the hard and fast factual evidence provided by concordance lines, native speakers simply do not talk or write about crowds or hosts of flowers, daffodils or otherwise. It could be, of course (to sound a cautionary note), that native speakers used to do so in Wordsworth's time in his native Lake District, so that

---

misguided since in giving less information about the relative usefulness of words, the dictionary obviously gives less guidance to learners as to which words are worth learning and which are not. Given the capability of the computer to specify frequency with a high degree of exactitude, and the over-riding importance of frequency for determining what language is to be learned, one might have expected that the number of frequency bands would have been increased, not reduced, with more black diamonds not fewer. It is to be hoped that this aberration will be corrected in future editions of the dictionary, and that descriptive precision will be restored in the interests of pedagogic relevance.

here the poet is in fact faithfully reflecting the regional native idiom of his day. Whether or not this is the case is a matter for historical dialectologists to determine. Be that as it may, it is obvious that what our students need is proper standard contemporary English and should, as a matter of principle be discouraged at all costs from adopting the idiom of eighteenth century country folk from Cumbria – or any other non-standard idiom, if it comes to that, rustic or otherwise. So we need to replace *crowd* and *host* with some other more collocationally appropriate term. *Bunch*, of course, immediately springs to mind, and the concordance confirms the normality of the collocation. Unfortunately it will not serve the poetic purpose here since the word would normally be used to refer to a relatively small number of flowers cut and bound together with little scope for any fluttering or dancing. Wordsworth, we must presume, does not suddenly come upon a bunch or bouquet of flowers beside the lake, beneath the trees. In the case of this text, therefore, we might propose *a lot of*, or *a mass of* golden daffodils, perhaps as a suitable replacement.

Actually, the lexical item *daffodil* itself poses a problem. Being a word of very rare occurrence (it does not figure at all in the Leech register of frequencies) it is of negligible potential value for language learners (with the obvious exception, of course, of those on ESP[4] courses for horticulturists, florists or possibly undertakers). This contrasts markedly with the superordinate term *flower*, which occurs at the very satisfactory rate of 56 in every million words in the Leech register, and so suggests itself as an attractive alternative. However, given the title of the poem, dispensing with daffodils would be a somewhat drastic measure, and we have always to bear in mind our principle that reversions should not be such as to undermine the aesthetic essentials of the original poem.

We come to the last line of the verse. On corpus evidence, neither *dancing* nor *fluttering* normally collocate with *daffodils*, nor indeed with flowers of any kind, and on those grounds we might wish to replace both expressions. Against this, with the lexical item *dance* there is the compensating factor that it is of relatively high frequency (four black diamonds in the *COBUILD* dictionary, and a reasonably respectable ratio of 37 per million words in the Leech register) and so it is clearly a useful word to retain. *Flutter,* on the other hand, is a sadly infrequent item: like *daffodil* it does not appear in the Leech register at all. It is not clear either that the sense of the poem actually requires both *dancing* and

---

[4] English for Specific Purposes. It will, of course, be more generally the case that on such courses there are likely to be words whose usefulness cannot be specified by general measures of frequency. The correspondence between frequency and usefulness depends on the entirely reasonable assumption that on the whole the purposes for which native speakers use their language are all much the same.

fluttering. The lexical item *dance* appears again in later verses of the poem (three times in fact), so it would seem that the poet attaches some particular significance to it, and again we might invoke aesthetic criteria for its retention. *Flutter,* on the other hand, makes no further appearance and really adds little if anything by way of substantive meaning to the poem, so it seems reasonable to reduce redundancy and eliminate it altogether.

With regard to redundancy, we might add that there is another expression in the poem that seems surplus to requirement, namely *on high* in line two. Where, after all, would the clouds float or pass over hills and valleys except on high. Furthermore, though *high* is itself extremely frequent, the phrase *on high* is of rare and restricted occurrence in contemporary English usage. Like *lonely as a cloud*, discussed earlier, though for slightly different reasons, it is decidedly not an expression we would wish our students to assimilate into their productive vocabulary. There are, then, good grounds for excising *on high* from the text. The criterion of frequency might also lead us to replace *all at once* with the commoner, and therefore more useful, expression *suddenly*.

With these various considerations in mind, and putting the proposed changes into place, we are now in a position to render the original as follows:

> I wandered like a lonely cloud that passes over valleys and hills and suddenly I saw a large mass of golden flowers beside the lake and beneath the trees, daffodils dancing in the breeze.

This, we venture to suggest, is a reformulation which captures the basic content of the original verse, makes its meaning more directly accessible and at the same provides an admirable model for the students' own language learning. But it is in prose, of course, and the purpose of our approach is not to reduce poems to prosaic form, but on the contrary to preserve their aesthetic integrity as poems while making them more accessible and relevant to the language-learning process. We need now therefore to move from revision to reversion, to recast the prose into verse by adding those features of rhyme and metrical regularity which are the essential *sine qua non* of poetry. These prosodic exigencies call for some minor adjustments to our prose version. These we have affected by the simply expedient of pluralizing the noun "mass" and replacing the verb "saw" with the phrase "caught my eye". In both cases, these adjustments serve the aesthetic purpose of maintaining the rhyme scheme while retaining their essential meaning. The latter, we venture to suggest, is particularly apt since it contributes not only to the aesthetic but to the pedagogic value of the poem in that it provides a very useful idiomatic expression which learners can add to their productive repertoire. The reversion process yields the following poetic text:

> *Like a lonely cloud that passes*
> *   Over hills and valleys, I*
> *Wandered, when suddenly large masses*
> *   Of golden flowers caught my eye*
> *Beside the lake, beneath the trees –*
> *Daffodils dancing in the breeze.*

We can now proceed to the next verse of the poem. The original runs as follows:

> *Continuous as the stars that shine*
> *   And twinkle on the milky way,*
> *They stretched in never-ending line*
> *   Along the margin of a bay:*
> *Ten thousand saw I at a glance,*
> *Tossing their heads in sprightly dance.*

A number of changes might be proposed here to bring the language in line with current conventions of English usage and make it less misleading for learners. Line 5 sets an unfortunate example for the aspiring student in that it reverses the normal subject/verb word order. This can be easily corrected to read:

> I saw ten thousand at a glance.

One might note in passing that it seems particularly perverse of the poet to indulge in such a grammatical aberration in the original line, since its correction has no affect whatever on the prosodic features of metre and rhyme. It might be suggested that the deviant grammar serves to disguise something else that is odd about this line. How, one might reasonably ask, can a glance enable the poet to be so precise about how many daffodils he saw, particularly since they were all fluttering and dancing about in the breeze? At a glance, he would no doubt see a lot of them, masses, even, as he tells us in the first verse, a host or crowd, but *ten thousand*? Hardly. And anyway, we are told earlier in this verse that the flowers were in continuous, never-ending line and so essentially infinite in number. Clearly the language is being used here in a very loose manner which we would certainly not want our students to emulate.

There are lexical difficulties in this verse as well. One of them is *milky way*, which calls for elimination on the grounds of low frequency and very limited usefulness. Another is *sprightly*. Here the difficulty is not only that it is an infrequent word (non-existent in fact as far as the Leech register is concerned) and so not really worth knowing, but that the collocational relations it contracts in its normal if infrequent, occurrence are inconsistent with its use in this context. A concordance reveals that on the rare occasions when the word occurs at all, *sprightly* is associated with old age. Thus in the most recent edition of the

Longman Dictionary of Contemporary English (corpus-based, of course) the entry for the word reads as follows:

> Sprightly adj *an old person who is sprightly is still active and full of energy.*

But in the poem, this geriatric association is quite out of place. There is no indication that what Wordsworth sees is a host of *old* daffodils, faded and wilting. On the contrary, we would venture to suggest, the impression the reader gets is of flowers in full bloom and in the flush of youth. Here is source of considerable confusion for the hapless student: the meaning of the word in the poem would seem to contradict the dictionary on whose authority he or she depends for learning proper English. We can remove this confusion easily enough by replacing *sprightly* with *lively*, which has the additional advantage of being a more frequent word anyway (it could hardly be less, since as we have noted *sprightly* is completely absent from the Leech register). Furthermore, as with our grammatical correction, the replacement involves no disruption of the prosodic regularity of the line in which it appears. So we might propose altering the last two lines of this verse to read:

> *I saw ten thousand at a glance,*
> *Nodding their heads in lively dance.*

This reversion does not, of course, remove the fundamental contradictions within the propositional content of this verse: the flowers being seen impressionistically at a glance as infinite and yet specified as an exact number. We need to get rid of the ten thousand and find a more general phrase, and one that fits into the metre of the line. *Large numbers* or perhaps *great masses* would do. But now we encounter a further difficulty. We have already been told in the first verse that the daffodils were present in great profusion, and that they were dancing, so these two lines tell us nothing new. Similarly, *along the margin of a bay* in line 3 is just another way of saying *beside the lake*. In fact, the only content that adds anything to what has been described in the first verse is the simile of the stars on the milky way, and even here *stretched in never-ending line* can be said to be just a gloss on *continuous*. Again, the lexical item *twinkle* (which itself is so infrequent as to find no place in the Leech register) is a hyponym of *shine*, and so there is no need for both. There is clearly a good deal of redundancy here, and that being so rather than attempt to produce a reversion which would remove them, it seems more reasonable to dispense with the verse altogether.

This might seem, at first sight, to be a somewhat drastic step to take. But the kind of textual adjustment we are proposing here, and which has long been practised in the production of simplified versions of prose literature on similar pedagogic grounds, cannot preclude abridgement. There can indeed be no hard and fast distinction between simplification and abridgement: it is simply a matter of what degree of revision is required to make a particular text more accessible, and more appropriate as an exemplar of contemporary native speaker usage. And of course whatever changes are made must preserve the essential literary quality of the original. Hence our insistence on reversion beyond revision. In the present case, the cutting of the second verse of Wordsworth's poem does not compromise the integrity of the whole, but rather, we would claim, enhances it by the removal of needless verbiage which otherwise interferes with the thematic continuity of the poem.[5] For the third verse (now the second) follows naturally on from the first. It runs as follows:

The waves beside them danced; but they
　　Out-did the sparkling waves in glee:
A Poet could not but be gay
　　In such a jocund company:
I gazed – and gazed – but little thought
What wealth the show to me had brought:

There is an aesthetically pleasing continuity of patterning here (disrupted, we venture to suggest by the obtruding second verse of the original) in that the opening line here makes a direct anaphoric connection with the last line of the first verse, by means of both lexical repetition (*dancing/danced*) and pronominal reference (*them*):

Daffodils dancing in the breeze.
*The waves beside **them danced**, but **they** ...*

There is, however, a difficulty with the second pronominal *they* in this line, for it would normally be taken to refer to the immediately preceding noun phrase *the waves*, but the next line makes it clear that it actually refers back to the daffodils. This clumsiness of phrasing can be easily corrected by reformulating the text to read something like:

The sparkling waves beside them danced, but they did not outdo the flowers in glee.

There remains however the very considerable difficulty with the lexical item *glee*. Not only is the word highly infrequent (there is no record of it in the Leech register), but on the authority of no less than three current corpus-based

---

[5] It is perhaps not without significance that this verse did not actually appear in the poem as originally published in 1807 but was added later when the poem was republished in *Miscellaneous Poems*, 1815.

dictionaries of English (the *Collins COBUILD Advanced Learner's English Dictionary*, the *Longman Dictionary of Contemporary English* and the *Macmillan English Dictionary for Advanced Learners*) the word signifies a sense of happiness, pleasure or satisfaction *at somebody else's misfortune*. Thus informed, the student will naturally be led to suppose that the dancing of the daffodils is in some way maliciously motivated, occasioned by a kind of *Schadenfreude*. Although this might suggest an interesting underlying significance in the poem, hitherto unsuspected, it seems unlikely that such a sense is intended here. A replacement is urgently required: a less semantically marked word like *happiness*, perhaps, or better *joy*, which has the additional advantage of being of similar syllabic structure and so readily accommodated within the metre of the original line.

But there are other lexical problems lurking in this verse. The word *jocund* in line 4, for example, occurs so rarely as to be effectively obsolete (the British National Corpus records only two instances). Indeed of the three dictionaries mentioned earlier, only one of them (the *Macmillan*) troubles to acknowledge its existence at all. Here is a word of extreme uselessness and we would certainly want to avoid any risk of our students acquiring it. Fortunately there are more frequent and useful words available to replace it, namely *happy, cheerful, joyful*. The most striking example of an unwanted word in this verse, however, is obviously the lexical item *gay*. It is interesting to note that lexical replacement in this case is warranted also by aesthetic considerations, by the need to protect the poetic integrity of the original. The difficulty with *gay* is not that word is uncommon: on the contrary, it is assigned no less than four black diamonds in the *COBUILD* dictionary and in the Leech register scores a fairly respectable 12 instances per million words. The problem is, of course, that it has acquired a contemporary sense it did not have in Wordsworth's time and so at odds with that which, we must suppose, the poet was likely to intend. In consequence, the students are likely to assign an entirely inappropriate interpretation to the lines in which it occurs – an interpretation that could, with some students, occasion ribald and irreverent mirth, fatal to the aesthetic appreciation of the poem. *Gay* will clearly have to go. As a replacement one might propose *happy*, or *joyful*.

The rest of this verse can be dealt with more briskly. All that is required is a relatively slight adjustment to correct the irregularity of the word order in the last line so that it reads:

What wealth the show had brought to me.

Further modification might be deemed desirable in the penultimate line, where the rather unusual construction *(I) little thought* might be rendered by a more currently conventional idiomatic phrase like *I did not realize*, or *I could not know (at the time)*.

Bearing all these considerations in mind, we are now in a position to propose a rewording of the original verse:

> The sparkling waves beside them danced as well but they did not outdo the flowers in joy. A poet could not but be happy in such cheerful company. I gazed and gazed but I could not know at the time what wealth the show had brought to me.

But we must now restore the poetic aesthetic of the original by means of reversion. This necessarily involves further readjustment to the wording to meet the dictates of metre and rhyme which, as we have pointed out earlier, of course constitute the essential artistic character of poetic utterance. This must be done, however, without compromising the basic propositional content of the prose. The following is one possible reversion:

> *The waves beside them danced no less,*
>   *Though the flowers danced more joyfully.*
> *Any poet would feel happiness*
>   *In such a cheerful company.*
> *I gazed and gazed but could not know*
> *What wealth was brought me by that show.*

There is one more verse in Wordsworth's poem:

> *For oft, when on my couch I lie*
>   *In vacant or in pensive mood,*
> *They flash upon that inward eye*
>   *Which is the bliss of solitude;*
> *And then my heart with pleasure fills,*
> *And dances with the daffodils.*

In the first line, the obsolete and currently non-existent word *oft* clearly calls for replacement and the abnormal grammatical word order needs to be regularized. In the next line ...

But our treatment of the preceding verses will have provided demonstration enough of our approach, and readers will anyway no doubt welcome the opportunity to try out these procedures for themselves to complete a reversion of the original poem.

To conclude, as we have indicated, the approach we propose has the dual purpose of purging poetry of its obscurity so as to make its meaning more intelligible, and of providing samples of proper English to serve as appropriate input for language learning. But the approach does not preclude the possibility that advanced students might not be subsequently exposed to the original texts from which reversions are derived, but indeed prepares them for that very possibility by providing an initiation into the mysteries of verbal art. Previously primed by a reversion, students are better prepared to cope with the linguistic difficulties of the original, and to appreciate whatever additional aesthetic effects, if any, it might have to offer.

Our final point concerns the nature of the reversion itself. Although we believe that the examples we have presented in this chapter have their own artistic merit as poetry, modesty forbids us to claim that they are masterpieces of verbal art, or even that they are, in some way, an aesthetic improvement on the origin. But we need to bear in mind that the original may well itself be a reversion, the revision of some earlier draft, and preferred by the poet, rightly or wrongly, as an improvement. We know, as a matter of fact, that Wordsworth was himself an inveterate textual tinkerer and producer of variants. It is perhaps not entirely fanciful to suggest, therefore, that our reversion here might bear some resemblance to an earlier draft of the poem composed by Wordsworth himself, when "in vacant or pensive mood" at the end of a hard day's wandering o'er vales and hills, but subsequently rejected and, regrettably, lost to posterity for ever.

References

Alatis, James E. (ed.). 1969. *Monograph series on languages and linguistics: Vol. 22. Report of the twentieth annual round table meeting on linguistics and language studies: Linguistics and the teaching of standard English to speakers of other languages or dialects*. Washington, D.C.: Georgetown University Press.

Alatis, James E. (ed.). 1991. *Georgetown university round table on languages and linguistics: Vol. 1991. Linguistics and language pedagogy: The state of the art*. Washington, D.C.: Georgetown University Press.

Aston, Guy, Bernardini, Silvia & Stewart, Dominic (eds.). 2004. *Studies in corpus linguistics. Corpora and language learners*. Amsterdam: John Benjamins Publishing Company.

Austin, John L. 1962. *How to do things with words. Oxford paperbacks: Vol. 234*. London: Oxford University Press.

Bachman, Lyle F. 1990. *Fundamental considerations in language testing. Oxford applied linguistics*. Oxford: Oxford University Press.

Bailey, Benjamin . 2007. Heteroglossia and boundaries. In Heller,Monica (ed.), *Bilingualism: A social approach*, 257–274. London: Palgrave Macmillan..

Bailey, Charles-James N. & Shuy, Roger W. (eds.). 1973. *New ways of analyzing variation in English*. Washington, D.C.: Georgetown University Press.

Baird, Robert, Baker, Will & Kitazawa, Mariko. 2014. The complexity of ELF. *Journal of English as a Lingua Franca* 3. 171–196. //doi.org/10.1515/jelf-2014-0007

Baker, Will. 2015. *Culture and identity through English as a Lingua Franca*. Berlin: de Gruyter.

Bazell, Charles E., Catford, John C., Halliday, Michael Alexander K. & Robins, Robert H. (eds.). 1966. *In memory of J. R. Firth*. London: Longmans.

Bell, Allan. 2001. Back in style: Reworking audience design. In Penelope Eckert & John R. Rickford (eds.), *Style and sociolinguistic variation*, 139–169. Cambridge: Cambridge University Press.

Berlin, Isaiah. 1953. *The hedgehog and the fox: An essay on Tolstoy's view of history*. London: Weidenfeld & Nicolson.

Berns, Margie. 2009. *Concise encyclopedia of applied linguistics*. Burlington: Elsevier Science.

Bernstein, Basil. 1990. *Class, codes and control: Volume IV*. The structuring of pedagogic discourse. London: Routledge.

Bex, Tony & Watts, Richard J. (eds.). 1999. *Standard English: The widening debate*. London, New York: Routledge.

Block, David. 2003. *The social turn in second language acquisition. Edinburgh textbooks in applied linguistics*. Edinburgh: Edinburgh University Press.

Brown, Penelope & Levinson, Stephen. C. 1987. *Politeness: Some universals in language usage* (Reissued 1987 with corrections, new introduction and new bibliography). *Studies in interactional sociolinguistics: Vol. 4*. Cambridge: Cambridge University Press.

Brumfit, Christopher. 1995. Teacher professionalism and research. In Guy Cook & Barbara Seidlhofer (eds.), *Principle & practice in applied linguistics: Studies in honour of H. G. Widdowson*, 27–41. Oxford: Oxford University Press.

Brumfit, Christopher. 1997. How applied linguistics is the same as any other science. *International Journal of Applied Linguistics* 7. 86–94. //doi.org/10.1111/j.1473-4192.1997.tb00107.x

Brumfit, Christopher & Carter, Ronald (eds.). 1986. *Literature and language teaching*. Oxford: Oxford University Press.
Brumfit, Christopher & Johnson, Keith. 1979. *The communicative approach to language teaching*. Oxford: Oxford University Press.
Bruthiaux, Paul, Atkinson, Dwight, Eggington, William, Grabe, William & Ramanathan, Vaidehi (eds.). 2005. *Multilingual matters: Vol. 133. Directions in applied linguistics: Essays in honor of Robert B. Kaplan*. Clevedon: Multilingual Matters.
Butler, Christopher & Fowler, Alastair (eds.). 1971. *Topics in criticism: An ordered set of positions in literary theory*. London, Harlow: Longman.
Bygate, Martin & Kramsch, Claire. 2000. Editorial. *Applied Linguistics*. 21. 1–2. //doi.org/10.1093/applin/21.1.1
Byrnes, Heidi (ed.). 2006. *Advanced language learning: The contribution of Halliday and Vygotsky*. London, New York: Continuum.
Caldas-Coulthard, Carmen R. & Coulthard, Malcolm (eds.). 1996. *Texts and practices: Readings in critical discourse analysis*. London, New York: Routledge.
Canale, Michael & Swain, Merrill. 1980. Theoretical bases of communicative approaches to second language teaching and testing. *Applied Linguistics*, I. 1–47. //doi.org/10.1093/applin/I.1.1
Carter, Ronald 2004. *Language and creativity: The art of common talk*. London: Routledge.
Carter, Ronald & McCarthy, Michael 1997. *Exploring spoken English*. Cambridge: Cambridge University Press.
Carter, Ronald & McCarthy, Michael 2006. *Cambridge grammar of English: A comprehensive guide to spoken and written English usage*. Cambridge: Cambridge University Press.
Carter, Ronald & Simpson, Paul (eds.). 1989. *Language, discourse and literature: An introductory reader in discourse stylistics*. London: Unwin Hyman.
Catford, John C. 1965. *A Linguistic theory of translation: An essay in applied linguistics. Language and language learning: Vol. 8*. London: Oxford University Press.
Chapelle, Carol A. 2012. *The encyclopedia of applied linguistics*. Hoboken, NJ: John Wiley & Sons.
Chatman, Seymour (ed.). 1973. *Approaches to poetics: Selected papers from the English institute*. New York: Columbia University Press.
Chatwin, Bruce. 1987. *The songlines*. London: Cape.
Chomsky, Noam. 1957. *Syntactic structures*. The Hague: Mouton.
Chomsky, Noam. 1965. *Aspects of the theory of syntax*. Cambridge, MA: MIT Press.
Chomsky, Noam. 1966. Linguistic theory. In R. G. Mead (ed.), *Language teaching: Broader contexts. Reports of the working committees*. New York: MLA Materials Center.
Chomsky, Noam. 1972. *Language and mind*. New York: Harcourt Brace Jovanovich.
Chomsky, Noam. 2001 *9–11*. New York: Seven Stories Press.
Cole, Peter & Morgan, John L. (eds.). 1975. *Syntax and semantics, Volume 3: Speech acts*. New York: Academic Press.
Cook, Guy. 2003. *Applied linguistics. Oxford introductions to language study*. Oxford: Oxford University Press.
Cook, Guy. 2010. *Translation in language teaching. Oxford applied linguistics*. Oxford: Oxford University Press.
Cook, Guy & Seidlhofer, Barbara (eds.). 1995. *Principle & practice in applied linguistics: Studies in honour of H. G. Widdowson*. Oxford: Oxford University Press.

Cook, Vivian. 2007. Chomsky's *syntactic structures* fifty years on. *International Journal of Applied Linguistics* 17(1). 120–131.
Council of Europe. 2018. *Common European framework of reference for languages: Learning, teaching, assessment: Companion volume with new descriptors*. Strasburg: Council of Europe
Coupland, Nikolas. 2000. Review Article: Sociolinguistic prevarication about "standard English". *Journal of Sociolinguistics* 4. 622–634. //doi.org/10.1111/1467-9481.00133
Cox, Charles B. & Dyson, Anthony E. 1963. *Modern poetry: Studies in practical criticism*. London: Edward Arnold Ltd.
Cox, Charles B. & Dyson, Anthony E. 1965. *The practical criticism of Poetry: A textbook*. London: Edward Arnold.
Crowley, Tony. 2003. *Standard English and the politics of language*, 2nd revised. Hampshire, New York: Palgrave Macmillan.
Davies, Alan. 2003. *The native speaker: Myth and reality*. London: Multilingual Matters.
Davies, Alan.& Elder Catherine. (eds.) 2004. *The handbook of applied linguistics. Blackwell handbooks in linguistics: Vol. 17*. Malden, Mass.: Blackwell.
Eagleton, Terry. 1983. *Literary theory: An introduction*. Oxford: Basil Blackwell.
Edmondson, Willis. 2005. Prejudice and practice in applied linguistics. *International Journal of Applied Linguistics* 15. 389–398.
Ellis, Nick C. 2012. Formulaic language and second language acquisition: Zipf and the phrasal teddy bear. *Annual Review of Applied Linguistics* 32. 17–44. //doi.org/10.1017/S0267190512000025
Ellis, Rod. 1994. *The study of second language acquisition. Oxford applied linguistics*. Oxford: Oxford University Press.
Ellis, Rod. 2003. *Task-based language learning and teaching*, 1st edn. *Oxford applied linguistics*. Oxford: Oxford University Press.
Ellis, Rod. 2008. *The study of second language acquisition*, 2nd edn. *Oxford applied linguistics*. Oxford: Oxford University Press.
Ellis, Rod.. 2009. Task-based language teaching: Sorting out the misunderstandings. *International Journal of Applied Linguistics* 19. 221–246. //doi.org/10.1111/j.1473-4192.2009.00231.x
Ervin-Tripp, Susan M. 1974. Is second Language Learning like the First. *TESOL Quarterly* 8. 111. //doi.org/10.2307/3585535
Ervin-Tripp, SusanM. 2001. Variety, style-switching, and ideology. In Penelope Eckert & John R. Rickford (eds.), *Style and variation*, 44–56. New York: Cambridge University Press.
Everest, Kelvin & Matthews, Geoffery (eds.). 2000. *Longman annotated English poets. The poems of Shelley: Volume Two 1817–1819*. London: Longman.
Fairclough, Norman. 1989. *Language and power. Language in social life series*. London: Longman.
Fairclough, Norman. 1992. *Discourse and social change*. Cambridge: Polity Press.
Fairclough, Norman. 1995. *Critical discourse analysis: The critical study of language*. London: Longman.
Firth, Alan & Wagner, Johannes. 1998. SLA property: No trespassing! *The Modern Language Journal* 82. 91–94. //doi.org/10.1111/j.1540-4781.1998.tb02598.x
Firth, Alan & Wagner, Johannes. 2007. Second/foreign language learning as a social accomplishment: Elaborations on a reconceptualized SLA. *The Modern Language Journal* 91. 800–819. //doi.org/10.1111/j.1540-4781.2007.00670.x

Firth, John R. 1957. *Papers in linguistics 1934–51*. Oxford: The Clarendon Press
Firth, John R. 1957/68 A synopsis of linguistic theory 1930–55. In F. R. Palmer (eds.), *Selected Papers of J.R. Firth 1952–59. Longman linguistics library: Vol. 7*. London: Longman.
Fish, Stanley. 1973. What is stylistics and why are they saying such terrible things about it. In Seymour Chatman (ed.), *Approaches to poetics: Selected papers from the English institute*, 109–152. New York: Columbia University Press.
Fishman, Joshua A. (ed.). 1968. *Readings in the sociology of language*. Berlin: De Gruyter. Retrieved from http://search.ebscohost.com/login.aspx?direct=true&scope=site&db=nlebk&AN=756402
Foster, Pauline. 2009. Task-based language learning research: Expecting too much or too little? *International Journal of Applied Linguistics* 19. 247–263. //doi.org/10.1111/j.1473-4192.2009.00242.x
Fowler, Roger. 1986. *Linguistic criticism. Opus book: 1986: 1*. Oxford: Oxford University Press.
Fowler, Roger. 1996. On critical linguistics. In Carmen R. Caldas-Coulthard & Malcolm Coulthard (eds.), *Texts and practices: Readings in critical discourse analysis*, 3–14. London, New York: Routledge.
Garfinkel, Harold. 1972. Remarks on ethnomethodology. In John J. Gumperz & Dell H. Hymes (eds.), *Directions in sociolinguistics: The ethnography of communication*, 301–324. New York: Holt, Rinehart and Winston.
Garfinkel, Harold. & Sacks, Harvey 1970. On formal structures of practical actions. In John C. McKinney & Edward A. Tiryakian (eds.), *Theoretical sociology: Perspectives and developments*, 337–366. New York: Appleton-Century-Crofts.
Gladwin, Thomas & Sturtevant, William C. (eds.). 1962. *Anthropology and Human Behaviour*. Washington, D.C.: Anthropological Society of Washington.
Granger, Sylviane. 2003. The international corpus of learner English: A new resource for foreign language learning and teaching and second language acquisition research. *TESOL Quarterly* 37. 538–546. //doi.org/10.2307/3588404
Grice, H Paul. 1975. Logic and Conversation. In Phillip Cole & John L. Morgan (eds.), *Syntax and semantics, Volume 3: Speech acts*, 41–58. New York: Academic Press.
Gumperz, John J. & Hymes, Dell H. (eds.). 1972. *Directions in sociolinguistics: The ethnography of communication*. New York: Holt, Rinehart and Winston.
Halliday, Michael AlexanderK. 1970. Language structure and language function. In John Lyons (ed.), *New horizons in linguistics*. Harmondsworth: Penguin Books.
Halliday, Michael Alexander K. 1973. *Explorations in the functions of language. Explorations in language study*. London: Edward Arnold.
Halliday, Michael Alexander K. 1975. *Learning how to mean: Explorations in the development of language. Explorations in language study*. London: Edward Arnold.
Halliday, Michael Alexander K. 1994. *An introduction to functional grammar*, 2nd edn. London: Edward Arnold.
Halliday, Michael Alexander K. & Hasan, Ruqaiya. 1976. *Cohesion in English*. London: Longman
Halliday, Michael Alexander K. & Matthiessen, Christian M. 2004. *An introduction to functional grammar*, 3rd edn. / rev. by Christian M.I.M. Matthiessen. London: Arnold.
Hammersley, Martyn 1996. *On the foundations of critical discourse analysis. Occasional papers, University of Southampton. Centre for Language in Education: Vol. 42*. Southampton: University of Southampton. Centre for Language in Education.

Heaney, Seamus. 1990. *The redress of poetry: An inaugural lecture delivered before the University of Oxford on 24 October 1989*. Oxford: Clarendon Press.

Herdina, Philip & Jessner Ulrike. 2002. *A dynamic model of multilingualism: Perspectives of change in psycholinguistics*. London: Multilingual Matters.

Hernández-Campoy, Juan M. & Cutillas-Espinosa, Juan A. (eds.) 2012, *Style-shifting in public: New perspectives on stylistic variation*. Amsterdam: John Benjamins,

Hogan Patrick C. 2010.*The Cambridge encyclopedia of the language sciences*. Cambridge: Cambridge University Press.

House, Juliane. 2009. *Translation. Oxford introductions to language study*. Oxford: Oxford University Press.

Housen, Abigail & Kuiken, Folkert (eds.). 2009. Complexity, Accuracy, and Fluency (CAF) in Second Language Acquisition Research [Special issue]. *Applied Linguistics* 30(4).

Huddleston, Rodney & Pullum, Geoffrey K. 2002. *The Cambridge grammar of the English language*. Cambridge: Cambridge University Press.

Hüttner, Julia, Mehlmauer-Larcher, Barbara, Reichl, Susanne & Schifter, Barbara. (eds.). 2012. *New perspectives on language and education: Vol. 22. Theory and practice in EFL teacher education: Bridging the gap*. Bristol: Multilingual Matters.

Hyland, Ken. 2005. *Metadiscourse: Exploring interaction in writing. Continuum discourse series*. London: Continuum.

Hyland, Ken & Tse, P. 2004. Metadiscourse in academic writing: A reappraisal. *Applied Linguistics* 25. 156–177. //doi.org/10.1093/applin/25.2.156

Hymes, Dell H. 1962. The Ethnography of Speaking. In Thomas Gladwin & William C. Sturtevant (eds.), *Anthropology and human behaviour*, 13–53. Washington, D.C.: Anthropological Society of Washington.

Hymes, Dell H. 1972. On Communicative Competence. In John B. Pride & Janet Holmes (eds.), *Penguin modern linguistics readings. Sociolinguistics: Selected readings*, 269–293. Harmondsworth: Penguin.

Hymes, Dell H. 1974. *Foundations in sociolinguistics: An ethnographic approach*. Philadelphia: University of Pennsylvania Press.

Jakobson, Roman. 1960. Closing Statement: Linguistics and Poetics. In Thomas A. Sebeok (ed.), *Style in language*. Cambridge, MA: MIT Press.

Kachru, Braj. 1985. Standards, codification, and sociolinguistic realism: The English language in the outer circle. In Quirk, Randolph & Henry G Widdowson (eds.), *English in the world*. Cambridge: Cambridge University Press.

Kaplan, Robert B. 2002*The Oxford handbook of applied linguistics*. New York: Oxford University Press.

Knapp, Karlfried & Seidlhofer, Barbara (eds.). 2009. *Handbooks of applied linguistics: Vol. 6. Handbook of foreign language communication and learning* (1. Aufl.). Berlin, New York: Mouton de Gruyter.

Kuhn, Thomas S. 1962. *The structure of scientific revolutions*. Chicago: University of Chicago Press.

Kuhn, Thomas S. 1970. *The structure of scientific revolutions*, 2nd edn. *International encyclopedia of unified science*. S.l.: University of Chicago Press.

Labov, William. 1969a. The logic of non-standard English. In James E. Alatis (ed.), *Monograph series on languages and linguistics: Vol. 22. Report of the Twentieth Annual Round Table meeting on linguistics and language studies: Linguistics and the teaching of standard

English to speakers of other Languages or dialects, 1–44. Washington, D.C.: Georgetown University Press.
Labov, William. 1969b. *The study of non-standard English*. Champaign, IL: National Council of Teachers of English.
Labov, William. 1970. The study of language in its social context. In *Studium Generale*, 66–87.
Labov, William. 1972. *Sociolinguistic patterns. Conduct and communication*. Philadelphia: University of Pennsylvania Press.
Labov, William. 1988. The judicial testing of linguistic theory. In Deborah Tannen (ed.), *Advances in discourse processes: Vol. 29. Linguistics in context: Connecting observation and understanding*, 159–182. Norwood, NJ: Ablex.
Lafford, Barbara A. 2007. Second language acquisition reconceptualized? The impact of Firth and Wagner (1997). *The Modern Language Journal* 91. 735–756.
Larsen-Freeman, Diane & Cameron, Lynne 2008. *Complex systems and applied linguistics. Oxford applied linguistics*. Oxford: Oxford University Press.
Lee, David. 1992. *Competing discourses: Perspective and ideology in language. Real language series*. London: Longman.
Leech, Geoffrey N., Rayson, Paul & Wilson, Andrew 2001. *Word frequencies in written and spoken English: Based on the British National Corpus*. Harlow: Longman.
Lessing, Doris. 1972. *The golden notebook*. London: Michael Joseph.
Li Wei. 2000. *The bilingualism reader*. London & New York: Routledge.
Lyons, John. 1966. Firth's theory of meaning. In Charles E. Bazell, John C. Catford, Michael Alexander K. Halliday & Robert H. Robins (eds.), *In memory of J. R. Firth*, 288–302. London: Longmans.
Lyons, John. (ed.). 1970. *New horizons in linguistics*. Harmondsworth: Penguin Books.
Mackey. William F. 1962/2000. The description of bilingualism. Originally published in *Canadian Journal of Linguistics* 7(2). 51–85. Cited in Li Wei (2000): 26.
McCarthy, Michael. 2001. *Issues in applied linguistics*, 1st edn. Cambridge: Cambridge University Press.
McKinney, John C. & Tiryakian, Edward A. (eds.). 1970. *Theoretical sociology: Perspectives and developments*. New York: Appleton-Century-Crofts.
Malinowski, Bronislaw. 1923. The problem of meaning in primitive languages. In Charles K. Ogden & Ivor A. Richards (eds.), *The meaning of meaning*, 296–336. London: Routledge and Regan Paul.
Martinez, Ron & Schmitt, Norbert. 2012. A phrasal expressions list. *Applied Linguistics* 33. 299–320. //doi.org/10.1093/applin/ams010
Maybin, Janet & Swann, Joan (eds.). Language creativity in everyday contexts. Special issue of *Applied Linguistics* 28(4)
Mead, Richelle G. (ed.). 1966. *Language teaching: Broader contexts*. Reports of the Working Committees. New York: MLA Materials Center.
Meunier, Fanny. 2012. Formulaic language and language teaching. *Annual Review of Applied Linguistics* 32. 111–129. //doi.org/10.1017/S0267190512000128
Millar, Neil. 2011. The processing of malformed formulaic language. *Applied Linguistics* 32. 129–148. //doi.org/10.1093/applin/amq035
Milroy, James & Milroy, Lesley 1991. *Authority in language: Investigating language prescription and standardisation*, 2nd edn. London: Routledge.

Mindt, Dieter. 1997. Corpora and the teaching of English in Germany. In Anne Wichmann, Swansea Fligelstone, Tony McEnery & Gianna Knowles (eds.), *Applied linguistics and language study. Teaching and language corpora*, 40–50. London, New York: Longman.

Nettle, Daniel & Romaine, Suzanne. 2000. *Vanishing voices: The extinction of the world's languages*. New York: Oxford University Press.

Niedzielski, Nancy A. & Preston, Dennis R. 2003. *Folk linguistics. Trends in linguistics. Studies and monographs [TiLSM]: Vol. 122*. Berlin: De Gruyter Mouton.

O'Halloran, Kieran. 1999. Draft chapters (PhD). University of London.

O'Malley, Joseph M. & Chamot, Anna U. 1989. *Learning strategies in second language acquisition*. Cambridge: Cambridge University Press.

Oxford, Rebecca L. 1990. *Language learning strategies: What every teacher should know*. New York: Newbury House.

Palmer, Frank R. 1968. *Selected Papers of J.R. Firth 1952–59. Longman linguistics library: Vol. 7*. London: Longman.

Pennycook, Alastair. 2001. *Critical applied linguistics: A critical introduction*. Mahwah, NJ: Laurence Erlbaum Associates.

Pennycook, Alastair. 2010. *Language as a local practice*. London: Routledge.

Phipps, Alison M. 2006 *Learning the arts of linguistic survival: Languaging, tourism, life. Tourism and cultural change: Vol. 10*. Clevedon, Buffalo: Channel View Publications.

Pitzl, Marie-L. 2018 *Creativity in English as a lingua franca*. Berlin: de Gruyter.

Pride, John. B. & Holmes, Janet (eds.). 1972. *Penguin modern linguistics readings. Sociolinguistics: Selected readings*. Harmondsworth: Penguin.

Quirk, Randolph & Widdowson, Henry G. (eds.). 1985. *English in the world: Teaching and learning the language an literatures*. Papers of an International Conference entitled 'Progress in English Studies' held in London, 17–21 September 1984 to celebrate the Fiftieth Anniversary of The British Council. Cambridge: Cambridge University Press for the British Council.

Rampton, Ben. 1990. Displacing the 'native speaker': expertise, affiliation, and inheritance. *ELT Journal* 44(2). 97–101

Rampton, Ben. 1997. Retuning in applied linguistics. *International Journal of Applied Linguistics* 7. 3–25.

Rogers, Neville (ed.). 1975. *The complete poetical works of Percy Bysshe Shelley: In four volumes*. Oxford: Clarendon Press.

Römer, Ute. 2004a. A corpus-driven approach to modal auxiliaries and their didactics. In John M. Sinclair (ed.), *Studies in corpus linguistics: Vol. 12. How to use corpora in language teaching* (185–199). Amsterdam, Philadelphia: John Benjamins.

Römer, Ute. 2004b. Comparing real and ideal language learner input: The use of an EFL textbook corpus in corpus linguistics and language teaching. In Guy Aston, Silvia Bernardini & D'Arrietta. Stewart (eds.), *Studies in corpus linguistics. Corpora and language learners*, Vol. 17, 151–168. Amsterdam: John Benjamins Publishing Company. //doi.org/10.1075/scl.17.12rom

Ryan, Ann & Wray, Alison (eds.). 1997. *British studies in applied linguistics: Vol. 12. Evolving models of language: Papers from the annual meeting of the British Association for applied linguistics held at the University of Wales, Swansea, September 1996*. Clevedon, England, Philadelphia, PA: British Association for Applied Linguistics in association with Multilingual Matters.

Sampson, Geoffrey R. 2007. Grammar without grammaticality. *Corpus linguistics and linguistic theory* 3 1–32. //doi.org/10.1515/CLLT.2007.001
Schneider, Edgar W. 2012. Exploring the interface between World Englishes and Second Language Acquisition – and implications for English as a Lingua Franca. *Journal of English as a Lingua Franca* 1. 57–91. //doi.org/10.1515/jelf-2012-0004
Scott. Mike.. 1997. WordSmith Tools. Oxford: Oxford University Press.
Scott, Mike & Tribble, Christopher 2006. *Textual patterns: Key words and corpus analysis in language education. Studies in corpus linguistics: Vol. 22.* Amsterdam, Philadelphia: John Benjamins Pub.
Searle, John R. 1969. *Speech acts: An essay in the philosophy of language.* Cambridge, UK: Cambridge University Press.
Sebeok, Thomas A. (ed.). 1960. *Style in language.* Cambridge, MA: MIT Press.
Seidlhofer, Barbara. 2001. Closing a conceptual gap: The case for a description of English as a lingua franca. *International Journal of Applied Linguistics* 11. 133–158. //doi.org/10.1111/1473-4192.00011
Seidlhofer, Barbara (ed.). 2003. *Controversies in applied linguistics.* Oxford: Oxford University Press.
Seidlhofer, Barbara. 2004. Research perspectives on teaching English as a lingua franca. *Annual Review of Applied Linguistics* 24 209–239. //doi.org/10.1017/S0267190504000145
Seidlhofer, Barbara. 2011. *Understanding English as a Lingua Franca. Oxford applied linguistics.* Oxford: Oxford University Press.
Seidlhofer, Barbara. 2012. Anglophone-centric attitudes and the globalization of English. *Journal of English as a Lingua Franca* 1. 393–407. //doi.org/10.1515/jelf-2012-0026
Seidlhofer, Barbara & Widdowson, Henry G. 2007. Idiomatic variation and change in English: The idiom principle and its realizations. In Ute Smit, Stefan Dollinger, Julia Hüttner, Gunther Kaltenböck & Ursula Lutzky (eds.), *Austrian studies in English: Vol. 95. Tracing English through time: Explorations in language variation. In honour of Herbert Schendl on the occasion of his 65th birthday,* 359–374. Vienna: Braumüller.
Selinker, Larry. 1972. Interlanguage. *IRAL – International Review of Applied Linguistics in Language Teaching* 10. 209–231. //doi.org/10.1515/iral.1972.10.1-4.209
Simpson, James. 2011. *The Routledge Handbook of applied linguistics. Routledge handbooks in applied linguistics.* Oxford, New York: Routledge.
Sinclair, John M. 1985. Selected issues. In Randolph Quirk & Henry G. Widdowson (eds.), *English in the world: Teaching and learning the language and literatures,* 248–254. Cambridge: Cambridge University Press for the British Council.
Sinclair, John M. 1991a. *Corpus, concordance, collocation. Describing English language.* Oxford: Oxford University Press.
Sinclair, John M. 1991b. Shared knowledge. In James E. Alatis (ed.), *Georgetown University Round Table on languages and linguistics: Vol. 1991. Linguistics and language pedagogy: The state of the art,* 489–500. Washington, D.C.: Georgetown University Press.
Sinclair, John M. 1997. Corpus evidence in language description. In Anne Wichmann, Steven. Fligelstone, Tony McEnery & Gerry Knowles (eds.), *Applied linguistics and language study. Teaching and language corpora,* 27–39. London, New York: Longman.
Sinclair, John M. (ed.). 2004. *Studies in corpus linguistics: Vol. 12. How to use corpora in language teaching.* Amsterdam, Philadelphia: John Benjamins.

Smit, Ute, Dollinger, Stefan, Hüttner, Julia, Kaltenböck, Gunther & Lutzky, Ursula (eds.). 2007. *Austrian studies in English: Vol. 95. Tracing English through time: Explorations in language variation*. In honour of Herbert Schendl on the occasion of his 65th birthday. Vienna: Braumüller.

Sperber, Dan & Deirdre Wilson. 1986. Relevance. Communication and cognition. Cambridge: Cambridge University Press.

Spolsky, Bernard. 1998. *Sociolinguistics. Oxford introductions to language study*. Oxford: Oxford University Press.

Spolsky, Bernard (ed.). 1999. *Concise encyclopedia of educational linguistics*. Amsterdam: Elsevier.

Steiner, George. 1975. *After Babel: Aspects of language and translation*. London, New York: Oxford University Press.

Stubbs, Michael. 1980. *Language and literacy: The sociolinguistics of reading and writing. Routledge education books*. London: Routledge & Kegan Paul.

Stubbs, Michael W. 1983. *Discourse analysis: The sociolinguistic analysis of natural language. Language in society: Vol. 4*. Oxford: Basil Blackwell.

Stubbs, Michael. 1996. *Text and corpus analysis: Computer-assisted studies of language and culture. Language in society: Vol. 23*. Oxford: Basil Blackwell.

Stubbs, Michael. 1997. Whorf's children: Critical comments on Critical Discourse Analysis (CDA). In Andrews Ryan & Alison Wray (eds.), *British Studies in Applied Linguistics: Vol. 12*, 100–116. Clevedon, England, Philadelphia, PA: British Association for Applied Linguistics in association with Multilingual Matters.

Stubbs, Michael. 2004. Review of Peter Verdonk: Stylistics. Oxford: OUP 2002. *Applied Linguistics* 25. 126–129.

Stubbs, Michael. 2005. Conrad in the computer: Examples of quantitative stylistic methods. *Language and Literature* 14. 5–24. //doi.org/10.1177/0963947005048873

Swain, Merrill. 2006. Languaging, agency and collaboration in advanced second language proficiency. In Heidi Byrnes (ed.), *Advanced Language Learning: The Contribution of Halliday and Vygotsky*, 95–108. London, New York: Continuum.

Swales, John. 1990. *Genre analysis: English in academic and research settings*. Cambridge: Cambridge University Press.

Swan, Merrill. 2005. *Practical English usage*, 3rd edn. Oxford: Oxford University Press.

Swan, Merrill. 2012. *Thinking about language teaching: Selected articles 1982–2011*. Oxford, UK: Oxford University Press.

Swann, Joan & Janet Maybin. 2007. Introduction:language creativity in everyday contexts. Applied linguistics vol 28. No 4: 491–496.

Tannen, Deborah (ed.). 1988. *Advances in discourse processes: Vol. 29. Linguistics in context: Connecting observation and understanding*. Norwood, NJ: Ablex.

Tannen, Deborah. 1990. *You just don't understand: Women and men in conversation*: New York Ballantine.

Trudgill, Peter. 1999. Standard English: What it isn't. In Tony Bex & Richard J. Watts (eds.), *Standard English: The widening debate*, 117–128. London, New York: Routledge.

Trudgill, Peter. 2002. *Sociolinguistic variation and change*. Edinburgh: Edinburgh University Press.

Trudgill, Peter & Hannah, Jean 2008. *International English: A guide to the varieties of standard English*, 5thedn. London: Hodder Education.

van Dijk, Teun. 2005 Critical discourse analysis. Ch 18. In Deborah Schiffrin, Deborah Tannen & Hugh Hamilton (eds.), *The handbook of discourse analysis*. Oxford:Blackwell

Verdonk, Peter. 2002. *Stylistics. Oxford Introductions to language study*. Oxford: Oxford University Press.

Vetchinnikova, Svetlana. 2015. Usage-based recycling or creative exploitation of the shared code? The case of phraseological patterning. *Journal of English as a Lingua Franca* 4. 223–252.

VOICE 2013. The Vienna-Oxford International Corpus of English (version 2.0 Online). Director : Barbara Seidlhofer; Researchers: Angelika Breiteneder, Theresa Klimpfinger, Stefan Majewski, Ruth Osimk-Teasdale, Marie-Luise Pitzl, Michael Radeka. http://voice.univie.ac.at

Webb, Steve & Kagimoto, Eve 2011. Learning collocations: Do the number of collocates, position of the node word, and synonymy affect learning? *Applied Linguistics* 32. 259–276. //doi.org/10.1093/applin/amq051

Weber, Jean J. (ed.). 1996. *The stylistics reader: From Roman Jakobson to the present*. London: Arnold.

Wenger, Etienne. 1998. *Communities of practice: Learning, meaning and identity*. Cambridge: Cambridge University Press.

Wichmann, Anne, Fligelstone, Steven, McEnery, Tony & Knowles, Gerry (eds.). 1997. *Applied linguistics and language study. Teaching and language corpora*. London, New York: Longman.

Widdowson, Henry G. 1975. *Stylistics and the teaching of literature* (1st publ). Applied linguistics and language study. London: Longman.

Widdowson, Henry G. 1980. Models and fictions. *Applied Linguistics* I. 165–170. //doi.org/10.1093/applin/I.2.165

Widdowson, Henry G. 1984. *Explorations in applied linguistics 2*. Oxford: Oxford University Press.

Widdowson, Henry G. 1986. The Untrodden Ways. In Chris Brumfit & Ronald Carter (eds.), *Literature and language teaching*, 133–139. Oxford: Oxford University Press.

Widdowson, Henry G. 1990. *Aspects of language teaching*. Oxford: Oxford University Press.

Widdowson, Henry G. 1992. *Practical stylistics: An approach to poetry*. Oxford: Oxford University Press.

Widdowson, Henry G. 1996. Reply to Fairclough: Discourse and interpretation: Conjectures and refutations. *Language and Literature* 5. 57–69.

Widdowson, Henry G. 1997. EIL, ESL, EFL: Global issues and local interests. *World Englishes* 16. 135–146. //doi.org/10.1111/1467-971X.00054

Widdowson, Henry G. 1998. The Theory and practice of critical discourse analysis. *Applied Linguistics* 19. 136–151. //academic.oup.com/applij/article-abstract/19/1/136/196602

Widdowson, Henry G. 2000. On the limitations of linguistics applied. *Applied Linguistics* 21. 3–25. //doi.org/10.1093/applin/21.1.3

Widdowson, Henry G. 2003. *Defining issues in English language teaching*. Oxford applied linguistics. Oxford: Oxford University Press.

Widdowson, Henry G. 2004. *Text, context, pretext: Critical issues in Discourse analysis*. Language in society: Vol. 35. Oxford: Blackwell.

Widdowson, Henry G. 2005. Applied linguistics, interdisciplinarity, and disparate realities. In Paul Bruthiaux, Dwight Atkinson, William Eggington, William Grabe & Ramanathan (eds.), *Multilingual matters: Vol. 133. Directions in applied linguistics: Essays in honor of Robert B. Kaplan*, 12–25. Clevedon: Multilingual Matters.

Widdowson, Henry G. 2006. Applied linguistics and interdisciplinarity. *International Journal of Applied Linguistics* 16. 93–96. //doi.org/10.1111/j.1473-4192.2006.00108.x

Widdowson, Henry G. 2009. The linguistic perspective. In Karlfried Knapp & Barbara Seidlhofer (eds.), *Handbooks of applied linguistics: Vol. 6. Handbook of foreign language communication and learning*, 1st edn., 193–218. Berlin, New York: Mouton de Gruyter.

Widdowson, Henry G. 2011. The marketing of academic expertise. *The Modern Language Journal* 95. 650–653. //doi.org/10.1111/j.1540-4781.2011.01248_11.x

Widdowson, Henry G. 2012a. Closing the gap, changing the subject. In Julia Hüttner, Barbara Mehlmauer-Larcher, Susanne. Reichl & Barbara Schiftner (eds.), *New perspectives on language and education: Vol. 22. Theory and practice in EFL teacher education: Bridging the gap*, 3–15. Bristol: Multilingual Matters.

Widdowson, Henry G. 2012b. ELF and the inconvenience of established concepts. *Journal of English as a Lingua Franca* 1. 5–26. //doi.org/10.1515/jelf-2012-0002

Widdowson, Henry G & Seidlhofer, Barbara 2003. The virtue of the vernacular: On intervention in linguistic affairs. In Britain, David Britten & Jenny Cheshire Schiftner (eds.), *Social dialectology (In honour of Peter Trudgill)*. Amsterdam: John Benjamins.

Wilkins, David A. 1972. *The linguistic and situational content of the common core in a unit/credit system*. Strasbourg: Council of Europe.

Wilkins, David A. 1976. *Notional syllabuses: A taxonomy and its relevance to foreign language curriculum development*. London: Oxford University Press.

Wimsatt, William K. 1970. *The verbal icon: Studies in the meaning of poetry*. University paperbacks: UP 333. London: Methuen & Co.

Wray, Alison. 2012. What do we (think we) know about formulaic language? An evaluation of the current state of play. *Annual Review of Applied Linguistics* 32. 231–254. //doi.org/10.1017/S026719051200013X.

Name Index

Arnold, Matthew 32

Bailey, Benjamin 225
Baker, Will 189
Ban Ki- Moon 236–238, 240, 243
Bell, Allan 226
Berlin, Isaiah 29, 30
Berns, Margie 51
Bernstein, Basil 43
Brown, Penelope 78
Brumfit, Christopher 53, 64
Bunyan, John 157
Bygate, Martin 37, 52

Caldas-Coulthard, Carmen 103
Carroll, Lewis 70
Carter, Ron 31, 104, 190, 239, 240
Catford, J.C. 208
Chatwin, Bruce 49
Chomsky, Noam 13, 15, 19, 21, 24, 25, 29, 31, 43, 70, 154–156, 158, 159, 161, 164, 167, 172, 180, 183, 184, 190, 214, 224, 226
Coleridge, S.T. 83
Conrad, Joseph 118, 119
Cook, Guy 24, 29, 31, 37, 52, 207, 212
Cook, Vivian 24
Coulthard, Malcolm 103
Coupland, Nikolas 183, 223, 228

Davies, Alan 51, 62, 223
Derrida, Jacques 43, 44
Donne, John 40

Eagleton, Terry 104, 105
Edmondson, Willis 52
Elder, Catherine 51
Eliot, T.S. 118, 127, 139, 152, 153, 203
Ellis, Nick 57
Ellis, Rod 57, 58, 168, 207, 215
Ervin-Tripp, Susan 214, 225

Fairclough, Norman 27, 43, 74, 75, 98, 113, 114
Farouk, Hamadi 197–204

Firth, J.R. 9, 19–30, 48, 57
Fish, Stanley 118–120, 127, 128, 232
Fittibaldi, Umberto 200
Forster, E.M. 1, 3
Foster, Pauline 58
Fowler, Roger 104, 105

Garfinkel, Harold 162, 163, 211, 212
Gorbachev, Mikhail 74–76
Grice, H.P. 12, 34, 35, 84, 85, 90, 92, 108, 112, 113, 132, 133, 142, 175, 176, 180, 191, 197, 226, 227

Halliday, Michael 10, 20, 26, 27, 36, 77, 88, 89, 166, 167, 169, 179, 240
Hannah, Jean 155, 158, 159, 183, 222
Hardy, Thomas 198, 199
Hasan, Ruqaiya 10
Heaney, Seamus 100, 101, 191
Hemingway, Ernest 110
Herdina, Philip 230
House, Juliana 207–209
Huddleston, Rodney 41
Hyland, Ken 87, 88, 92–94
Hymes, Dell 13, 22, 23, 36, 54, 130, 165–167, 175, 214–216, 229–231

Jakobson, Roman 22, 23, 31–36
Jefferson, Thomas 69
Jessner, Ulrike 230

Kachru, Braj 155, 174
Kagimoto, Eve 216
Kaplan, Robert 37, 51, 52
Kramsch, Claire 37, 52
Kuhn, Thomas 42, 153

Labov, William 10, 21, 22, 28, 38, 39, 42, 43, 46, 154, 160, 171–175, 180, 215, 216
Lantolf, James 53
Leech, Geoffrey 246–248, 250–253
Lee, David 114
Lessing, Doris 71, 72, 79
Levinson, Stephen 87

Name Index

Li Wei 225
Lyons, John 20

Mackey, W.F. 228
Malinowski, Bronislaw 9, 22
Martinez, Ron 60, 216, 217
Maybin, Janet 31
McCarthy, Michael 59, 238–240
Mortimer, John 156–158

Narayan, R. K. 111
Nettle, Daniel 38, 41
Niedzielski, Nancy 39, 40

Obama, Barack 79

Palmer, Frank 20, 21, 25
Pennycook, Alastair 47, 98, 179
Pinter, Harold 163
Pitzl, Marie-Luise 183, 189, 193
Preston, Dennis 39, 40
Pullum, Geoffrey 41

Rampton, Ben 48, 223
Romaine, Susanne 38, 41
Römer, Ute 60

Sampson, Geoffrey 156–158, 161
de Saussure, Ferdinand 172, 222
Schmitt, Norbert 60, 216, 217
Schneider, Edwin 174
Scott, Mike 119
Searle, John 9, 23, 24, 33
Seidlhofer, Barbara 1, 36, 41, 48, 61, 93, 94, 152, 153, 178, 183, 186, 188, 193, 196, 217, 219, 240, 243, 244
Selinker, Larry 54, 55

Shakespeare, William 2, 40, 66, 129, 131, 132, 134, 137, 138, 140, 189, 195
Shelley, P.B. 200–204
Simpson, John 51, 104
Sinclair, John 35, 39, 46, 59, 60, 61, 77, 170
Spolsky, Bernard 43
Steiner, George 99, 152, 153, 211
Stevens, Wallace 96
Stoppard, Tom 132
Stubbs, Michael 43, 77, 115, 118–123, 125, 127, 128
Swales, John 92, 93, 179
Swan, Michael 59, 235
Swann, Joan 31

Tannen, Deborah 82
Tennyson, Alfred 164, 195
Thomas, Dylan 32, 192, 196, 197, 199
Tribble, Chris 119
Trudgill, Peter 38, 41, 154, 155, 158, 159, 183, 222–224

van Dijk, Teun 78
Verdonk, Peter 128, 129

Webb, Stuart 216
Wenger, Etienne 93, 179
Whewell, William 109
Widdowson, Henry 26, 27, 29, 36, 41, 42, 47, 51, 56, 58, 59, 62, 77, 89, 103, 108, 110, 115, 116, 126, 160, 163, 166, 168, 169, 181, 184, 199, 212–214, 218, 219, 238, 239
Wilde, Oscar 142
Wimsatt, W.K. 198
Wordsworth, William 106, 111, 112, 116, 245, 247, 248, 251–255
Wray, Alison 60, 61, 181, 182

Subject Index

Academic discourse 95
Actes de parole 97
Adaptive variability 172, 183–188
African American English 172, 173
Ambiguity 2, 6, 34, 76, 77, 192, 227
Analysis 42, 45, 59, 66–69, 76–80, 88, 103–105, 115, 128, 158, 162, 163
– interpretation 66, 68
Applied linguistics 18–64, 101, 216
– linguistics 18, 21, 150
Appropriateness 164, 229
Authenticity 15, 16, 56, 61, 181

Bank of English 191
Bilingual competence 222–232
– lingual capability 222–232
Bilingualism 222, 225, 228, 230
British Association of Applied Linguistics (BAAL) 37–39
British English 155, 183, 222
British National Corpus (BNC) 119, 191, 217, 247, 253

Capability 13, 14, 101, 169, 174, 179, 220, 222–243, 247
– competence 233–243
Characterizing 131
– contextualizing function 131
COBUILD Dictionary 235, 246, 247, 248, 253
Code switching 225, 226, 228
Coherence 10, 11
– cohesion 10, 11
Collocation 10, 24, 28, 32, 33, 115, 177, 178, 216, 247, 248, 250
Common European Framework of Reference (CEFR) 180, 230
Communal identity 36, 173, 174, 187
Communication 6, 8, 9, 11, 13, 15, 16, 18, 21, 23, 28, 33, 34, 35, 60, 61, 66, 67, 68, 70, 74, 79, 81–86, 88, 91, 92, 95, 112, 113, 150, 154, 160, 165–168, 172–182, 187–189, 191, 193, 194, 200, 212, 214, 219, 224, 228, 231, 232–234, 236, 237, 240, 242, 243

Communicative competence 1, 13, 36, 54, 55, 194, 213–215, 228, 229, 234
Communicative language teaching (CLT) 168, 181, 214, 215, 217, 236
Community 13, 15, 21, 36, 70, 90, 92–95, 98, 99, 150, 152–154, 165, 173–176, 178–180, 184, 185, 187, 189, 190, 194, 195, 199, 206, 214, 224, 229, 239
Community membership 93, 178
Community of Practice 179
Competence 13, 14, 233–243
Complexity, accuracy, fluency (CAF) 58
Complexity theory 64, 152, 171, 172, 224
Conceptual space 83, 84, 95
Conformity 31, 32, 34, 92, 93, 100, 150, 154, 162, 166, 167, 173, 180–182, 186–188, 190, 194, 196, 199, 234, 240, 246
– creativity 15, 31–36, 150, 180, 190–197, 199
Context 8, 9, 134, 137
Context of situation 9, 22, 24–26, 107
Contextual conditions 16, 61, 115, 116
Contextualization 25, 131, 133
Contextualizing 131, 132, 138
– characterizing function 131
Conventions of usage 14, 213, 227, 228, 231, 235
Convergence 9, 12, 54, 66, 70, 84, 86
Conversation analysis 64, 162, 163
Co-operative imperative 12, 86, 87, 90, 91
Co-operative Principle 12, 34, 35, 84, 85, 108, 112, 113, 117, 132, 134, 176, 177, 191, 193, 194, 197, 226, 227
Corpus analysis 1, 56, 63, 97–99, 118–128
Corpus linguistics 7, 10, 28, 35, 42, 51, 56, 57, 59, 62, 64, 66, 96, 97, 118, 159, 160, 170, 181, 223, 235, 245
Co-text 8–10, 26, 33
Council of Europe 54, 230
Creative incompetence 150, 196–204
Creativity in language use 191
Critical discourse analysis (CDA) 27, 47, 67, 68, 74, 77, 78, 80, 98, 103, 104, 115, 116, 139

Critical linguistics 77, 99, 103, 117
– literary criticism 103
Cultural factors in communication 33
Culture 25, 94, 164, 170, 189–192, 194, 195, 227
Culture and creativity 195

Data 28, 29, 39, 42, 44, 45, 47–50, 54–56, 59, 60, 62, 63, 76, 80, 97, 116, 119, 120, 153, 155, 157–163, 169, 177, 208–211, 213, 216, 218
– evidence 28, 54, 162, 211, 218
Disciplinarity 37–50, 52, 57, 61, 63
Disciplinary expertise 29, 40, 45, 49
– folk experience 29, 44, 45, 49
Discipline 13, 18, 28, 38–48, 50, 62–64, 93, 171, 189
– domain 40, 46, 50
Discourse 6–11, 27, 28, 47, 51, 66–68, 73, 74, 77, 78, 84, 86–101, 103–105, 116, 120, 160, 162, 163, 209–212, 218, 219, 226
– text 6–8, 66
Discourse analysis 7, 27, 47, 51, 64, 67, 74, 77, 78, 80, 88, 98, 103, 104, 116, 139
Discourse community 95, 98, 178
Discourse interpretation 1, 11, 66, 67, 78
Domains of use 43, 226

Ebonic English 173
Encoding principles 14, 15, 185–187
English as a Foreign Language (EFL) 60, 167, 206, 216, 234, 235, 242
English as a Lingua Franca (ELF) 14, 16, 36, 149, 152, 153, 161, 169, 171, 183, 189–195, 204, 206, 217, 227, 230, 236, 238, 240, 242, 243
English as a native language (ENL) 233–238, 242, 243
English taught as a foreign language (ETFL) 236, 238, 239, 242
– English learned as a foreign language (ELFL) 236, 239, 242
Equivalence 32, 33
Example 165, 166, 218
– sample of language 165, 218

Factors in the speech event 22, 23, 31, 35
Feasibility 166
Folk linguistics 40
Formalist 19, 21, 26–28, 32, 33, 35, 42, 88, 154, 190
– functionalist linguistics 21, 22
Formulaic expressions 60, 61, 216
Function 9, 10, 22–28, 31–36, 41, 42, 54, 72, 88, 90, 106–108, 120, 137, 164, 166–170, 178–182, 190, 210, 215–217, 224–226, 235, 239, 240, 245
– in systemic functional grammar 179
– in speech events 22, 90

Genre 3, 82–85, 87–95, 105, 106, 120
Genre conventions 82–95
Grammar 13, 14, 16, 20, 24, 25, 27, 41, 71, 89, 155, 156, 159, 167, 168, 172, 179, 182, 183, 185, 190, 198, 222, 234, 235, 240, 250
Grammaticality 155, 156

Identity factors 164
Ideological investment 74–76
Ideology 46, 47, 67, 98, 104, 139
Idiomaticity 28, 35, 177, 178, 217
Idiom principle 35, 36, 177, 186, 187, 217
Illocutionary force 9, 11, 33, 83, 130, 142, 209
Implicature 34–36, 132–134, 176, 180, 191–193, 197, 198, 227
Impositioning 84, 91
Individuality 98, 101
– social role 98
Interactive encounters 84
Inter-community communication 174
Interdisciplinarity 37–50, 52, 57, 61, 63
Interdisciplinary collaboration 38, 39, 43–45, 47
Interlanguage 54, 55, 57, 58, 168, 169, 196, 211
Interpersonal positioning 82–95
Interpretation 1, 2, 8, 11, 20, 27, 66–81, 99, 103–120, 127, 128, 191, 198, 209–218, 253
– analysis 66, 68

Language community 36
Language events 9, 22, 26, 29, 30
Language learners 63, 168, 169, 212, 216, 218, 228, 229, 238, 247, 248
– teachees 182, 213, 218
Language learning 18, 38, 45, 46, 53, 54, 61, 151, 168, 171, 180, 207–221, 230, 240, 249, 255
– language teaching 207
Language learning
– as translating
Language learning process 45, 249
– language learning objective 54
Languaging 219, 220, 243
langue 26, 28, 97, 185, 222, 228
Leech register 246–248, 250–253
Levels of discourse 91
Linguistic competence 54, 55, 160, 168, 190, 246
Linguistic diversity 41, 42
Linguistics 18–64, 206–255
– applied linguistics 21, 150
Literature teaching 79, 80
Literary criticism 2, 66, 103, 104, 117
– critical linguistics 117
Literary texts 2, 8, 66, 71, 79, 80, 103, 104, 110, 113, 115, 116, 118, 128, 210, 244

Meaning indeterminacy 2, 79, 116, 119, 120, 124, 150, 210, 223, 225
Meaning potential 14, 26, 27, 36, 89, 179, 180, 199
Medium 6, 7, 189
– means of communication 16, 74, 154, 172, 180, 182, 188, 189, 236
Metadiscourse 87–90
Meta-functions 89
Monolingual language teaching 213, 220, 230

National Rifle Association (NRA) 72, 78
Native speaker 13–16, 28, 36, 39, 42, 54–56, 58, 60, 61, 94, 150, 154, 157, 158, 160–162, 164, 165, 167–169, 176, 177, 180–185, 187–189, 192–196, 198–204, 214–220, 223, 225, 227–238, 241, 244–248, 252

Native speaker competence 55, 58, 161, 162, 164, 165, 168, 169, 183, 184, 196, 219, 220, 235
Norms of usage 174, 188, 213

P1, P2 participants 12, 67–71, 82, 83, 85, 86, 89, 210
Paradigm 42, 95, 153, 170, 173, 174
Patterns of usage 187, 192, 235
Performance 7, 13, 34, 95, 129, 130, 153, 154, 159–164, 167, 170, 172, 190, 216, 228, 230, 235, 237
Perlocutionary effect 23, 35, 83, 142, 191, 209
Personal space 66, 86
Phraseological patterns 187
Poetic function 31–36
Poetry teaching 100, 101
Politeness 87
Positional convergence 84
Positioning 12, 82–95
Pragmatic creativity 36, 190–192, 194, 195
– poetic creativity 31, 190–192
Pragmatic meaning 8, 9, 12, 23, 66, 74, 80, 90
Pragmatics 2, 10, 11, 23, 24, 26, 51, 64, 80, 83, 85, 88, 171–182, 187, 228, 232
– semantics 10, 23–27, 80
Pragmatic significance 73, 77
– semantic signification 77
Pragmatics of variation 175, 180, 182
Pretext 11, 12
Pretextual conditions 70, 76, 79
Pretextual purpose 11, 68, 70, 71, 73, 76, 78, 80, 81, 83, 163

'Real' English 16, 183, 240
Real world problems 29, 37–39, 45, 47, 52, 53, 57, 62–64
Reference 1–3, 6, 10, 13, 14, 16, 18–22, 24, 26, 31, 34, 41, 44, 46, 48–50, 64, 68, 72–75, 84, 85, 90, 95, 114, 121, 134, 142, 157, 180, 209–219, 222, 230, 238, 253
– denotation 68–70
Referential scope 69
Renewal of connection 28, 29, 48
Representation 9, 41, 44, 50, 74, 77, 88, 109, 119, 126, 131–134, 137, 138, 153, 161, 163, 164, 191

– reference 41, 44, 74, 109, 126, 131–134, 164
Representations of reality 9, 44, 153, 163, 164
Reversions 244–255

Sample 13, 59, 61, 162, 165, 214, 218, 238, 254
– example 165, 166, 218
Second Amendment 72
Second language acquisition (SLA) 31, 45, 46, 53, 55, 57–63, 104, 169, 184, 230
Schematic construct 9, 22, 24, 25, 193
Semantics 8, 10, 19, 23–25, 27, 70, 113
– pragmatics 10, 23, 24
Semantic signification 77
– pragmatic significance 73, 77
Social level 24, 90–92, 95
– individual level of positioning 90–93, 95
Socio-cultural conventions 9, 86
Speech acts 9, 23, 24, 33
Speech community 21, 154, 184, 214, 224, 229
Speech event 22, 23, 31, 33, 35, 90, 91
Standard English 14, 94, 155, 156, 158, 167, 172–174, 179, 183–186, 188, 222, 223, 227, 234, 235
Stylistic analysis 104, 127, 128
Stylistics 103, 104, 116–129, 138–148, 244
Systemic functional grammar 179

Task-based language teaching (TBLT) 57, 207, 215, 217, 218, 220, 234, 236
Teachees 182, 213, 218
– Learners 181, 182, 212, 213–222
Teaching English as a Foreign Language (TEFL) 233, 242, 243
Teaching English to Speakers of Other Languages (TESOL) 241
Teaching poetry 100, 101
Territorial imperative 12, 86, 87, 90, 91
Text 6, 7, 73, 78, 79, 105–110, 210
– discourse 6, 7
Text analysis 7, 79
– discourse interpretation 78
Textualization 11, 25, 73, 92, 131, 133, 211
Threshold Level 55, 56, 60
Translaters 211, 212, 218–220
– translators 210–212, 219
Translation 207–221

Variable interpretation 20, 71, 72, 79, 80, 117
Variation 15, 171–184, 188, 224, 225, 228
– Change 41, 42
Variety 15
Vienna Oxford International Corpus of English (VOICE) 178, 193
Virtual language 14, 15, 36, 166, 169, 180, 183–188, 231
– *langue* 185

World Englishes (WE) 173, 174, 180

www.ingramcontent.com/pod-product-compliance
Lightning Source LLC
Chambersburg PA
CBHW031802220426
43662CB00007B/502